Child Labor in America

A History

CHAIM M. ROSENBERG

McFarland & Company, Inc., Publishers

Jefferson, North Carolina, and London

LIBRARY OF CONGRESS CATALOGUING-IN-PUBLICATION DATA

Rosenberg, Chaim M.
Child labor in America ; a history / Chaim M. Rosenberg.
p.   cm.
Includes bibliographical references and index.

ISBN 978-0-7864-7349-6
softcover : acid free paper ∞

1. Child labor — United States — History.   2. Child labor —
Government policy — United States — History.   3. Child
labor — Law and legislation — United States — History.   I. Title.
HD6250.U3R67 2013   331.3'10973 — dc23   2013025614

BRITISH LIBRARY CATALOGUING DATA ARE AVAILABLE

On the cover: young doffers in Elk Cotton Mills,
Fayetteville, Tennessee, November 1910 (photograph
by Lewis Wickes Hine, Library of Congress)

Manufactured in the United States of America

*McFarland & Company, Inc., Publishers
Box 611, Jefferson, North Carolina 28640
www.mcfarlandpub.com*

To my wife, Dawn,
who has encouraged me and
read every word I wrote.
And to Daniel, Naomi, Natan and Hadas
Rebecca and Colin
Amber and William.
The children we love.

Acknowledgments

Above all I thank my wife, Dawn, for her patience and support and for reading every word I wrote. My family, David, Linda and Adrienne, helped shape the book. Professor Susan Ware of Harvard University discussed with me the role of Florence Kelley, Jane Addams, Julia Lathrop and Lillian Wald in drawing public attention to the use of child labor in America. These remarkable women championed the belief that the years of childhood are for play, study and maturation, but not for labor. Professor Eric Edmonds of Dartmouth University sent me data on the state of child labor today, particularly in Asia and Africa. Michael Kravitz of the Wage & Hour Division of the U.S. Department of Labor sent me information on present day child law violations.

The public libraries of Boston, Wellesley, Newton, Winchester and Needham as well as the remarkable archives of the *New York Times* have provided much of the material for this book. That modern day resource, Google Books, brings the scholarship of the ages, housed in the great libraries of the world, to our computer screens at the touch of our fingers, saving time and countless journeys.

Photographs showing children at work, particularly for the period from 1908 to 1918, enrich my book. Most come from the camera of Lewis Wickes Hine when the National Child Labor Committee employed him. These photographs are a national treasure, now in the custody of the Library of Congress.

Table of Contents

Preface

Soon after the War of Independence, the United States entered the industrial age. Machines installed in large factories, powered first by water and later by steam, did the work formerly done by hand. Child labor was cheap labor, and large numbers of children were put to work in the mills and mines. Little children worked on the farms picking fruits, vegetables, cotton and tobacco. Children as young as five or six were put to work in tenement industries making ink, artificial flowers, paper and clothing. Little boys dug deep underground for copper and coal. Many boys worked the furnaces of the bottle factories; others rolled cigars. Telegram boys pedaled their bicycles to deliver messages. Small girls worked as domestic servants or sold flowers on street corners. Children peeled tomatoes, shucked oysters, and cut shrimp and sardine in the canning factories. With the growth of cities, children were out early in the morning selling newspapers and tending pushcarts selling fruit and vegetables. Young boys walked the streets offering to shine shoes or worked in shoeshine parlors. By 1900, over two million children under the age of sixteen held jobs, earning low pay for long hours.

Manufacturers and their lobbyists mobilized powerful forces to keep the age-old practice of child labor, arguing that without the discipline of work idle hands led to mischief and that children needed to work to support their sick and disabled parents. Opposition to child labor grew vocal during the Progressive Era arguing that child labor was an evil, destroying the physical and mental health of the children. Child labor led to illiteracy and stunted the intellect, dooming the children to dull lives. Furthermore, cheap child labor replaced adult workers and kept wages low. The child's place, argued the reformers, was at school to acquire the skills needed for good citizenship and a varied and productive life. A quartet of forceful women — Florence Kelley, Jane Addams, Julia Lathrop and Lillian Wald — led the battle to abolish child labor as well as the fight for women's rights, a minimum wage, and eight-hour workdays, health care and insurance against disability. They insisted that children had rights and were not mere appendages of their fathers. By their advocacy of education, these women were determined to lift poor children, home-born and immigrant alike, out of the slums and into the mainstream of American life. Their example motivated many others to join in the half-century battle that played out in the press, state and federal legislatures as well as in the courts. Through the efforts of these four women the National Child Labor Committee and the United States Children's Bureau were founded to ensure a childhood of play, education and hope, but free of toil.

The indefatigable photographer Lewis Wickes Hine documented an important part of the story of child labor in the United States. From 1908 to 1918, Hine traveled the length and breadth of the nation carrying with him his large box camera, taking pictures of children at work in the mills, on the farms, in the glass houses, on the streets and down the mines. The Hine pictures, preserved in the Library of Congress, record better than words the image of child labor in America. Most of the pictures reproduced in this book were selected from the Hine collection of over five thousand images. Child labor increased during the Great Depression but at the expense of jobs for adults. It took the New Deal legislation to put a legal end to child labor. Frances Perkins — a disciple of Florence Kelley — served as secretary of labor in the Franklin D. Roosevelt administration that saw the Fair Labor Standards Act of 1938 into law.

This book describes the many types of child labor in the United States and follows the struggle to keep children in school and out of the workforce. Rising prosperity and labor saving technology such as canning machinery, office machines, bowling alley machines, vacuum cleaners, clothes washing and drying machines and dishwashers eliminated many of the jobs once done by children.

Taking children out of the workforce and keeping them in school is a measure of a country's social and economic advancement. A sound education, the reformers argued, is the necessary foundation to good citizenship of a democracy. In the United States most children now complete high school and many go on to college. Despite strong laws, child labor still finds ways of coming back, such as migrant farm labor. In under-developed countries, especially in parts of Asia and Africa, child labor is still endemic.

Introduction

The children of the very poor have no young times.—Essays to Elia,
Charles Lamb, 1823

Probably no segment of the progressive crusade engaged more fully the
moral energies of the reformers than the battle against the exploitation
of children in mine, factory, street and field.
— Clarke A. Chambers, 1963

George Washington lived sixty-seven years, twice as many as of the average American of his time. The next five presidents lived even longer: John Adams to ninety, Thomas Jefferson to eighty-three, James Madison to eighty-five, James Monroe to seventy-three and John Quincy Adams to eighty. Wealth and position in early America, however, did not ensure a long life. The rich Boston merchant-turned-manufacturer Francis Cabot Lowell died at forty-three, his mother at twenty-three, his sister at forty-one, his wife at forty-two, his older son, John Jr., at thirty-six, his daughter, Susanna, at twenty-six and his younger son Edward at only twenty-two.[1] During the course of the nineteenth century life expectancy in America rose slowly to reach forty-seven years for men and fifty years for women in 1900. In the twentieth century life expectancy climbed steadily and at the start of the twenty-first century reached almost eighty years for men and a few more years for women.

In colonial times only the plantation owners in the South and merchants in the North had the means to give their sons a college education. For the vast majority in America it was a hand-to-mouth existence. Father, mother and all able children had to help. When a boy reached thirteen his father put him to work on the farm or placed him as an apprentice to a local craftsman or tradesman. The terms promised he would be housed, fed, clothed and trained in return for his obedience and his labor. The more ambitious boys left home to follow the expansion of the nation south and west. The girls of the household stayed home until they married. Tragedy struck frequently with the death of a father or mother, leaving the family destitute. Following the Poor Law of England, orphaned or abandoned children in America became wards of the local parish. When they reached thirteen years these children were apprenticed out, the boys to learn a trade and the girls into domestic service.

The Puritan ethic praised the virtue of work and scorned the sin of idleness. In 1640, the Great and General Court of Massachusetts directed "what course may be taken for

3

teaching boys and girls in all towns the spinning of yarn." The court instructed that it "will be expected that all masters of families should see that their children and servants should be industriously employed so as the mornings and evenings and other seasons may not be lost as formerly they have been." The scarcity of hired labor gave value to large families. It was the duty of children to help their parents, even into old age. There was much work to do and the labor of many children was needed. The older the children — boys and girls — the more work they did. There were trees to fell, land to plow, seeds to sow, fields to cultivate, and the fruits of labor to gather. The corn was separated from the chaff and ground into flour. The chickens, cows, sheep and horses were fed. The eggs and milk were collected and butter churned. There were homes and barns to build, fences to erect and wood to chop for the cold winters. Wool and flax were collected and spun into thread, woven into cloth or linen and sewn into sheeting and clothes. Each household had a spinning wheel and a handloom. Leather was tanned, cut and made into shoes. Water was gathered from the streams and carried into the house. Long, straight trees were cut and floated down river to the shipyards. The ships went to sea in search of fish, which was then salted and dried. To do these many tasks the citizens used the wind, the flow of water and the strength of their horses, but most work used human power and traditional tools. In 1790, America was still rural, with only one in thirty Americans living in towns or cities with over eight thousand inhabitants.

The Industrial Revolution began late in the eighteenth century in England with cotton textiles using power machinery to do the work done for millennia by hand. Many machines were needed to convert raw cotton into finished cloth. The factories and machines destroyed the craft guilds and the apprenticeship system, reducing the mill worker to a servant of the machine, repeating a task over and over again. Some of these tasks required a man's strength and judgment, but others were better suited to the nimble fingers and fleetness of foot of children.

Early in the history of the industrialization of the United States, prominent men saw the value of putting children to work. In a speech delivered in Carpenter's Hall, Philadelphia, in 1775, Daniel Roberdeau, president of the Pennsylvania Society for the Encouragement of Manufactures, said: "The expense of manufacturing cloth will be lessened from the great share women and children will have in them." Cheap labor from children would permit the new nation to compete against British textile imports.[2] George Washington wrote in his diary, October 28, 1789, that while on a tour of Boston he visited a sailcloth factory where "they have 28 looms at work, and 14 girls spinning with both hands.... Children (girls) turn the wheels for them. And with this assistance each spinner can turn out 14 lbs. of thread per day when they stick to it."[3] Washington was enthusiastic about new machinery and encouraged the development of industry. After examining a new threshing machine, he wrote in his diary, January 22, 1790: "Two boys are sufficient to turn the wheel, feed the mill, and remove the threshed grain. Women, or boys of 12 or 14 years of age, are fully adequate to the management of the mill or threshing machine."[4] In his *Report on Manufactures* (1791), Alexander Hamilton, secretary of the treasury in the Washington administration, noted that more than half of the workers in the cotton mills of Great Britain were children. He maintained that in an industrial America "women and children are rendered more useful, and the latter more early useful, by manufacturing establishments, than they would otherwise be." Furthermore, children "who would otherwise be idle" could become a ready source of cheap labor.[5] Tench Coxe of Philadelphia supported Alexander Hamilton in the belief that labor was good for children. "It was perceived," he wrote in 1794, "that children, too young for labour, could be kept from idleness and rambling, and of course from early temptations to vice, by placing them for a time in manufactories."[6]

When the Industrial Revolution in the United States took wing in the 1820s only five million people lived in the country. The expansion of industry brought in millions more and by the start of the Civil War, the American population exceeded thirty million. At war's end America entered its Gilded Age in which the few became immensely wealthy off the labor of the many. The mine owners, railroad moguls, factory owners and steel barons lived opulent lives. Workers' wages, by contrast, were so low that it took the work of both parents and their children to pay the rent and put bread on the table. These children left school early to work long hours for very little money, and they handed the pay envelopes to their parents. In 1890, most families in America earned less than $400 a year, with $550 needed for a decent life. Dire necessity drove parents, especially immigrant parents, to send their under-age children to work.

Mass immigration brought many more children into the workforce who were willing to work for low wages. Little people worked as bobbin boys and girls in the textile mills and breaker-boys and mule handlers in the mines. There were telegraph boys, rushing around town on their bicycles delivering messages. Little boys without shoes sold newspapers early in the morning or set up shoeshine stands. Children worked in canneries, shucked oysters or cleaned shrimp. Children worked with their sharecropping parents picking cotton, fruit or vegetables. They worked in the hosiery mills, glass factories, and in the tenement house industries, making paper flowers, baskets or sewing clothes. They were employed in department stores as sales girls and in hotels as bellhops. Children cleaned chimneys, smoked as they made cigars and worked as domestic servants. Leaving home early in the morning they carried their tin lunch pails to the factory or mine where they toiled twelve or more hours a day. They went on strike with the grownups. Little miners crept on their hands and knees working a coal vein only three feet high. They contracted black lung disease. Winter and summer their little fingers removed the slate and rock from the coal or picked cotton or cut sardines. Their hands hardened, cracked and bled; their faces were pale and sad. Without shoes they scampered on and off the spinning machines to remove full bobbins of cotton thread and replace them with empty ones; all for forty to ninety cents a day. Working children ran high risks of being maimed or killed at work. Many youngsters burned to death or leaped out of the windows of burning factories.

Child labor pervaded American life, especially from 1870 to 1920. The 1870 United States Census showed that 765,000 children aged fifteen years or younger worked, comprising one in seventeen of all persons gainfully employed. The 1880 Census noted an increase in child labor. Rather than attend school, the children of the poor worked in agriculture, the mills and mines to aid their parents. By 1890, one child in five under the age of sixteen years was put to work, comprising one-fifth of the total work force. By the 1880s both Germany and England had reduced child labor to below 5 percent of all workers. The United States, with 6.43 percent of its work force below age fifteen, was slightly better than Italy with 7.08 percent.

In 1900, the population of the United States reached 70,212,108. The United States Census of that year listed 1,752,187 children under the age of sixteen gainfully employed, comprising 6 percent of the nation's workforce; one child in five under the age of fifteen, boys and girls alike, was at work. Two-thirds of these children were engaged in agriculture, mostly working with their parents. The other concentrations of child labor were laborers, clerks, messenger and office boys, miners, cotton mill operatives, sweatshop workers, and cigar and cigarette makers. In all likelihood the official counts of laboring children in the censuses were underestimates as they did not include children working at home or children whose parents lied that they were older.

The last two decades of the nineteenth century saw a rise in child labor. In Philadelphia by 1900 15 percent of 13-year-old boys had left school and entered the labor force. (Among immigrant children up to a third of the 13-year-olds were working.) Among the 15-year-old boys more than half were working and among those over 17 years 70 percent were on the job and only 10 percent at school.[7] At the start of the twentieth century the streets of American cities were filled with children selling newspapers, shining shoes, hawking fruits and vegetables, selling flowers and baskets, delivering messengers or setting out early to work in sweatshops or cigar factories.

From the beginning of industrialization American firms faced stiff competition from imported goods, and sought to raise the tariffs against foreign goods. Companies repeatedly cut costs and employed cheaper labor. Immigrants followed the patterns of their native countries by insisting that their sons and daughters enter the mills and mines at an early age. Parents perjured themselves by claiming that their little children were of age to work. Many justified child labor as building character and the antidote to idleness. Horatio Alger Jr. wrote a series of popular rags-to-riches novels about determined youngsters who worked their way out of poverty into middle-class respectability and even wealth. Benjamin Franklin, Andrew Carnegie and Thomas Edison succeeded brilliantly, but most child workers soon lost their dreams and were dulled by a lack of education and long hours of repetitive work.

The Progressive Era, starting late in the nineteenth century, sought to uplift the poor, improve the lot of the workers, give votes to women, extend education, abolish child labor and offer hope to children of the poor. Mining and mill disasters included children among the dead and injured. Reformers regarded child labor as an evil akin to slavery that deprived children of the joy of play, learning and character development, dooming them to remain illiterate and sick in body and mind. These reformers championed the rights of children and battled for stricter state and federal child labor laws, and demanded that children remain full time in school at least until age sixteen. In 1904 activists from the South and the North formed the National Child Labor Committee (NCLC) and hired the photographer Lewis Wickes Hine to document the practice of child labor. He crisscrossed the country taking five thousand pictures of children as young as five years at work. The Hine archive is a national treasure illustrating the plight of the working child.

After 1900 the number of children in the United States who were gainfully employed began to decline, falling to 1,622,000 in 1910, 1,437,000 in 1920, and only 667,000 in 1930, being 1.37 percent of the total labor force. Child labor was tenacious, particularly in the South. It rose again during the Great Depression. The battle to end child labor continued until 1938 with the New Deal and passage of the Fair Labor Standards Act. Child labor is the cheapest form of labor and the mill and mine owners fought long and hard to justify the practice. When labor became too expensive in New England the mill owners — wealthy, college educated, the cream of the Northern elite — moved production to the South, where labor came cheap and the child labor laws were much less restrictive. Years later these jobs left the United States and were outsourced to low wage nations.

The story of child labor in America begins with the picking of cotton in the South, and the spinning of cotton into thread and weaving it into cloth, done in the cotton mills of the Northeast.

1

Cotton and Cotton Mills

*But in the picking of cotton, men, women and children, both white and
black, are employed exactly as they were in the days before the invention
of the cotton gin.... Pickers usually carry a sack strapped over their shoul-
ders and as they walk or crawl along the rows the cotton is picked from
the stalk by hand and dropped into the sack.*
— Eugene Clyde Brooks, 1911

Oh! Isn't it a pity, such a pretty girl as I,
Should be sent to a factory to pine away and die.
Oh! I cannot be a slave,
I will not be a slave!
For I'm so fond of liberty,
That I cannot be a slave.
— Song of the striking Lowell mill-girls, 1836

Picking Cotton

Sugar cane needs a hot climate year round but cotton can tolerate cooler weather. That
is why slaves were shipped to the Caribbean to grow cane and to the American South to
grow cotton. Cotton was brought to Virginia in 1607. The ripe cotton boll opens into four
sections to expose its white, fluffy fibers. Imbedded among the fibers are some fifty black
cottonseeds to a boll. Growing cotton for profit was difficult because the seeds stick so
firmly to the fibers. It took a day's work to remove by hand the seeds from two pounds of
cotton. In 1792 Eli Whitney, a graduate of Yale, moved to Mulberry Grove near Savannah,
Georgia, to teach the children of Catharine Greene. This large plantation was awarded by
the State of Georgia to her husband, Rhode Island-born general Nathanael Greene, the lib-
erator of the South at the close of the Revolutionary War. After seeing the slaves laboring
hard to remove the cottonseeds by hand, Whitney invented the cotton gin — a hand-churned
wooden roller with wire spikes that dislodged the seeds. Whitney's crude invention soon
led to larger cotton gins powered by draught animals or flowing water, capable of de-seeding
500 pounds of cotton a day.

The cotton mills of England and Scotland were the main customers for Southern cotton, especially the strong, long and silk-like Sea Island fiber. In 1784, 71 bales of American
cotton were shipped to the port of Liverpool. In 1800, 72,730 bales were shipped. At the
start of the American Civil War, shipments of cotton from the South to England had reached
a colossal 2,400,527 bales. The textile mills of New England were another large and growing

market for Southern cotton. In 1860, the South produced 1,918,701,000 pounds of raw cotton, which, at 15 cents a pound seemed enough money to separate from the Union. From 1790 until the start of the Civil War, the slave population of the South was about one-half that of the free white population. In 1860, the South had eight million free whites and four million black slaves. One-half of the slaves were engaged in planting, cultivating, and picking, de-seeding, bailing and shipping raw cotton.

In slavery, little children and adults alike picked cotton. In 1800, advertisements for ginners appeared "calling for Negro boys and girls ten or twelve years old to help at the machines." Basil Hall, the Scottish naval officer who toured America in 1827 and 1828, considered that among plantation owners and their overseers whipping slaves "is not more strict than necessary for the maintenance of a proper degree of authority, without which the whole framework of society would be blown to atoms." Another observed: "The only whipping of slaves that I have seen in Virginia has been of those wild, lazy children as they are being broke in to work."[1] In 1839, the American Anti-Slavery Society published its account, *American Slavery, As It Is: Testimony of a Thousand Witnesses*, depicting slavery's cruelty. In the cotton fields the overseers "ascertain how much labor a slave can perform in a day.... The slaves work very hard; that the lash is almost universally applied by the end of the day, if they fail to perform their task in the cotton-picking season. You will see them with their baskets of cotton, slowly bending their way to the cotton-house, where each basket is weighed.... Here comes the mother, with her children; she does not know whether herself, or her children, or all of them, must take the lash. "Slave children aged nine to twelve were kept busy from dawn to dusk during the cotton picking season — August to the

Itinerant family, father, mother and five children, picking cotton c. 1910; the more children there are, the more the family earns picking cotton.

end of December. Early in the season the cotton bolls low on the stalk are the first to open, requiring constant stooping. The little children worked the row, emptying their bag at the end for weighing.[2]

The Civil War left the South broken and impoverished. The plantation owners and gentry soon regained their property, leaving most, black and white alike, without land. By necessity they became tenant farmers and sharecroppers — renting for cash or a share of the crops owned by the landlord. With wages from cotton-picking so low a large family, with many children to do unskilled work, was an absolute necessity to survive. In his 1941 report on tenant farmers in the Deep South, James Agee wrote, "And children come into the world chiefly that they may help with the work and through their help the family may increase itself." These children did not regularly attend school and had little for clothing or food. Sharecropper and tenant families used all available hands to work the cotton fields to earn enough money for a shack, basic clothing and barely enough food. Poorly endowed orphanages in the South, originally built to house children left on their own by the Civil War, sent out the little ones to pick cotton.

The Industrial Commission of the U.S. Congress on agriculture and agricultural labor in 1901 learned that "on the cotton plantations of the South it is customary for women and children to hoe and pick cotton. Children as young as six years of age sometimes pick cotton, and boys of ten become plowmen. The child labor on farms is not confined to negro children."

One witness gave the following matter-of-fact responses to the questions of the incredulous congressmen:

Q: You say a boy of 10 is a good plow hand?
A: Yes, sir.
Q: And from 8 up they work on the farm?
A: Yes, sir, and they pick cotton from 6 up.
Q: Do girls pick cotton?
A: Yes, sir, and chop cotton too; that means they use the hoe to cultivate the cotton.
Q: You say it is nothing unusual to see boys plowing at 10 years of age?
A: No, sir, oh, no.
Q: Is that general in both races — colored and white — working the children as young as that in the fields?
A: Yes, sir.
Q: Is it found to be a matter of necessity, is it?
A: Yes sir, on account of low prices and the families they have to feed.[3]

In their provocative 1914 book *Children in Bondage,* Edwin Markham, Benjamin Lindsay and George Creel report sarcastically that "a quarter of a million children are in the cotton fields of Texas. Even a baby of four, properly prodded and losing no time with teddy bears or afternoon naps, can pick from six to eight pounds a day; and a boy of five, not fooling away his hours in a kindergarten, can pick thirty pounds. Four children in one family from four to sixteen, have the proud record of picking in a day four times their own weight. A boy of ten, who spends no precious time at school or swimming-hole, and who has a proper appreciation of the high commercial end he serves in helping on a bumper crop of cotton, can pick one hundred pounds a day. Think of the vacuum in a mind engaged in gathering together this nothingness all day long, from blistering August to bitter December."[4] Whole families continued this impoverished way of life well into the twentieth century until the work was taken over by cotton-picking machines and the families migrated to work in the factories of the North.

Cotton Mills

The American Industrial Revolution began at the close of the eighteenth century with the use of water-powered machines to spin cotton thread. Samuel Slater, who introduced the Arkwright power cotton-spinning machine to America, was a product of the English apprenticeship system. He came from Belper, county of Derbyshire in England, where his father farmed his own land. Their neighbor was the illustrious Jedediah Strutt, who grew rich by his invention of the Derby Ribbed Stocking Machine, a foot- and hand-powered knitting machine. This invention boosted the number of craftsmen in the English Midlands making socks and mittens by machine, stimulating the demand for spun cotton. Strutt formed a partnership with the venerable Sir Richard Arkwright, the inventor of the spinning frame, to spin cotton into thread using water power — one of the great inventions that launched the Industrial Revolution.

When Samuel was fourteen he was bound out to Jedediah Strutt as an apprentice and over the next seven years learned all there was to know about the power cotton spinning machines. He was a bright and inventive lad and found ways to make the machines work more efficiently. At age twenty-one and at the end of his indentures, Samuel Slater left England with the hope of using his knowledge of spinning machines to make his fortune in America. In 1790, he joined the wealthy merchant Moses Brown to open a cotton-spinning mill in Pawtucket, Rhode Island. He paid poorly; Samuel employed children aged seven to twelve to work full days, six days a week. These children came from local poor families with little learning. They were Smith Wilkinson (ten years old and Slater's future brother-in-law); the Jenks children, Jabez, John and Sylvanus; the Turpin children, Charles, Arnold, Eunice and Ann; and Otis Burrows. To improve their education and to assuage his conscience, Slater set up for the children a Sunday school in his home where he taught religion as well reading and writing. In 1793, after three years of hard work, Slater opened a new and larger mill with an Arkwright machine and seventy-two spindles powered by the flow of the Blackstone River, ready to produce cotton thread.

George Savage White was born in Bath, England, and trained as an Episcopal minister before coming to Rhode Island. He wrote several books on religious questions and one, published in 1836, on the life of Samuel Slater as "The Father of American Manufactures." White believed that "multitudes of women and children have been kept out of vice, simply by being employed, and thus, instead of being destitute, provided with an abundance of comfortable sustenance." Too much money, he thought, was a bad thing since "many a youth has been ruined by beginning with high wages." A man of moderation, the Reverend White sought a balance between wealth that "can lead to idleness (and) poverty that feels the burden of degradation while the power is lost to remove it." Having observed child labor both in England and the United States, in 1827 he sent a twenty-one-item questionnaire about child labor to "several heads of manufacturing establishments in New England." His study would not meet modern standards of scientific inquiry, and he did not ask the opinions of the children, but the responses were interesting nonetheless.

Smith Wilkinson of Pomfret, Connecticut (an early employee and a relative of Samuel

Slater), responded that it is good for children to work. In his mill children were put to work twelve hours a day, six days a week, leaving them "no time to spend in idleness or vicious amusements." Another responded that "children under ten are generally unprofitable at any price, and it is seldom that they are employed, unless their parents work in the mill, and they are brought in to do light chores such as setting the spools on the frame." The Wilkinson factory of Pomfret was so dependent on child labor that in 1806 it bought a thousand acres of farmland "to give employment to the parents of the children employed in the factory."[5] A factory in Newmarket, New Hampshire, employed two hundred and fifty females, five males and twenty overseers. Only nine girls and two boys were under fifteen years, and "in every instance the children under fifteen reside with the parents or guardians in the village." The children attended school six months of the year and worked six months in the mill.

On March 25, 1793, Ebenezar Hall of Bethlehem, Connecticut, advertised for four apprentices to work in his cotton manufactory. On December 30 of that year he advertised for "two or three lively lads as apprentices" to learn weaving and cutting of cotton cloth. On May 16, 1795, the firm of Livingston, Dickson & McIntosh of Connecticut advertised for "boys and girls from the age of ten to fourteen" to work in their cotton mill. The *Federal Gazette* of Baltimore on January 4, 1808, carried an advertisement from the Baltimore Cotton Manufactory for "a number of boys and girls from eight to twelve years ...to whom constant employment and encouraging wages will be given."

Others in America followed the example set by Samuel Slater of establishing cotton spinning factories and employing children to work in them. John Ewing placed an advertisement in the *Connecticut Journal* of May 4, 1795 for "any number of boys and girls from the age of ten to fourteen to serve as apprentices" in his New Haven cotton and woolen manufactory. In return for "good and comfortable maintenance, clothing and schooling" the children would receive "instruction in the various branches of the factory." In Maryland, the Union Manufacturing Company opened in 1810 with 2,800 spindles. "From the beginning there was a system of apprenticeships for bringing into the service of the company children and youths, and providing for them a school and religious instruction, clothing and board." In 1794, the Englishman Henry Wansey toured the Dickson Cotton Factory, near New York City. "They are training up women and children to the business," he recalled, "of whom I saw 20 or 30 at work."[6] Their lot was not an easy one. When Josiah Quincy, future mayor of Boston toured southern New England in 1801, he saw many little children at work in mills. "In the process of turning cotton from its rough into every variety of marketable thread, such as cleaning, carding, spinning, winding etc., are here performed by machinery operating by water wheels only by children from four to ten years old, and one superintendent. Above one hundred of the former are employed at the rate of from 12 to 25 cents for a day's labor." Compassion "calls us to pity these little creatures, plying in a contracted room, among flyers and cogs, at an age when nature requires for them air, space and sports. There was a dull dejection in the countenance of all of them."[7]

The American Industrial Revolution evolved in Waltham, Massachusetts, where, in 1814, Francis Cabot Lowell built his Boston Manufacturing Company, in which cotton shipped from the South was spun into thread and woven into cloth by machinery powered by the flow of the Charles River. Lowell assembled a talented team to make his mill a success. Nathan Appleton was one of Boston's leading and wealthiest merchants; Patrick Tracy Jackson, Lowell's brother-in-law, managed the mill; and Paul Moody, a mechanical genius, built and ran the machinery. Waltham was then a small village. To attract workers, Francis Cabot Lowell built boarding houses close to his mill. Young women between the ages of seventeen and twenty years old, largely the daughters of New England farm families, were attracted to Waltham by the promise of cash payments for their work. The success of the Boston Manufacturing Company encouraged the owners to build a second, then a third mill at Waltham using all the power of the river to turn the waterwheels and the machinery.

The domestic cotton textile industry of the United States was spurred by the War of 1812 that cut off British imports and by the resounding success of the Boston Manufacturing Company. By 1816, one hundred thousand people in the United States were employed in the cotton textile industry with capital in excess of $40 million. According to *A History of the American Manufactures from 1608 to 1860,* there were 10,000 men over seventeen years, 60,000 women and girls and 24,000 "boys under seventeen years of age," suggesting that more than half of all textile workers then were children under seventeen years. "Manufacturing was considered favorable to morale, as the education of children was attended to in most large factories, particularly by Sunday school."[8] The Boston Manufacturing Company was the exception as most of the early American cotton mills hired little children. By 1809, a total of eight-seven mills operated, mostly in New England, each employing about "five men and thirty-five women and children."

Francis Cabot Lowell died in 1817, aged forty-three years. The profits of the Waltham mill attracted other Boston merchants to shift their money from cloth imported from Great Britain and India, to investing in domestic production. Appleton, Jackson and Moody saw their opportunity for expansion by harnessing the power of the mighty Merrimack River close by the Pawtucket Falls at the village of East Chelmsford. The Merrimack River was used to float logs from the forests of New Hampshire to the shipbuilding town of Newburyport. To prevent the logs being smashed to pieces by the falls, they had to be taken out of the fast flowing waters, transported by ox-cart beyond the falls and rolled back down river. Late in the eighteenth century the Pawtucket Canal was dug to the south of the river to circumvent the falls and allow the logs a continuous passage down river. The Embargo of 1807 and the War of 1812 against the British destroyed ship building in Newburyport and made the Pawtucket Canal redundant.

Through their agents, Nathan Appleton, Paul Moody and Patrick Tracy Jackson bought the water rights, the Pawtucket Canal and four hundred acres of land between the canal and the river. Here they built America's first industrial city of Lowell, named in honor of Francis Cabot Lowell. In 1822, the Merrimack Manufacturing Company was the first of the great mills of Lowell, followed over the next two decades by the Hamilton, Appleton, Lowell, Lawrence, Massachusetts, Boott, Suffolk and Tremont mills, making Lowell an American manufacturing powerhouse. Other New England towns copied the Lowell example, boosting the region to the nation's leader in textile manufacture.

Each of the great Lowell mills built boarding houses to house the young Yankee women coming off the farms to earn money. At first Lowell followed the example of Waltham by hiring workers seventeen and older, mostly young women, known as the Mill Girls of Lowell. Soon, however, competition from abroad as well as between the domestic mills put pressure on salaries; the Lowell mills cut wages and hired children as young as nine.

Born in Boston in 1825, Harriet was one of four children of William and Harriet Hanson. When the girl was six years old her father died leaving her mother to find a way to keep the family together. Mother Harriet opened a small shop selling food, candy and firewood. Times were very hard with the family living in one room above the shop, sharing a single bed "two at the foot and three at the head." The earnings from the shop barely sustained the family and Mrs. Hanson decided, when Harriet was age ten, to move to Lowell to take charge of a boarding house at the Tremont Mill, where she took care of forty mill girls. Little Harriet attended school and helped her mother in the boarding house. "Needing money which I could earn," wrote Harriet in her book *Looms and Spindles*, her mother allowed Harriet "at my urgent request (for I wanted to earn money like the other little girls), to go to work at the mill. I worked first in the spinning-room as a 'doffer.' The doffers were the very youngest girls, whose work was to doff, or take off, the full bobbins, and replace them with the empty ones." Many years later, Harriet Hanson wrote:

> I can see myself now, racing down the alley between the spinning-frames, carrying in front of me a bobbin-box bigger than I was. These mites had to be very swift in their movements, so as not to keep the spinning frames stopped long. And they worked only about fifteen minutes in every hour. The rest of the time was their own, and when the overseer was kind they were allowed to read, knit or even go outside in the mill-yard to play ... .We were paid two dollars a week and how proud I was when my turn came to stand up on the bobbin-box and write my name in the paymaster's book, and how indignant I was when he asked me if I could "write." "Of course, I can," said I, and he smiled as he looked down at me.[9]

The work hours for the girls regardless of age was from five in the morning to seven at night, with a half hour for breakfast and for dinner. "Even the doffers were on duty," continues Harriet Hanson, "nearly fourteen hours a day and this was the greatest hardship in the lives of these children." Not until 1842 were the hours of children under twelve years working in the Lowell mills reduced by law to ten hours a day. When not working in the mill, Harriet helped her mother in the boarding house, read books and tried her hand at writing stories. She considered herself fortunate, especially when compared with the children working in English mills, who "were treated badly and were whipped by the cruel overseers."

By 1836, the growth and optimism of the city of Lowell was shattered when the mills, in fierce competition with each other and with imports from Europe, lowered wages by 15 percent and took more from the workers for board and lodging. Harriet, only eleven years old at the time, remembers taking part in the strike where some 1,500 girls walked out and closed down production. "Naturally," she wrote defiantly, "I took sides with the strikers." The 1836 Lowell strike did not succeed and the workers had to accept lower wages and benefits. Harriet's mother was warned by the mill agent not to allow her to join strikes with the older girls. "Your daughter is a child, and her you could control." Starting in 1840, Harriet and others in a quest for self-improvement and literary expression, joined together to write for *The Lowell Offering*. In 1848, she married William Robinson and left the mills to start a life as mother, housewife and writer. Later in her life, with the support of her daughter Hattie, she joined the National Woman Suffrage Association and campaigned for the right of women to vote.

Lucy Larcom, born in the port town of Beverly, Massachusetts, in 1824 describes in her book *A New England Girlhood* her life in Lowell, where she lived and worked at the same time as Harriet Hanson. Lucy was the ninth of ten children. Her father, Benjamin Larcom, was a sea captain who died when Lucy was eleven years old. "It was a hard time for my mother and her children," wrote Lucy. Like Harriet Hanson's mother, Mrs. Larcom moved to Lowell to run a boarding house, for the Lawrence Mill workers.

Lowell suited the Puritan mindset of the Larcom family, as the town "had a high reputation for good order, morality, piety and all that was dear to the old-fashioned New England heart." Lucy, with her interest in poetry and books, was sent to the local grammar school and also helped her mother with the cleaning of the boarding house. But money was very short and it was decided that "the children will have to leave school and go into the mills. The mill-agent did not want to take us little girls, but assented on condition we should be sure to attend school the full number of months prescribed each year." The first job of the eleven-year-old Lucy Larcom was at the Boott Mill "just to change the bobbins in the spinning-frames every three-quarters of an hour or so, with half a dozen other little girls. When I came back at night, the family began to pity me for my long, tiresome day's work, but I laughed and said: 'Why, it is nothing but fun. It is just like play.'" Lucy's early enthusiasm wore off once she learned the "mysteries of the dressing-room and the weaving room." She tried to hide the smell of the oil by bringing in flowers. She "never cared much for machines. The buzzing and hissing and whizzing of pulleys and rollers and spindles and flyers around me often grew tiresome." It was forbidden to bring books into the mill. Lucy wanted a life of the mind, poetry, verse and nature. She wrote such delightful poems and stories that a relative advised her mother to "keep what she writes till she grows up, and perhaps she will get money for it."

Lucy Larcom found a literary outlet by writing for *The Lowell Offering*. She left the mill at age twenty-one and moved to Illinois. Later she returned to Massachusetts to write and teach. She died in 1893, the year of the World's Columbian Exposition, held in Chicago.

Harriet Hanson and Lucy Larcom published their accounts of their working childhoods when they were mature adults and well-published authors. There are also many letters, less eloquent but heartfelt, from youngsters writing to parents or friends showing their loneliness and struggles to survive. Mary Paul came to work in Lowell when she was fifteen years old. On December 21, 1845, she wrote to her father in Bernard, Vermont:

Dear Father.

I am well which one comfort is. My life and health are spared while others are cut off. Last Thursday one girl fell down and broke her neck, which caused instant death. She was going in or coming out of the mill and fell down it being very icy. Last Thursday we were paid. In all I had six dollars and sixty cents, paid $4.68 for board. With the rest I got a pair of rubbers and a pair of 30-cent shoes. Perhaps you would like something about our regulations about going in and coming out of the mill. At half past six the bell rings for the girls to get up and at seven they are called to the mill. At half past 12 we have dinner, are called back again at one and stay till half past seven. I get along very well with my work. I can doff as fast as any girl in my room. If any girl wants employment I advise them to come to Lowell.

Three years later (November 5, 1848) despair was creeping into Mary's letters.

The work is very hard indeed and sometimes I think I shall not be able to endure it. I never worked so hard in my life but perhaps I shall get used to it. I suppose you have heard before this month that the wages are to be reduced on the 20th of this month.... The companies pretend they are losing immense sums every day and therefore are obliged to lessen the wages, but this seems perfectly absurd to me for they are constantly making repairs ... I expect to be paid two dollars a week but it will be dearly earned.

The Child at the Loom, drawing in the September 1906 issue of *Cosmopolitan Magazine*, by Warren Rockwell.

Mary Paul left the mill after four years of hard work and moved to New Jersey where she married and raised a family.

In 1832, reported the Reverend George S. White, American textile factories (largely in New England), employed 18,539 men who received on average $5 a week in pay, the 38,927 women received $2 and the 4,697 children (less than 8 percent of the labor force), only $1.75 a week. Colonel David Humphreys, once aide-de-camp to General Washington and a graduate of Yale, employed "a considerable number of children, many of them apprentices from New York almshouses."

As early as 1832 there were rumblings against the long hours of work inflicted on little children employed in the Massachusetts textile mills. The New England Association of Farmers, Mechanics and other Workingmen — an early trade union — resolved that "children should not be allowed to labor in factories from morning to night, without any time for healthy recreation and mental culture (because it) endangers their well-being and health." In 1836, Massachusetts ordered that children between the ages of twelve and fifteen years working "in manufactories shall attend school three months in each year."[10] In 1842, Massachusetts became the first state to limit the workday of children from fourteen to ten hours a day. In 1876, the commonwealth voted to prohibit children under ten from working in the mills. In 1883, the age was upped to 12 years, in 1888 to 13 years and in 1898 no children under 14 was permitted by law to work in the mills. Older children could work up to a maximum of fifty-eight hours a week. Instead of work at an early age, the commonwealth proposed "to give children better opportunities for education and enjoyment." Children fourteen to sixteen years old were permitted to work only if they could read or write and produce a certificate of school completion. Massachusetts employed inspectors to enter the mills to ensure that the children were hired according to the law. Liberal laws such as these were fought every inch of the way by the mill owners who argued that without work little children would become idle, and that they preferred work to school and wanted to help their families. Similar laws were passed in other states but were rarely enforced and young children continued to work in New England mills. In 1870, the mighty Pacific Mills of Lawrence, Massachusetts, employed 3,600 workers of whom 410 (over 11 percent) were children, many as young as 10 to 12 years of age.

Established by the Massachusetts General Court, the Bureau of Statistics of Labor kept detailed reports on workers and their wages. Henry F. Bedford tabulated these statistics for the years 1860, 1872, 1878 and 1881. Wages rose gradually over the years. Wages were highest in the boot and shoe industry and in the building trades and lowest in the cotton mills. In every category of work in the cotton mills, boys and girls earned half as much as adults. Adult openers and pickers earned $5 to $8 a week, while boys earned only $2.60 to $4. Cloth room males earned $5.50 to $8 a week, but boys and girls in the same category made only $4 to $5 a week.[11]

By the 1820s, the use of machinery to spin cotton into thread and weave it into cloth spread from the Northeast into the Mid-Atlantic States. The Manayunk section of Philadelphia, situated along the Schuylkill River, became a major textile center, with ten mills in 1828, increasing to twenty-four mills by 1850. It became known as the Manchester of America. Manayunk was far more exploitative than Lowell and got rid of most of the high price male labor, hiring instead women and young children. Half the labor force was made up of children younger than fifteen years of age, many as young as seven or eight. As elsewhere in industrialized America, children's wages in Philadelphia were low. According to Charles Parrow, conditions were so bad that an 1837 commission was unable to ban the employment of children ten years or younger. Ten-year-old children earned an average of 72 cents a week, twelve-year-old children 96 cents, fourteen-year-old children $1.20 and sixteen-year-olds, who could do the work of adults, earned only $1.44 a week, a pittance for a sixty-hour work week.

The textile industry moved from New England to the Mid-Atlantic States and then to the South. The Virginian William Gregg (1800–1867) advocated that the South should not only grow cotton but build the factories to make textiles. In 1844, he visited mills in Massachusetts and on his return established in South Carolina the Graniteville Manufacturing Company, based on what he had learned in the North. Gregg recruited managers and purchased machinery from Massachusetts to operate his mill, built houses for the workers and a school for their children. Cotton textile manufacture in the South barely survived the Civil War and remained depressed for a decade after. In 1878, a small town in Gaston County, North Carolina, was renamed Lowell in the hope that it would follow the path of its Massachusetts namesake. Due to the efforts of Edward Atkinson of Boston, the International Cotton Exposition was held in Atlanta, Georgia, in 1881 and attracted many New England companies, which displayed the latest machinery. The fair gave a great boost to the South not only to use machines to plant and reap cotton, but also machines to manufacture textiles. New textile mills in the South benefited from low priced land, low taxes, low fuel costs, cheap local cotton, and especially, a docile labor force, coming off the farms, willing to work long hours for little pay. After the Whitfield Mills of Newburyport, Massachusetts, failed in 1889 its machinery was sold to the Spartan Mills in the village of Spartanburg, South Carolina. Within ten years Spartanburg had twenty cotton mills and was known as "The Lowell of the South."

The exclusive Arkwright Club of Boston, formed in 1880, was made up of the treasurers of the leading cotton mills of northern New England. Named for Richard Arkwright, the inventor of the water-powered spinning machine, the club lobbied the legislatures of Massachusetts, New Hampshire and Maine against rising wages, the ten-hour work day and restrictions on child labor. No longer able to hold back the pressures of local labor, members of the club cast covetous eyes to the unrestricted South where mill wages were 40 percent lower.

In 1894 the Massachusetts Cotton Mills of Lowell built a subsidiary plant in Lindale, Georgia. The Dwight Manufacturing Company of Chicopee (incorporated in 1841) opposed new Massachusetts laws allowing only 48 hours of work weekly against sixty and over in the South. In 1894, Dwight sent the 23-year-old Howard Gardner Nichols, born in Haverhill and a graduate of Harvard University, to supervise the construction of its new mill in the South. Two years later, Nichols completed the mill with 150 workers cottages in Alabama City, Alabama, offering work to 500 people.

In 1899, William Croad Lovering, representative from Massachusetts in the United States Congress from 1897 to 1910, introduced a bill supported by the Arkwright Club to amend the federal Constitution by establishing a nationwide eight-hour workday in factories. The Lovering family was the owner of the vast Whittenton cotton mill in Taunton, Massachusetts. The family also owned a controlling share in the Merrimack Manufacturing Company and Massachusetts Cotton Mills of Lowell at the very time these mills were expanding to the South. A federally mandated standard workweek would reduce the labor cost advantage of the South. Representative William Lovering failed in his attempt to establish a level playing field between North and South cotton mills by an amendment to the Constitution.

Both Dwight and Massachusetts Cotton were soon making more money from their new mills in the South than the older ones in Massachusetts. "Georgia Cotton Mills Ahead: Massachusetts Owners Decide to Extend the Business to the Detriment of Lowell's Industry," ran the 1898 headline. The annual meeting held in Boston was told that "certain products of the Massachusetts Cotton mill at Lowell can be produced at the mill in Lindale, Ga., for a lower cost ...owing to the lower cost of manufacture due to cheaper wages, longer working hours, lower taxation, and lower cost of power." The shareholders voted to instruct the directors "to consider the possibility of an extension of the business in Georgia" and curtailing activities in Massachusetts.[12] Next came the announcement that "the Merrimac mills of Lowell, one of the largest and oldest cotton manufacturing plants in the United States, will be moving South," putting 3,600 jobs at risk.[13] On July 9, 1900, the Merrimack Manufacturing Company opened its subsidiary in Huntsville, Alabama, with employment for 750. A second mill opened in Huntsville in 1903, employing 1,100 more. The company built 279-workers' cottages, offered at low rents from 50 to 75 cents a week. The village associated with the mills grew and the company erected Merrimack Hall as a community center, with a school (following the company's practice in Lowell), two barber shops and a bicycle store. Reporting in 1901, the Merrimack Mills and the Massachusetts Cotton Mills detailed the advantages of producing cotton textiles in the new Southern mills over the

A group of boys working as doffers and sweepers at a cotton mill, Newberry, South Carolina, February 10, 1908. Newberry mills were among the first in the United States to use steam-power.

older Northern mills. The machinery costs were the same but fuel and cotton were cheaper in the South, wages 30 percent less, yet workers in the South put in eight hours more work each week than workers in Lowell.

Elbert Green Hubbard, born 1856 in Bloomington, Illinois, a true son of capitalism, worked as a traveling salesman for the Larkin Soap Company. Later, he changed his views by espousing anarchic and leftist ideas. He reacted against factory-made products by founding Roycroft, an Arts and Crafts movement in East Aurora, New York, where individual expression was encouraged. Hubbard, a charismatic figure, established a press and published books and magazines to propagate his ideas. Hubbard noted in 1905, "Next to Massachusetts, South Carolina manufactures more cotton cloth than any other state in the nation. The cotton mills of South Carolina are mostly owned and operated by New England capital." The companies claimed that they had moved to the South to be closer to the cotton, "but the actual reason is that in South Carolina there is no law regulating child labor ...the result is child labor of so horrible a type that African slavery was a paradise compared with it." The overwrought Hubbard claimed, "Boys and girls from the age of six years and upwards are employed. They usually work from six o'clock in the morning until seven at night." Most of the children went barefoot and wore tattered clothes. To keep the little children awake, the supervisors resorted to "shaking the sleepers, shouting in their ears, lifting them to their feet, and in a few instances kicking the delinquents into wakefulness." By moving to the South and employing many children, a cotton mill saved $2,000 a week. "This means a saving of $100,000 a year, and a mill having a capital of $1,000,000 thus gets a gain of 10 percent per annum." Capitalism is king, wrote Hubbard, not cotton. "The shareholders live in Boston and all they want is their dividends."[14]

Irene Ashby, a slender, vivacious Englishwoman, graduate of Westfield College, a women-only school in Hampstead, London, became a passionate advocate for poor children. She was a woman "of good social standing who enjoyed a life of garden parties, theatres and balls" who decided after graduation "to help the masses by living amongst them and working in the West London Social Guild, a settlement house." In 1900 she was hired by Samuel Gompers of the American Federation of Labor to come to the United States and report on child labor in the Southern textile mills, where she found conditions "too horrible for belief." Her 1902 report created shockwaves. Ashby wrote:

> There are American children dragged into the mills when scarcely out of their babyhood, without education, without opportunity, being robbed of health morally and physically and forced to labor ... Mattie, the little one standing beside me, is six years old. She is a spinner inside a cotton mill twelve hours a day. She stands in a four-feet passageway between the spinning frames where the cotton is spun from coarse to finer thread. From daylight to dark she is in the midst of the ceaseless throb and racket of the machinery.... I found a tiny child of five years in the spinning room, her hair was covered with threads that had fallen back into her hair from the frame as she worked. She was helper to her sister. Neither child knew her age, but, a girl of eight, standing near, told me that they were seven and five, and worked there all day long. It is a common sight to see children of cotton operatives stretched on the bed dressed as they come from the mills in the morning, too weary to do anything but fling themselves down to rest.

Working in a mill endangered the health of the children, some of whom suffer "a horrible form of dropsy." Irene Ashby continued: "A doctor tells me that ten percent of the children who go to work before 12 years of age, after five years contract consumption. The lint forms in their lungs a perfect cultivating place for tuberculosis, while the change from the hot atmosphere of the mill to the night chill or morning air often brings on pneumonia, which frequently, if not the cause of death, is the forerunner of consumption."[15]

Irene Ashby returned to England, married Alfred Newt MacFadyen, a British army officer, and moved to South Africa, where he joined the staff of the prime minister, Sir Alfred Milner. Surrounded by arch-colonialists, Irene changed her focus from the rights of children to the enfranchisement of women. For years she was president of the Women's Enfranchisement League of the Cape Colony. Her acceptance of the franchise for white women only alienated liberals like Olive Schreiner who wanted the franchise extended to all women, regardless of race. White women in South Africa had to wait until 1930 to enjoy rights equal to white men. Universal suffrage in that country only came in 1992 after the fall of apartheid.

More and more mills cut production and jobs in New England and transferred work to the South. These Southern factories were built with New England money, designed by New England architects, staffed by managers from New England, and were engineered and fitted with machinery made in New England. The company towns in the South were built in the New England tradition of providing housing for the workers, a company store, schools, libraries, sports and health facilities, and churches.

In 1904 the average male worker in the cotton mills of New England was earning $440 a year, women $340 and children under sixteen years $230. In North Carolina and other

Southern states wages of men, women and children were half as much. These figures are all the more remarkable since the mill workers in the Northeast were largely immigrants, while native-born workers dominated in the South. By the start of the twentieth century, the mills in the Northeast and Mid-Atlantic states had largely done away with child labor (children under fourteen years) while in the South one in eight cotton mill workers was a child. According to the statistician Isaac A. Hourwich (writing in 1921) these differences in labor costs accounted for the decline of the Northern mills and the growth in the South. The accelerated transfer to the South devastated the New England textile industry. The vast Boott Cotton Mills of Lowell started to fail early in the twentieth century, the Lowell Manufacturing Company closed in 1916, and the Assabet mills of Maynard in 1930. The Dwight Manufacturing Company of Chicopee, the town's largest taxpayer, shut down in 1927 with the loss of 2,000 jobs. The machine shops in Lowell were demolished in 1932. The Merrimack Manufacturing Company in Lowell limped along until it was finally shut down in 1958 and the buildings were demolished. The Whittenton Mills of Taunton shut down its mill, leaving 350,000 sq. ft of space empty. In 1923, Lowell Bleachery, founded in 1832, set up Lowell Bleachery South in Griffin, Georgia.

New England mill owners faced restrictions in the use of child labor and were confronted by militant trade unions fighting for shorter hours of work, better conditions and higher pay. In 1880, 14 percent of all the mill workers in New England were younger than age sixteen. Laws restricting child labor were taking effect and by 1890 the percentage

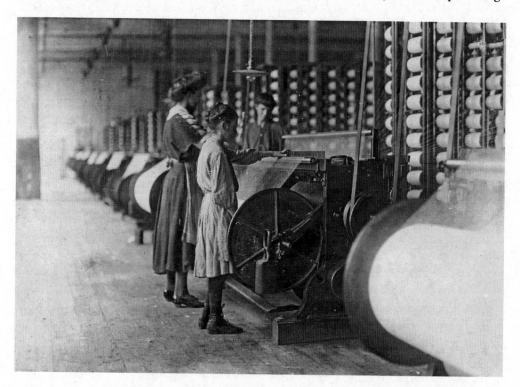

Girl tending a warping machine in a mill in Gastonia, North Carolina. The town of Gastonia grew from 256 in 1877 to over 30,000 in 1930. The workers in the 130 cotton mills were largely mountain folk leaving their exhausted farms for jobs in the mills.

Boys covered with lint, leaving work at a Gastonia cotton mill, c. 1909. Jobs in the South were scarce and the locals were leery of outsiders. Children like these ten- to twelve-year-old boys were willing to work. In 1909, W.T. Love of the Spencer Mountain Cotton Mill said: "I think boys should be allowed to work after they are ten years old.... My observation is that the majority of cotton-mill boys get into all kinds of mischief and many develop into hoboes before they are twelve years old, if not at school or at work."

dropped to 7 percent and by 1905, to 6 percent. In the South, unions did not yet exist or were weak. The new jobs in the South went to impoverished white tenant and sharecropping families, with over a quarter of the jobs going to the cheapest workers, children under fifteen years of age. From 1880 to 1905, one-quarter of all the workers in the fast expanding Southern textile industry were less than sixteen years old. Employing children in the South kept all wages low, further encouraging the shift of the American textile industry from New England to the Southern states.

In 1908, the photographer Lewis Wickes Hine began his momentous work for the National Child Labor Committee documenting the employment of children in American factories and farms. He took pictures of child workers at the Merrimack Manufacturing Company in Lowell and at its subsidiary, the Merrimack Manufacturing Company of Huntsville, Alabama. He also snapped pictures outside the Massachusetts Cotton Company of Lowell and its subsidiary, the Massachusetts Cotton Company of Lindale, Georgia.

On June 18, 1898, the United States Congress authorized an investigation by the U.S. Industrial Commission into the work and wages of women and children. The detailed investigation found that "child labor is employed most extensively in textile factories.... Fully

Fourteen- and fifteen-year-old workers at the Granite textile mill, Fall River, Massachusetts, 1915. The mill was the site in 1877 of a tragic fire that claimed many young lives. In 1915, despite stringent laws, children still found jobs in the Granite and other northern textile mills.

one-third of the cotton factory operatives in a certain town of Georgia are under 14 years of age.... In the Southern cotton mills, 12 appears to be the age at which children are ordinarily expected to begin work; but some of the mills employ children under that age — sometimes as young as 9, 8 or even 7 years."[16] By the start of the twentieth century the South, chiefly Alabama, Georgia and the Carolinas, had gained 83,000 textile mill jobs, of which some 25,000 (thirty percent) were filled by children under fifteen years of age, and many from six to nine years. Textiles were fast becoming a major industry in the South. Parents and their children — almost all white — worked in the Southern cotton mills. Joseph Winters worked in the same mill as Estelle, his fourteen-year-old daughter. Caumine Roberts and his thirteen-year-old daughter worked in the Florence cotton mill. Dilard Mathies was a spinner as was his oldest daughter, thirteen-year-old Eva. In New England, there were still 11,000 children age fifteen or younger, comprising only 6 percent of a larger labor force. In the Mid-Atlantic States there were some 4,300 children in the mills (12.5 percent of the total labor force). These children earned only 30 to 40 cents a day, a major factor in holding down labor costs.

The issue of child labor was hotly debated late in the nineteenth century and for years to come. In 1901, the United States Industrial Commission, headed by Senator James H. Kyle of South Dakota, held hearings on the industrial health of the nation in general and child labor in particular. It was the position of the U.S. Department of Labor that "children are employed in Southern textile mills at entirely too early an age. Many go to work at 8 years of age. Farmers come from the country and naturally seek to put all the members of their families into employment also." A Southern mill owner, Mr. McAdam, told the committee that "children learn very rapidly — much better than grown parents — and some of them become very good hands." In several states the efforts to pass laws forbidding child labor in the mills "have not succeeded." Governor Allen D. Chandler of Georgia testified that "widows cannot support themselves and their children without the children's help." Another witness told of a man earning $2 a day who was fired and replaced by his own son at $1 a day.

Kensington, Pennsylvania, lies a few miles northeast of the center of Philadelphia. In the nineteenth century it was one of the largest textile producing centers in the United States, especially carpets and hosiery. Labor grew militant with demands for higher pay, reduced hours of work, and end to the practice of child labor. On June 1, 1903, seventy-five thousand textile workers went out on strike, of whom "at least ten thousand were little children." The strike shut down six hundred factories. Mary Harris Jones (1837–1930), better known as Mother Jones and well into her 60s, took up their cause. Mother Jones was famous as a tenacious labor organizer, much feared by the mill owners. She arrived in Kensington on June 14, when the strike entered its third week. In her autobiography, Mother Jones described the children who joined the Kensington strike.

> Everyday little children came into the Union Headquarters. Some with their hands off, some with a thumb missing, some with their fingers off at the knuckle. They were stooped things, round-shouldered and skinny. Many of them were not over ten years of age, the state law prohibited their working before they were twelve years of age.

The laws were poorly enforced and the impoverished parents lied about the age of their children. It was a question of "starvation or perjury."[17]

Mother Jones assembled a group of the children for a public demonstration. She chose especially "the little boys with their fingers off, and hands crushed and maimed ...I held up their mutilated hands and showed them to the crowd ...I called upon the millionaire manufacturers to cease their moral murders." Ever the dramatic organizer, Mother Jones obtained permission from the parents to take the children on a protest march from Kensington to Oyster Bay, New York, the opulent summer home of President Theodore Roosevelt, in the hope that the president would "have Congress pass a law prohibiting the exploitation of childhood."

Carrying knapsacks "in which was a knife and a fork, a tin cup and a plate" the children set out by foot with Mother Jones in the lead. The children carried placards denouncing child labor and announcing "We want to go to school." The crusade of two hundred children and adult supporters passed through Trenton, Princeton, Newark and Paterson in New Jersey and east into New York. Along the way kindly farmers gave food, clothing and shelter to the children, train drivers stopped their locomotives and allowed the children to travel free. After several weeks on the road the bedraggled children reached Oyster Bay, but the president refused to meet with them. The mill owners in Kensington stayed united and the strike failed, but two years later the Pennsylvania legislature passed a law restricting child labor.

Mother Jones recalled seeing the little workers during her visits to the cotton mills.

> Little girls and boys, barefooted, walk up and down between the endless rows of spindles, reaching their little hands into the machinery to repair snapped threads. They crawled under the

machinery to oil it. They replaced spindles all day long, all day long; night through, night through. Tiny babies of six years old with faces of sixty did an eight-hour shift for ten cents a day. If they fell asleep, cold water was dashed in their faces. And the voice of the manager yelled above the ceaseless racket and whirl of the machines.... At five-thirty in the morning long lines of little grey children come out of the early dawn into the factory, into the lint-filled rooms.

With their control of the press, the captains of industry were able to thwart the demands for more stringent child labor laws. Speaking at the annual meeting of the National Association of Hosiery Manufacturers held in Philadelphia in May 1908, the appropriately named Joseph S. Rambo, president of the Pennsylvania Manufactures Association, "voiced his opposition to further child labor legislation." Mr. Rambo complained about magazine articles "written by sentimental and impractical persons ...against this very necessary branch of our industry." After all, society "must have masses and classes, and hewers and carriers. We cannot all be captains of industries." How quickly he forgot! Joseph S. Rambo himself was the son of a shoemaker and one of twelve children of a poor family. He started as a laborer in a cotton mill but worked his way to owning his own mills, including the Globe Knitting Mills, Norristown, Pennsylvania.

In 1910, the United States Bureau of Labor completed an extensive investigation on the *Condition of Woman and Child-Wage Earners in the United States*. Running nineteen volumes the report makes interesting reading. In 1905, the cotton industry in the United States employed 310,458 people of whom "40,020 were children under 16 years of age." New England, then still dominant in cotton textiles, employed 9,385 of these youngsters (6 percent of the total workforce in these states), New York, New Jersey, Pennsylvania and Maryland mills employed 2,765 (8.7 percent of their workforce), while the South employed 27,538 children under the age of 16 (22.9 percent of the workforce.) A quarter-century earlier New England mills employed many more youngsters (17,774) but their numbers declined year after year in response to ever-stricter state laws governing child labor. In the South the number of workers under 16 years of age increased year after year. As the industry moved from North to South, so grew the number of children employed. In 1900, the Southern States employed two out of three of all children under 16 working in the cotton industry. Most were aged 14 and 15, but children as young as 9 were employed in the mills of the South. In North Carolina "the cloth mills in the smallest towns had the highest proportion of child workers." The little children were employed as doffers, cleaners, and ring spinners. Many of the young ring spinners were "as skillful as adults" and much cheaper to hire.

Some believed that the number of youngsters working in the mills was even higher, since many parents lied about the age of their children. One inspector noted: "The girl (age given as 15) does not look to be over 13. She is a little girl with dresses to her knees." Another reported: "The next two children, twin boys, were little fellows in short trousers, apparently not more than 13 years of age. The mother said they were 17. When I expressed surprise she simply said: They are small." Yet another inspector reported: "I believe there are children as young as 10 years in this mill. I counted 28 who were undeniably under 11 years of age," but their parents claimed they were at least seventeen.

Over the years, the stricter enforcement of the child labor laws in the New England states reduced the number of children under sixteen working in the mills. Children seeking work had to produce a birth certificate, a school leaving certificate and pass a test in reading and writing. But in the South child labor laws then were "flagrantly violated," allowing children as young as seven years to work. In 1908, one worker in three in the cotton mills of Georgia and the Carolinas was a child between ten and fifteen years of age. In South Carolina alone there were 1,500 children under twelve years working in the mills. In Mississippi, one worker in four was under fourteen years of age. The State of Georgia in 1910 allowed a child as young as ten years "to be legally employed if it is an orphan and depended on its own labor for support or if it had a widowed mother or disabled father depended upon it." North and South Carolina had child labor laws similar to Georgia but Mississippi had no age or school restrictions. In Alabama a young child was permitted to work "if said child shall attend school for eight weeks in every year of employment."

In the textile industry grown men earned on average $6 to $7 a week, women $4 to $5 a week, but children could be bought at $2 a week. Where did their money go? "It was usually paid to the father or the envelope is turned over to the parent unopened." Before reaching puberty these thin and frail looking children worked fifty-eight hours a week in the Northeast and sixty-seven hours a week in the South. Many worked the night shift. For a meager wage, children worked in overcrowded mills with poor lighting, dust and lint, dirty washrooms, spitting on the floor, and the constant din of dangerous machinery. But their work was not yet all done. On returning home these children helped care for younger siblings, and did family chores. Child labor in the South was an economic necessity. The

Boy and girl workers at the Whitnell Cotton Manufacturing Company, North Carolina. The mill superintendent, T.A. Wright, told Lewis Hine in 1909 that the parents were to blame for the large number of children working in the mill. "Father loafs just as soon as children get old enough to work.

average income of a Southern mill family in 1905 was $975 of which the working children contributed $330. The families were too large and too poor to manage on the fathers' and mothers' wages alone and, in order to put them to work, parents lied about the age of their children.

Southern states encouraged cheap labor as an inducement to Northern companies to relocate. Alabama in 1901 "has no legislation as to hours of labor or for the protection of women and child labor. There were formerly such laws but they were repealed to encourage the establishment of mills."

On January 12, 1912, nine months after the Triangle Shirtwaist fire in New York, the workers in the mills of Lawrence, Massachusetts, went on strike protesting a cut in pay. The strike became ugly with charges of cruelty, clubbing of women and children, huddling strikers' families in jail and taking children from their homes to the Lawrence poor house. Known as the Bread and Roses Strike, it involved 30,000 textile workers, most of immigrant stock. Hundreds of children of the strikers were evacuated by train from Lawrence to be sheltered by sympathetic families in New York.

Despite the strict Massachusetts laws against child labor, there were many children working full-time in the mills. The most notable of them, Camella Teoli, was invited to appear before the Rules Committee of the House of Representatives in Washington. Asked how she started working so young in the mill she replied:

The Loudon Hosiery Company in Tennessee was established in 1906. There were many children among its 400 workers. The knitting machines, driven by electric power, posed dangers to small children. Picture 1908.

I used to go to school (until the 6th grade), and then a man came up to my house and asked my father why I didn't go to work, so my father says I don't know if she is 13 or 14 years old. So the man says you give me $4 and I will make the papers come from the old country saying you are 14. So, my father gives him $4, and in a month came the papers that I was 14. I went to work and about two weeks got hurt in my head.

Only two weeks on her job as a doffer Camella was getting ready to go home after a long workday. She unpinned her long hair and began to comb it. The hair got caught up in the spinning machine, which grabbed her, tearing off a large piece of her scalp. A friend turned off the machine, found the piece of scalp and wrapped it in newspaper. Camella spent seven months in the hospital, paid for by the company, but she received no pay. She was left with a bald patch, which she attempted to cover with her remaining hair. For need of money, Camella returned to work but at a different mill. With all the others she went on strike in January 1912.

Helen Taft, the wife of President William Howard Taft, attended a number of the hearings of the Rules Committee, showing particular interest in Camella Teoli and other children. A frightened Camella told the committee that she was working at the Washington mill at the time of her accident.

Q: What part of your head (was injured)?
A: My head.
Q. Well, how were you hurt?
A: The machine pulled the scalp off.

Replying to a question why she went on strike, Camella responded: "Because I didn't get enough to eat at home."

Several other children from Lawrence who started working before age fifteen appeared before the committee and told about the harsh conditions in the Lawrence mills and why they had to leave school and go to work. Pearl Schinberg, born in Lawrence, went to work at fourteen to help support a household of ten. She worked as a burler, taking the knots off the cloth, earning $3.50 a week. Charles Vasiersky's family lived off bread and molasses, with meat a rare luxury. "What would we eat if I went to school?" Charles left school in the seventh grade to start working in the mill. "I got my hand all hurt in the Everett mill; when I started up the frame the belt catches me and smashed my hand all up."

Q: What do you do evenings?
A: I go out and play and go home and fall asleep.
Q: Do you read any books?
A: No sir. I have not got any money to spend to buy any.

Samuel Goldberg was the oldest of five children. His father worked at a mill earning $9 a week. Born in Lawrence, Samuel left school and at fourteen years and two months started working in a different mill. He told the committee that in his work as a doffer he took "off full bobbins and put empty bobbins on," earning $5.10 during the busy months but in the slack summers his earnings dropped as low as $1.65 a week. If he was late, even by five minutes, he was docked an hour's wage. A worker who was late three times was fired. The workers had to pay 5 cents a day for drinking water and received no lunch. Samuel started work at 6:45 in the morning and continued until 5:30 at night, with a half-hour for lunch.[18]

The Bread and Roses Strike was settled on March 14, 1912, with a promise of increased wages and a bonus for overtime. The immigrant workers had taken on the mighty American Woolen Company and won. But the writing was on the wall. In the 1920s the vast Pacific Mills of Lawrence began moving work to the South and built a mill and a village of 375 workers' cottages at Lyman, South Carolina. During the first half of the twentieth century the great mills of Lawrence and other Northern cities shut down or moved to the South for cheaper labor and fewer restrictions on child labor.

The shift of textile mills from North to South continued and by 1970 was virtually complete. Of the 6,000 textile mills in the United States, three-quarters were located in the Southeast. But the success of the South did not last long. Dwight in Alabama shut down in 1959. Merrimack mill in Huntsville, Alabama, closed in 1989 and the buildings were demolished three years later. J. P. Stevens & Company started in North Andover, Massachusetts, in 1813, moved to Great Falls, South Carolina, but closed in 1986. Pepperell Manufacturing Company of Biddeford, Maine, moved to Alabama in 1920; its successor, WestPoint, filed for Chapter 11 in 2003 and closed its mills in the South. The Pacific mills of Lyman, Georgia, closed in 2005. The vast Cannon mills of Kannapolis, North Carolina, that once employed 18,000 workers declared bankruptcy in 2003. Hundreds of thousand textile jobs moved offshore in search of cheaper workers, including the cheap labor of children.

2

Apprenticeship System

To be idle and to be poor have always been reproaches, and therefore every man endeavors with his utmost to hide his poverty from others, and his idleness from himself.
— Samuel Johnson, 1781

[Johnny Tremain] was a rather skinny boy, neither large nor small for fourteen. As an apprentice [to a Boston silversmith] he was little more than a slave until he had served his master seven years. He had no wages. The very clothes upon his back belonged to the master.
— Esther Forbes, *Johnny Tremain: A Story of Boston in Revolt*, 1943

In Colonial Times

One of the most famous apprenticeships in colonial America was that of Benjamin Franklin. He was born in Boston in 1706 and lived long enough to be one of the Founding Fathers. Franklin was part of a large litter and his "elder brothers were all put apprentices to different trades" while he was considered for the church. His parents could not afford the expense of a college education and instead sent young Benjamin "to a school for writing and arithmetic." After only two years of schooling, Benjamin later wrote in his autobiography, at "ten years old I was taken home to assist my father in his business, which was that of a tallow-chandler and soap-boiler." Benjamin cut the wicks for the candles, filled the dipping mould, attended the store and went out on errands. "I disliked the trade, and had a strong inclination for the sea, but my father declared against it." Fearful that Benjamin would run away to sea, his father took him to see "joiners, bricklayers, turners, braziers etc. at their work, that he might observe my inclination, and endeavor to fix it on some trade or other on land." His father "at last fixed upon the cutler's trade," working for his cousin Samuel. But Samuel's request for a fee did not please the father and Benjamin returned home. It was Benjamin's love of books that settled him for a life as a printer, like his older brother James. Only twelve years of age, he signed the indentures to serve an apprenticeship until he reached the age of twenty-one. A quick learner at things he liked, Benjamin was "a useful hand to my brother." Benjamin composed ballads as well as learned the craft of printing. With his brother's support he wrote *The Lighthouse Tragedy,* which "sold wonderfully."

In 1720, his brother started a newspaper, the *New England Courant,* the second to appear in America. James employed his literary friends to write for his newspaper. Having quietly improved his spelling and grammar, and sharpened his ideas, Benjamin "was excited to try my hand" at writing for the paper but feared his brother's scorn. He sent in anonymous contributions, which were judged to come from an unknown "character among us for learning and ingenuity." When James found out that the mystery author was none other than his little brother his anger was matched by Benjamin's self-confidence, causing a rift between them. When Benjamin broke his indentures James made sure that no other printer in Boston would hire him. At age seventeen Benjamin left Boston for New York and then Philadelphia. Boston lost and Philadelphia gained an author, printer, scientist, inventor, diplomat, statesman and politician — in short, a great man.[1]

Samuel Sewell, born in 1652 in Bishopstoke, Hampshire, England, at age nine settled with his family in Newbury, Massachusetts. He was a bright boy and was admitted to Harvard College with the intention of becoming a minister. Instead he entered business, married, and sired eleven children. From 1673 until shortly before his death he kept a diary recording the trials and tribulations of his large family, various events in colonial America and his participation as a judge in the notorious Salem witch trials. For our purposes we will concentrate on his efforts to find a proper calling for his son, Samuel Jr. Sixteen-year-old Sam had been apprenticed to Captain Checkly, a general merchant, but was "weeping and much discomposed and loath to go" to work in the store. "I prayed with Sam alone," recorded the father on February 26, 1696, "that God would direct our way as to a calling for him." Their prayers were answered, as shortly thereafter Mr. Wilkins agreed to take the boy as his apprentice, and Sam was happy learning to become a bookseller. In 1717, Samuel Sr. was appointed chief justice of Massachusetts. He died in Boston aged seventy-seven, having outlived most of his children.[2]

Thomas Hancock, born in 1703, came from Lexington to Boston at age thirteen to start an apprenticeship under Mr. Henchman, bookseller and bookbinder. His indentures, signed and witnessed on May 20, 1717, stipulated that his apprenticeship would last seven years. The boy promised his master and mistress that he "faithfully shall serve, their secrets keep, their commands (lawful and honest) everywhere gladly do and perform; hurt to his said master or mistress he shall not do, not of others or know to be done.... Fornication he shall not commit. Matrimony he shall not contract. Taverns and alehouses he shall not frequent. At cards, dice or any other unlawful games he shall not play." Thomas promised further never to leave the premises without permission and always to obey his master and mistress. The wording on this indenture agreement closely follows that of Nathan Knight, who agreed in 1666 to become apprentice to Samuel Widden, mason of Portsmouth, New Hampshire, suggesting it was then the standard legal document for indentures, at least in New England.

These restrictions did not prevent Thomas Hancock from marrying Lydia, his master's daughter. Once his indentures were complete he opened his own bookstore and set about to make his mark in the world. When Mr. Henchman died, Thomas acquired "a nest egg out of which he hatched the greatest fortune in New England." His wealth came from the whale oil trade and foreign trade. Thomas Hancock built one of the grandest houses on Beacon Hill, but he and Lydia were childless. After his brother died, Thomas took in his nephew John to live with him and Lydia, giving the boy a far easier start to life than he had enjoyed. John attended Boston Latin School and Harvard College before joining his uncle's business, soon becoming a full partner. When Thomas died at age sixty-one he left his fortune of seventy thousand dollars to John Hancock, catapulting the young man into the ranks of the wealthiest in the American colonies. John Hancock enjoys lasting fame as an American patriot, bold signer of the United States Declaration of Independence, and as first and third governor of the Commonwealth of Massachusetts.[3]

The apprenticeship system that developed in colonial America was based on the guild and municipal laws enacted in England during the thirteenth and fourteenth centuries. A 1201 London ordinance forbade "one master to entice away another's apprentice and fixed the period of service to ten years." Copies of the indenture agreements between master and apprentice were kept in the Guildhall. By 1350, the fishmongers, bricklayers, hatters, masons, barbers, brewers, carpenters, clockmakers and other guilds had established regulations for the employment of apprentices. During his training with a skilled master, the apprentice was entitled to housing and food and a small money allowance. In return he promised to be loyal, obey commands and abstain from gambling and heavy drinking. For a boy the period of indentures was usually seven years from age fourteen to twenty-one. For a girl the period was until age eighteen or when she married. After completing the terms of indenture, the apprentice could apply to the authorities to practice his craft independently and call himself a full-fledged master. The Statute of Artificers, a group of English laws (1558–1563) regulating the wages and qualifications of the various craft guilds, established the rules of apprenticeship.

The close of the sixteenth century was an especially difficult time in England. The monasteries were shut, the coinage was debased, agriculture was in decline and unemployment was rife. Families split up leading to hungry and abandoned children. The Elizabethan Poor Law of 1601 gave the local parishes across England the responsibility to house, feed, and clothe poor children and provide them with a guardian. The law also empowered churchwardens and overseers to "bind any such children to be apprentices ... till such man-child shall come to the age of four and twenty and such woman-child to the age of one and twenty, or the time of her marriage." In 1767 the terms for parish-apprentices was revised to "seven years only or until the age of twenty-one." These laws were applied with varying degrees of flexibility or rigidity, goodness or evil.

Poor and orphaned English children were sent to the Virginia colony as early as 1619 "to be apprentices." William Cockaine, a prominent London merchant, collected five hundred pounds to transport one hundred children to Virginia. Aged from twelve and up, "they shall be apprentices, the boys till they come to 21 years of age, the girls till a like age or till they are married." After completing their indentures they would be awarded Crown land, with horses and animals. So successful was this venture that another group of one hundred children was sent to Virginia the following year. In 1622, the Council of New England, following the example of the Virginia Company, agreed to take one hundred poor children, some of them "boys and girls to be taken up out of the streets of London as vagrants," and sent to the New World as apprentices.[4]

The Industrial Revolution that began in England late in the eighteenth century undermined the apprenticeship system. William F. Willoughby, who worked for the United States Bureau of Labor, pointed out that in early nineteenth-century England, "The growth of child labor is inseparably connected with the introduction of machinery." Orphans from the workhouses of London and Birmingham were sent to the factories in the north, where "children of all ages, down to three and four, were found in the hardest and most painful labor, while babes of six were commonly found in large numbers in many factories. Labor from twelve to thirteen and often sixteen hours a day was the rule."[5]

Charles Dickens rampaged against the cruelty and greed of the system of workhouses that gave the children little love or food but demanded their obedience and gratitude. His fictional orphan boy, Oliver Twist, was "a victim of a systematic course of treachery and deception" by the authorities. Underfed and badly treated, at his ninth birthday poor Oliver was "a pale thin child, somewhat diminutive in stature and decidedly small in circumference." For daring one day to say, "Please, sir, I want some more," he was beaten, isolated and offered up for sale for five pounds "to any man or woman who wanted an apprentice to any trade, business or calling." Oliver was first offered to Mr. Gamfield, the chimney sweep, even though chimney sweeping was "a nasty trade" and boys sometimes suffocated in the chimneys. Next Oliver was sold to Mr. Sowerberry, the undertaker, where he was given leftover food to eat and required to sleep in the shop among the coffins. Abused and exploited, poor Oliver ran away to London where he met the Artful Dodger, "one of the queerest looking boys that Oliver had ever seen. He was a snub-nosed, flat-browed, common-faced boy enough; and as dirty a juvenile as one would wish to see; but he had about him all the airs and manners of a man. He was short of his age: with rather bow-legs, and little, sharp, ugly eyes. His hat was stuck on the top of his head so lightly, that it threatened to fall off every moment." Learning that Oliver was "very hungry and tired," the Dodger took him to meet Fagin to begin his apprenticeship in thievery. Soon, Oliver was hard at work on the streets of London accompanying Dodger and Charley Bates as they pinched pocketbooks, handkerchiefs, shirt-pins, watches, spectacle-cases and snuffboxes off unsuspecting gentlemen.[6]

Charles Dickens wrote from his own experience. When his father was imprisoned for debt, the twelve-year-old Charles went to work at Warren's Blacking Factory, 30 Hungerford Stairs, the Strand, gluing labels to bottles of shoe blacking. This experience was bitterly retold in his 1850 novel *David Copperfield*. After his mother died, David's cruel stepfather, Edward Murdstone, set him to work in the Murdstone & Grinby's wine company, washing the bottles, on a diet of bread, butter and water.[7]

In *Great Expectations,* Dickens tells how the desiccated Miss Havisham arranged for Pip to be bound over as apprentice to Joe Gargery, blacksmith and timid husband of Pip's older sister. Joe asks if Pip has any objection "to the business — such as its being open to black and sut or such-like." Despite his shame and embarrassment, Pip replies that he has no objection. "Pip "took the indentures out of his hand and gave them to Miss. Havisham." To seal the agreement, she gives Pip twenty-five guineas and instructs him: "Give it to your master." After his indentures "were duly signed and attested" young Pip was bound to Joe Gargery to learn the blacksmith's trade. Pip remained in Joe's house and workshop until he learned of his great expectations, that he would be sent to London to become a gentleman.[8]

Signing himself as Alfred, the Reverend Samuel Kydd, author of *The History of the Factory Movement,* published in London in 1857, sets out the harrowing conditions of the apprenticeship system as it shifted from the workshop to the factory floor. Instead of learning a trade from a master, now whole groups of abandoned children were taken from the poorhouses of England and sent to the far away cotton mills, breaking links with family, village and church. These poor and unfortunate children were "used up as the cheapest raw material in the market." Clothed in rags, poorly fed, and given the briefest of training, they operated machines, doing the same task over and over again. The factory system "impaired the strength and destroyed the vital stamina of the rising generation." Vulnerable to disease and without education or moral instruction, the children of the early mills in England were doomed to a bleak and short life.[9]

Children had always worked, wrote John Spargo in 1906, "but it is only since the reign of the machine that their work has been synonymous with slavery." English-born Spargo came to America in his mid-twenties and was active in socialist circles. In addition to *Bitter Cry of the Children* (1905), he wrote other books on the plight of poor children in the United States and Europe. In 1912, he published a biography of Karl Marx. Later in life he softened his politics and moved to Vermont to become an expert in ceramics.[10]

Katarina Honeyman, late professor of social and economic history at the University of Leeds, England, devoted much of her academic career to the study of child labor at the start of the Industrial Revolution. In her 2007 book, *Child Workers in England, 1780–1820*, she describes the effects of the Industrial Revolution, especially on the children of the poor. Before the age of power machines (that is before 1780), English craftsmen, helped by their children, spun thread, wove cloth and knitted socks and mittens in their cottages, using hand- and foot-operated machines. The industrial revolution destroyed this long-established way of life, severely disrupted family ties, and left many poor, orphaned and abandoned children seeking relief from the financially stretched parishes. The answer was to put the children to work to earn their keep. In 1790, Mr. Vaux, a lace maker, proposed building textile factories around London to employ children and so "prevent the habitual idleness and degeneracy so common and so destructive to that most exposed and neglected part of the community." Larger parishes hired agents to seek out factories willing to hire the pauper children as apprentices. These factories generally wanted little girls in preference to boys because they adjusted quickly to the monotony of the work and were easier of temper. Honeyman cites examples of the arrangements reached between the parishes and the burgeoning industrial world. In 1790, the St. Clement Danes chapel bound out seventy-three children to John Birch of Backbarrow at three to four guineas per child "providing Birch with a useful capital sum of 250–300 pounds, enough to build an apprentice house." In 1802, the parish of St. Martin in the Fields bound out two hundred children, "the average age was just under 11," to textile mills. In 1844, the Leicester Board of Guardians received an offer from Mr. Chambers, owner of a cotton mill in Mayfield, for girls "to train as doublers ... and would provide them with food, lodging and clothing." St. Pancras Parish bound out twenty-two children to Thomas Garnett's mill. Similar deals between parishes and mills continued well into the nineteenth century.[11]

In colonial America, the placement of apprentices depended on the wealth and well-being of the family. Parents of lesser means placed their children at age thirteen years as apprentice apothecaries, printers, bookbinders, coach makers and the like, where they could move up in the world. The care of children of the poor, orphans, illegitimate or abandoned, was the responsibility of the local authorities, which bound them over to positions — pauper apprentice — suited to their station, such as farm laborers and fishermen. Apprenticeships were introduced during the earliest days of the British settlement of America. On July 26, 1631, a Boston court registered "Lucy Smith is bound to apprentice with Roger Ludlow for 7 years." On July 3 the following year John Smithe was bound over to John Wilson for five years. The demand for labor in colonial America was so great that the terms of indenture were reduced to as few as three years before setting up as an independent craftsman. This shortened term of training, however, was deemed too brief and on June 20, 1660, a town meeting in Boston determined that "no person shall henceforth open a shop in the town, or occupy any manufacture or science, till he has completed 21 years or served seven years apprenticeship." Unlike Europe, there were no organized craft guilds in America, rather an apprentice learned from a single master and after seven years of training was free to start out on his own.

Colonial America comprised largely rural farmers and fishermen with many villages but few towns. Philadelphia, New York and Boston in the 1770s were very small compared with London and Paris. Poverty was rampant; the care of poor, abandoned or orphaned children followed the English Poor Laws. The General Court of the Colony of Plymouth passed a law in 1641 to make the care of these unfortunate children a public responsibility. Such children could be "placed out into families where they might be better brought up and provided for." The master was required to house, clothe, feed and educate his ward and to teach him a useful trade. These children rarely saw their own family. In 1642, the General Court of the Massachusetts Bay Colony, sitting in Boston, passed a similar law. In 1848, a Salem town meeting ordered "the eldest children of Reuben Gubby be placed out, the boy until age 21 years and the maid until age 18 years." Legislation in New England and New York permitted boys to be held as apprentices until the age of twenty-one and girls until age eighteen years.

In 1720, a town meeting in Boston voted to buy twenty spinning wheels for the use of children in its almshouse. The merchant Daniel Oliver, chairman of the overseers of the poor, donated money to build a spinning school. It took another fifteen years before the spinning school opened on Tremont Street, opposite where the Park Street Church was later built. In 1754, the Manufactory Building was erected at 120 Tremont Street, Boston, to house poor women and children in return for spinning linen. This effort failed. After the Battle of Bunker Hill in 1775 the British army commandeered the building and used it as a hospital. In 1769, the Boston merchant William Malineux was concerned over the "deplorable circumstances of the poor" and proposed setting up spinning wheels so that "all, or as many of the children in the town, as might be inclined to learn to spin might learn that useful and interesting knowledge." Poverty in colonial Boston motivated its most prominent citizens like Nicholas Boylston, Harrison Gray, Thomas Hancock and Josiah Quincy to establish The Society for Encouraging Industry and Employing the Poor.

As in England, the system of care for poor children in America was sometimes kind but often cruel. In New York, Stephen Ward, age twelve, was bound out until age twenty-one as an apprentice to John Deffer. A few years into Stephen's indentures his uncle petitioned to take charge and train him in husbandry. The court agreed. In 1725, the widow Mary Anderson took out a complaint against Benjamin Bake for the abuse of her daughter, who was his apprentice. The court discharged her apprenticeship. Apprentices who ran away, if caught, were returned to their masters and forced to serve "double the time of such their absence."

The terms of indenture in colonial New York and New England closely followed the wording of their English model. For example, the church wardens and overseers of the poor of the city of New York "placed and bound William Reade, a poor fatherless and motherless child of five years unto Robert Nisbert, tailor, until he the said William Reade shall come

Shoemaker and apprentice, when shoes were made one pair at a time. Library of Congress, Photographs and Prints. Call # Lot 4397-T. Artist unknown.

into the full age of twenty-one years." The range of apprenticeships for boys ran from baker, barber, blacksmith, and carpenter all the way down the alphabet to tailor, turner, weaver and wheelwright. In colonial America poor girls were taught housewifery, including cleaning, dusting, polishing, knitting, sewing and spinning.

The laws relating to poor children were modified to deal with new circumstances. Virginia in 1657 considered a child recently arrived who did not have indentures. Such a child "if under fifteen would serve till he or she shall be one and twenty of age, and the courts to be the judges of their age." In the early years of the Virginia settlement young and adult English indentured servants made up the large part of the colony's population. In return for the price of a ticket, they were bound to wealthy planters. Indentured service was different from slavery only by the period of service being limited to four to seven years. After completing their indentures, the servants were free to take up land grants. A few of these servants later became rich in the New World, but most managed only to eke out a modest living. The first of the black Africans to come to Virginia arrived in 1619. At first they were treated like the white indentured servants, but these small freedoms were soon taken away. As the slave trade expanded, Virginia and other southern colonies preferred Africans to white Englishmen. The black slaves were life-long property without the prospect of freedom.

The apprenticeship was an integral part of the labor system in colonial Boston, New York, Baltimore and Philadelphia. Masters and apprentices, whether local or imported, came before the courts to have the terms of the apprenticeship recorded. By 1770, Philadelphia with 30,000 residents was one of the major trading centers of the British crown. The thriving economy created a great demand for cheap labor. The office of the mayor kept records of children arriving from London, Rotterdam, Lisbon and other ports to take up apprenticeships. Between October 1771 and October 1773 over fifteen thousand children came through Philadelphia. Most of the children came to be servants in homes, but others were to be taught a trade, such as carpentry, tailoring, boat building and masonry. In each case the master paid a fee for transportation, and was obligated to house, clothe and feed his apprentice, and teach him to read and write in return for a period of service lasting two to eleven years. When the child reached the age of twenty-one he was free of his indentures.[12]

The Boston Massacre

In October 1768, the 14th and 29th regiments, two thousand British troops, arrived in Boston to keep the order and to help the customs officials collect taxes levied on colonists by Parliament. Rather than restore calm, the presence of British soldiers inflamed the passions of the 16,000 residents of Boston, who refused to house the troops or cooperate with them. On the evening of March 5, 1770, Edward Garrick (or Gerrish), a wig-maker's apprentice, happened upon Captain John Goldfinch passing by and yelled at him: "There goes the fellow that won't pay my master for dressing his hair." The captain walked on and Garrick, backed by a dozen of his fellow apprentices, turned his scorn on Private Hugh White, the solitary British sentry on duty outside the Custom House, taunting him with words, sticks, pieces of ice and snowballs, and defying him to "fire and be damned." The sentry, "muttering and growling," struck Garrick on the side of the head with the butt of his musket, knocking the crying boy to the ground. Garrick got back on his feet, telling people that the soldier had beaten him about the head. Other soldiers came rushing to help Private White as the gathering crowd of angry Bostonians grew to four hundred, forming a menacing semi-circle facing the troops. Captain Thomas Preston, the officer of the day, tried to settle the crowd and support his men. Someone in the crowd shouted "Fire" and the soldiers fired into the crowd, killing three instantly with two others soon to die from their wounds and a number seriously injured. Two of the dead were young apprentices.

In what became known as the Boston Massacre, the news of the dead and injured exacerbated the angry mood of the colonists against British rule. Captain Preston and his men were formally charged with murder and put on trial at the Suffolk County Court. Believing that everyone deserved a fair trial, lawyer John Adams, assisted by Josiah Quincy II, agreed to defend the British soldiers, who claimed they acted in self-defense. Testimony for the trial was collected from over sixty witnesses, nearly all of whom were "of legal age," with very little testimony coming from the boys, many of them young apprentices, who threatened and insulted the British soldiers.

James Caldwell was seventeen years old when he was killed by two balls into his back. He was not from Boston but was a sailor on the brig *Hawk* under the command of Captain Thomas Morton. The ship carried from the Caribbean a cargo of molasses to be made into rum at one of the Boston rum distilleries. The second youngster killed was Samuel Maverick, also aged seventeen, an apprentice to ivory-turner and dentist Isaac Greenwood, who lived near Clark's Wharf in Boston. Young Maverick boarded with the Greenwood family, where he received his meals and a little money in return for his labor. Samuel heard the shouting and went out on King's Street near the Custom House to see what the excitement was about. He worked his way to the front of the crowd taunting the British soldiers. Caught up in the excitement, Maverick yelled out: "Fire away, you damned lobsterbacks." Hit in the stomach, Maverick yelled out to his friend: "Joe, I am shot." The wounded boy ran down Royal Exchange Lane to Dock Square, where he collapsed. He was carried to his mother's boardinghouse on Union Street where he died the next morning. Maverick Square in Boston is named for him.

Christopher Monk and John Clark, both seventeen years old, were badly wounded.

Yet another young man involved in the Boston Massacre incident was Henry Knox. Born on Long Lane, Boston, Henry was the seventh of ten sons, only four of whom reached manhood. He attended Boston Latin School where he studied Greek, Latin, arithmetic and history. His father died when Henry reached age twelve, requiring him to leave school to support his mother and his younger brother. According to his 1873 biography, the clever Henry Knox "was fortunate in being employed by Messrs. Wharton & Bowes, booksellers, in Cornhill. The excellent Mr. Nicholas Bowes supplied the place of a father to him, keeping a strict eye upon his morals and forming him in early age to habits of industry and regularity." Knox, a nineteen-year-old bookseller's apprentice, tried to separate the crowd from the soldiers and warned Captain Preston "for God's sake to take his men back again, for if they fired his life must answer for the consequences."

The jury acquitted six of the soldiers but found two guilty of manslaughter. The Boston Massacre convinced Knox to take sides in the battle between the king's men and the colonists. In 1771, when he reached the age of twenty-one, he completed his apprenticeship and opened his own shop, the London Book Store. At the time of the Battle of Lexington and Concord he left Boston to join the militia. Knox saw action in the Battle of Bunker Hill. He was selected by General George Washington to bring the cannons from Fort Ticonderoga to Dorchester Heights, forcing the British to evacuate Boston and sail for Halifax. Knox served as a major general during the Revolutionary War and, from 1785 to 1794, as the first United States secretary of war.

Apprentices and Wards After Independence

In the young and independent country of America the rules governing the apprenticeship system differed from one state to another. Metalwork, especially silversmith, was the most prestigious of the craft apprenticeships. Paul Revere began his apprenticeship in this lucrative trade when he was thirteen years old. In the middle of esteem were the apprentice blacksmith and carpenter; lowest in esteem were the apprentice tailor and shoemaker. Through the apprenticeship system, the craft skills were passed down from one generation to the next. The craft apprentice system in America never reached the level of development as in England. The Revolutionary War cast aside existing agreements as many youngsters volunteered to fight against the British. With the coming of peace, the states of America were faced with the care of orphaned or abandoned children. Poverty was also rife even among families that managed to stay whole.

In the United States the methods to care for orphaned, poor or abandoned children were influenced by the Elizabethan Poor Laws and the introduction by Sir John Peel the

Elder of the Health and Morals of Apprentices Law of 1802. These laws limited the working day for children to twelve hours. Boys and girls were to be housed in separate dormitories, with no more than two children to a bed. Education, at least in reading, writing and arithmetic, was mandatory. Each apprentice was to receive two suits of clothing and was required to attend religious classes on Sunday. The law passed despite the doomsday clamor of industrialists that it would cause their economic ruin.

The apprenticeship system in America was strongest from 1720 until 1820. Early in the nineteenth century the bounding out of children to farmers or craftsmen began to give way to placing children in orphanages or community homes.[13] In 1814, the Boston Asylum for Indigent Boys was established and during its first eight years received 146 boys. The society bought a large building with an extensive playground in Boston to house up to sixty boys. Benjamin Greene and his son Gardiner, who made their fortunes trading in cotton, sugar, coffee and rum, established the society. Gardiner married the daughter of the Boston-

Thompson Island is one of the Boston harbor islands. In 1838 the Boston Farm School opened, housing up to 300 boys, orphaned or abandoned, on the island. In addition to school, the boys worked the farm and were taught trades to prepare them for work on the mainland. In 1907, it was renamed the Boston Farm and Trades School (courtesy the University Archives & Special Collections Department, Joseph P. Healey Library, University of Massachusetts Boston: "Thompson's Island Collection: Records, 1814–1990").

born painter John Singleton Copley. Under their leadership the society attracted patrons from among the leading families of Boston, including the brothers Amos and Abbot Lawrence, Patrick Tracy Jackson, Senator James Lloyd, Nathan Appleton, William Appleton and Thomas Handasyd Perkins, all prominent merchants who became the principal backers of the textile mills in Lowell and elsewhere in New England. The largest single benefactor of the Asylum for Indigent Boys was the estate of Abraham Truro, which donated $5,000, fully one-fifth of all the funds collected to launch the home. Truro also donated large sums to build the Bunker Hill Monument and the Truro synagogue in Newport, Rhode Island.

The cost of running the home soon exceeded the society's income leading to a plan to purchase a farm "on which the boys might labor, and thus partly support themselves, and be better fitted, at less expense, to enter the next stage of life." In 1833, a second group of prominent Boston citizens formed the Boston Farm School Society and bought Thompson's Island in Boston Harbor, lying three and a half miles from Long Wharf. In 1838 the two societies merged. The purpose of the farm school was to save through work those abandoned boys who "are in danger of becoming vicious and dangerous or useless members of society." Boys aged three to twelve years became wards of the societies and were sent to the island where they were housed, fed and taught reading, writing and arithmetic. Up to 300 boys could be housed on the island at any one time. Under adult supervision the boys "cultivated the farm between school hours."

In 1857, Superintendent William Morse heard some of the boys amusing themselves with singing and makeshift instruments. He bought them proper musical instruments and formed a school marching band. At age twelve the boys were bound out as apprentices to farmers. In 1881, an industrial school was built on the island to teach the boys a trade such painting, carpentry, printing or to be a blacksmith. In 1907 the island school was renamed the Boston Farm and Trades School.

The terms of an apprentice's indentures were tested in October 1831 in a case before the Supreme Court of Massachusetts. John G. Easton, a master cooper, took on an apprentice with the promise to instruct him in the trade of the coopersmith. Claiming to follow a "custom for master coopers to send their apprentices to sea in whaling ships," Easton, with the agreement of the boy, arranged for him to go on a voyage around Cape Horn, a journey of many months. In return for the boy's services on board the whaling ship, Easton would receive one sixty-fifth of the ship's earnings, a total of $576.60. The Supreme Court ruled that the "custom for a master cooper to send his apprentice aboard a whaling voyage is bad, being repugnant to the objects and terms of the contract of apprenticeship." Since Easton had broken the terms of indenture, he was denied the money.

The heavy concentration of apprentices in Philadelphia led in 1820 to the founding of the Apprentices' Library, the oldest free circulating library in America. Its goal was "to promote orderly and virtuous habits, diffuse knowledge and the desire for knowledge." By 1875, the library had 21,000 books and was used by 2,000 boys and girls, who came on separate days. The idea spread and Boston and New York had apprentices' libraries of their own. The combination of schooling and training for work was also applied to children who had run afoul with the law. A number of these children had committed serious crimes, but many were sent away by the request of their own parents for "stubbornness." In 1846 the Commonwealth of Massachusetts opened the Lyman School for Boys in the country town of Westborough. The reform school, the nation's first, was named for its benefactor,

Theodore Lyman, a former mayor of Boston who gave $72,000 to build the twelve cottages, each large enough to house thirty-five boys. The daily life of the school comprised religious and moral instruction, reading and writing and learning a trade such as carpentry, plumbing, masonry, printing and dairying. By law, the boys could be held at the school until age twenty-one, but if they behaved well they were placed outside as apprentices, under the control of the parole department.

As in Western Europe, the craft guilds and apprenticeship system began to totter as manufacturing gained force. The economic depression of 1837 heralded the demise of the American craftsman and the craft apprentice system. Increasingly machines were taking over the work of craftsmen. Children no longer learned how to make a pair of shoes from start to finish or to spin cotton into thread and weave it into cloth. The crafts of spinning weaving, cabinetmaking, shoemaking and others were being lost. Instead, the worker tended the machine. American cities were filling with unemployed and impoverished craftsmen and their families.

In 1856, the Massachusetts legislature established the Industrial School for Girls in the village of Lancaster, "the first separate reformatory for girls in the United States." Ten cottages were built to house up to thirty girls each, who could be kept until they reached twenty-one years. The curriculum aimed to build character, discipline and humility through kitchen work, pantry, dining room, laundry, cooking, bread making, sewing and basket making. The girls who conformed to the strict standards of the school were "placed in other families at work for wages."

As the apprenticeship system weakened along the industrialized eastern seaboard of America, it gained strength in the west. In 1858, California passed An Act to Provide for Binding Minors as Apprentices, Clerks and Servants. With the permission of his father, a boy aged fourteen or older could enter into an agreement with a master to pay for his passage to California in return for one year's labor. The term of apprenticeship could last seven years (from age fourteen to twenty-one). The master was obliged by law to "send the child to school three months of each year" to learn reading, writing and arithmetic. In return for his work and obedience, the child would also receive board and lodging, clothing and medical attention. Enforcement of the California apprenticeship and child labor laws was poor. Children younger than fourteen years were put to work for nine or more hours a day. A study done in 1870 found 2,214 California children aged ten to fifteen years engaged in "gainful employment," but only 393 of them were covered by an apprenticeship contract. Only in the early years of the twentieth century did California achieve the level of control over child labor comparable to the Northeast.

In 1790, the population of Manhattan was only 33,131. New York City grew immensely with the opening in 1826 of the Erie Canal, making it the nation's gateway for immigration and commerce. For most, dreams of success soon turned to despair creating a vast underclass living in overcrowded tenements. In 1845, an estimated 35,000 street children competed with poor children from intact families selling newspapers, begging, stealing, running errands, or finding menial work in the countless small businesses that had sprung up all over New York City. Reverend Charles Loring Brace was born in Litchfield, Connecticut, in 1826 and studied religion and moral philosophy at Yale. While attending the Union Theological Seminary he was shocked by the poverty in the bustling city, with thousands of children homeless or living in hovels. Rather than accept a comfortable pulpit, Brace moved to the slums of Five Points and in 1853, with financial support from the city's wealthy families, established the Children's Aid Society. The society set up industrial schools with the aim of converting street urchins "into self-reliant members of society" through education and gainful employment.

By 1890, the Children's Aid Society was operating twenty-two industrial schools. The society set up a home for newsboys, a sewing workshop for girls and even the Crippled Boys Brush Shop. Believing that they needed a more wholesome environment than the mean streets of New York, Brace established the Orphan Train to transport children to start new lives with farm families across the land. Brace rationalized that in the rural West, "the demand for children's labor is practically unlimited." From 1853 to 1929, the Orphan Train (later called euphemistically the Placing-Out Department or the Foster-Home Department,) removed up to two hundred and fifty thousand children from the slums of New York, sometimes with and often without the permission of their parents. Many of the Orphan Train children were settled among warm, accepting families, but others landed up working in mines or lumber camps.

By no means were all of these children orphans; many belonged to single mothers or to couples who could not afford to care for them. In 1904 the New York Foundling Hospital—a Catholic institution—arranged to send forty Irish children, aged two to six years, with names like Katherine Fitzpatrick and Jerome Shanley, to be adopted by Mexican families living in a remote Arizona copper-mining town. On reaching the town the children and accompanying nuns and nurses were set upon by an angry mob of "Anglos" who refused to allow the white children to be adopted by the Mexican Catholic families. In the infamous case known as the Arizona Orphan Abduction, the children were taken by force and sent to Anglo homes. The Foundling Hospital filed suit against the abductors. In 1906 the case reached the U.S. Supreme Court, which decided that the Mexican families were unfit "by mode of living, habits and education" to be given the custody of the white children.

Henry Bergh (1823–1889) of New York City was determined to protect animals, founding in 1866 the American Society for the Prevention of Cruelty to Animals. Chosen as legal counsel was Elbridge Thomas Gerry (1837–1922) a New York lawyer who carried the illustrious name of his grandfather, a signer of the Declaration of Independence, governor of Massachusetts and fifth vice-president of the United States. Gerry Senior is also remembered for his "gerrymandering"—manipulating electoral boundaries to the advantage of one political party over another. In 1875, from the model of the animal organization grew the New York Society for the Prevention of Cruelty to Children (SPCC). Bergh and Gerry recruited the elderly and wealthy leather merchant John D. Wright as president to establish a society aimed at providing food, shelter, medical care and legal aid to battered children as well as preventing the sale of alcohol to children. SPCC sought to establish children's courts, prevent children from working in sweatshops and reduce their hours of work to sixty per week. After Wright died in 1879, Gerry was elected president and the SPCC became known as the Gerry Society.

Despite the efforts of Brace, Bergh, Gerry and others the demand for cheap child labor in the basement and tenement workshops of New York continued apace and by 1900, an estimated 100,000 children under fifteen years were at work selling newspapers, making paper flowers, clothing, cigars, cigarettes, spinning flax or making envelopes.

The experience of Massachusetts in establishing farm and industrial schools and reformatories was applied across the nation. By 1900, most of the American states had apprenticeship laws on their books. These institutions were based on the Puritan premise that redemption came through work and idleness was the breeding ground for evil. Whether Alabama, Colorado, California, Delaware or New Hampshire these laws stipulated that the father had the right to bind out his son or daughter to serve as an apprentice. If the father were dead or incompetent, the authority rested with the mother or legal guardian. The overseers of the poor had the authority to place the abandoned or deprived children in institutions or in apprenticeships. It was a barter system. The master was required by law to see that the child was taught a trade, learned to read and write, and was provided with food, housing and clothing and any necessary medical attention. The apprentice or the child in an institution was bound to obey his master and mistress and earn his keep. If he transgressed the master had the legal power to "enforce obedience and good behavior by such moderate corporal punishment" as was commonly administered. Except for the insane or feeble-minded, the child was expected to pay his own way through gainful employment.

The indentured apprenticeship system broke down in the textile mills, farms, glassworks and mines where there was little training, leaving the child workers stuck in rote, mindless jobs like doffing bobbins, breaking coal, shucking oysters or picking cotton or tomatoes. The new industries such as the railroads and the electric companies tried to remedy matters by introducing apprenticeship systems. At the start of the twentieth century the General Electric Company developed a four-year apprenticeship system to train youngsters to understand its machines, be able to read and comprehend mechanical drawings and to sketch out new machinery. The apprentices earned 9 cents an hour for the first year, 12 cents in the second year, 14 cents in the third year and 16½ cents for the final year together with a cash bonus of $100 on completion of the apprenticeship. At the end of his apprenticeship the youngster was hired to work in the company with the prospect of advancement and long-term employment.

3

Florence Kelley

Florence Kelley was one of a galaxy of wonderful women with whom she worked — Jane Addams, Julia Lathrop, Lillian D. Wald ... among others. Florence Kelley seemed at the time, and remains in memory, the most salient, salty character of them all.... She dedicated her life to the well-being of others.... She was an inextinguishable flame. [She] had probably the largest single share in shaping the social history of the United States in the first thirty years of this century.
— Felix Frankfurter, U.S. Supreme Court, 1953[1]

A quartet of remarkable women — Florence Kelley, Jane Addams, Julia Lathrop and Lillian Wald — played key roles in America's Progressive Era, from 1890 to 1920, and continued into the years of the Great Depression. In addition to their fight against child labor and for children's rights, they championed women's suffrage, civil liberties, the rights of people of color, better care for the mentally ill, a separate court system for juvenile offenders, and a fair deal for working people. Julia, born in 1858, was older than Florence by a year, than Jane by two years, and Lillian by nine years.

Florence Kelley was born in 1859 in the shadow of Independence Hall in Philadelphia. She was the daughter of William Darrah Kelley (1814–1890), who started work at age eleven years as an errand boy in a bookstore and later as an apprentice to Rickard & Dubosq, jewelers of Philadelphia. Through prodigious effort William rose to become a lawyer, judge and was re-elected fourteen times as a member of the U.S. House of Representatives, serving from 1860 until his death. A forceful speaker with progressive ideas, William D. Kelley advocated on behalf of the weak and the downtrodden. "The spirit of commerce," he said in 1866, "is essentially selfish." Wealth is collected in a few hands, leading to overproduction that reduces the laboring classes "to want and pauperism." William Kelley had a profound impact on his daughter's political thinking. One of Florence's earliest memories was a visit with her father to a glass factory where she saw little boys, frightened and haggard from long hours of grueling work.

Florence entered Cornell University at age sixteen but missed several years of schooling because of illness. Before she graduated from Cornell University she did research in the Library of Congress to complete her senior thesis on *Some Changes in the Legal Status of Children after Blackstone.*[2] The eighteenth-century English jurist William Blackstone wrote that a child is the property of his father. In the opinion of Florence Kelley, even illegitimate and poor children deserve their separate legal status and are not mere appendages of their parents.

After Cornell, she hoped to study law but, because she was a woman, Florence was denied admission to do graduate work at the University of Pennsylvania. Instead she traveled in 1883 to Switzerland to study at the Zurich Polytechnicum, one of the colleges in Europe open to women. Florence was among a few American women studying in Zurich; nearly all the women students were Russians, studying the sciences or medicine.

In Zurich, Florence attended lectures by Julius Platter (1844–1923), professor of economics at the university of Zurich, where she met Lazare Wischnewetzky, a Jewish-Russian medical student, born in Taganrog, a Black Sea port. Florence described Lazare as "a charming Russian gentleman who has been very kind in bringing me books on the National Economy lectures that we both hear." During her four years abroad, she met German socialists, banned by Bismarck and living in exile in Switzerland. In Zurich, Florence also attended lectures by Eduard Bernstein, editor of the newspaper of the German socialist party and a confidant of Karl Marx and Friedrich Engels. The impressionable Florence joined the Socialist Party, convinced that she was entering "the World of the Future." She read reports of bloody clashes between workers and militia in the United States, and believed that a full-scale revolution was soon to come, with victory to the working classes. In May 1884, she wrote to her father expressing concern that "the American workingman must ever more and more compete [against] the labor of women and children and imported contract laborers and ever-improving, man-superseding machinery." On October 14, she married Lazare Wischnewetzky.

Karl Marx died in March 14, 1883, and was buried in London's Highgate cemetery, with only eleven mourners present. Fired by socialist zeal, Florence Kelley wanted to educate the American workers on the writings of Marx and Engels. The following year, when only twenty-four years old, Kelley contacted Friedrich Engels to ask his permission to translate his classic *Condition of the Working-Class in England in 1844* from the original German into English. Engels was busy collecting, deciphering, and analyzing Marx's voluminous notes into what would be volumes 2 and 3 of *Das Kapital*. Writing from his comfortable home at 122 Regents Park Road, London, Engels was enthusiastic in having his earlier book translated for an American audience at a time when America's industrial evolution "corresponds at the present moment as nearly as possible to the English status in 1844."[3] America was following the European economic pattern, wrote Engels to Kelley, despite bourgeois opinion "that America stood above class antagonisms and struggles."(4)

In 1887, under her married name, the book was available in England and the United States. Kelley wrote Engels that 20,000 copies of *Condition of the Working-Class in England* had been printed with the aim "to make it accessible immediately to the greatest possible number of readers, since it bears directly upon the conditions of the labor movement in America at the present moment."[5] Two months later the excited Kelley informed Engels: "We have many orders in advance from all parts of the country and hundreds and hundreds of copies have been sent in all directions yesterday and today."[6] In addition, she had sent word about the American publication of the book "to every American organization of workingmen." Kelley-Wischnewetzky lauded Engels's book as "an amazing achievement." Hers remained until 1958 the only English-language translation of Engels' classic work

Friedrich Engels (1820–1895) was the son of a wealthy Prussian cotton manufacturer. At age twenty-two, he was sent to Manchester to manage the family's cotton interests at a time when that English city was at the height of its economic power. What captured his imagination was the plight and degradation of the workers — once self-employed craftsmen, now mere appendages to the power machinery of the Industrial Revolution. Engels wrote a series of articles that were published in a journal edited by Karl Marx. In 1845, these articles were assembled into a German-language book, *Die Lage der arbeitenden Klasse in England* (*The Condition of the Working-Class in England*) published in Leipzig. Friedrich Engels' brilliant indictment of capitalism at work in Manchester would form one of the prime pillars of communist theory. In the textile mills, wrote Engels, "machinery more and more supersedes the work of men. The human labor involved in both spinning and weaving consists chiefly in piecing broken threads and the machine does all of the rest. This work requires no muscular strength, but only flexibility of finger. Men are, therefore, not only not needed for it, but ... are less fit for it than women and children, and are, therefore, naturally almost superseded by them ... and, as women and children work more cheaply ... they take their places." Grown men earning nine shillings a week were replaced by little children paid half as much. As a result, "husbands were thrown out of employment." In Florence Kelley's translation, Engels piles on details of how badly working children were treated. In the English industrial towns, education "is upon a very low plane." Engels claimed that "from the beginning of manufacturing industry, children have been employed in mills.... Even children from work-houses were employed in multitudes, being rented out for a number of years to the manufacturers as apprentices. They were lodged, fed, and clothed in common, and were, of course, completely the slaves of their masters." Only a third of the children were able to read or write, because "children were taken from school in the seventh, and, at the very latest, in the twelve year.... A mass of children work the whole week through in the mills or at home and therefore cannot attend school." Working children have soft bones, which "make narrow chests universal." These children are "lean, pale, feeble and stunted" from malnutrition and lead poisoning. "The children," wrote Engels, "work in small, ill-ventilated, damp rooms.... They usually die of consumption after suffering the severest forms of digestive disorders."

Engels described the use of child labor also in the coal and iron mines of England, where "children of four, five and seven years are employed," In these mines, "opening and shutting the doors the smallest children are usually employed, who thus, pass twelve hours daily, in the dark, alone sitting usually in damp passages without even having work enough to save them from the stupefying, brutalizing tedium of doing nothing." In the mines, little children "crawl upon their hands and knees, fastened to a tub by a harness and chain," dragging coal through low-roofed tunnels. Working in noisy confined spaces, for twelve or more hours a day, leaves the children miserable in spirit and in body. These poor children lack "the usual mobility, liveliness and cheeriness of youth," but are sickly, depressed, enfeebled by illness, and after returning from work, wanting only "to be quiet at home." Engels, in Kelley's vibrant translation, has a special criticism about children working the night shift. Night work causes "irritation of the whole nervous system, with general lassitude and enfeeblement [leading to] drunkenness and unbridled sexual indulgence."

The British textile industry grew huge. By 1850, there were 4,340 textile mills in England, Scotland and Wales, with a total of twenty-six million spindles and over three hundred thousand power looms. These factories employed 596,082 workers of whom 40,775 were children under thirteen years of age.

Florence Kelley's translation of *The Condition of the Working-Class in England in 1844* was reprinted several times. In the 1892 edition Friedrich Engels wrote the preface, nearly fifty years after the original appeared in German. During that period, Engels wrote, the leading capitalists had become more skillful and cunning. They no longer battled the workers head-on but "were now at the forefront to preach peace and harmony ... all these concessions of justice and philanthropy were nothing else but means to accelerate the concentration of capital in the hands of a few ... and to crush all the quicker and all the safer their smaller competitors." Engels saw evidence of the class struggle not only in England but also across the continent and now in the United States. 'The cause of the miserable conditions of the working class is to be sought," he wrote in 1892, "in the *Capitalistic System itself*" (his emphasis). "The classes are divided more and more sharply, the spirit of resistance penetrates the workers, the bitterness intensifies; the guerilla skirmishes become concentrated in the more important battles," concluded Engels, four years before his death, "and soon the slightest impulse will suffice to set the avalanche in motion."

Paraphrasing Engels, Florence Kelley later wrote about how "the limitations of our bourgeois philanthropy, whatever form it may take, is really only an effort to give back to the workers a little bit of that which our whole social system, systematically robs them of, and so to prop up that system yet a little longer."[7]

Florence Kelley Wischnewetzky also translated Friedrich Engels' *The Labor Movement in the United States,* written in London in January 1887. Based on news reports of strikes shutting down American factories and mines, Engels foresaw the coming of a workers' revolt that, in Kelley's stirring translation, "burst out with such irresistible force, would spread with the rapidity of a prairie fire, [and] would shake American society to its very foundations." Kelley wrote to Engels bemoaning that Americans abroad who regard "what is admirable for Germany or England will not do at all for America — and Socialism remains for them a European product." Upon returning to America, Florence found, "We have almost no English speaking Socialists worthy of consideration or capable of influencing anyone favorably."[8] Engels advised her to reach out to labor groups such as the Knights of Labor which "ought not to be pooh-poohed from without but to be revolutionized from within."[9]

With a Russian husband, fluent German and her absorption of socialist doctrine, Florence Kelley had moved far from her American roots. She was not motivated principally by humanitarian concerns for the poor, but viewed their struggle in scientific terms — as defined by Marx and Engels. Her biographer Kathryn Kish Sklar wrote: "No other American student who later emerged to prominence in the Progressive Era ventured so fully into European Socialism; none left American political culture so far behind." Florence saw it as her task to use her skills as a translator and public speaker to spread the socialist doctrine on American soil. After completing the translation into English of *The Condition of the English Working Class in 1844,* Florence Kelley, husband Lazare Wischnewetzky and son left Switzerland in 1886 to settle in New York City. Lazare failed to establish his medical practice and by 1889 the marriage, now with three children, was failing.

The great debate in the 1888 presidential election was the issue of tariffs, with Benjamin Harrison favoring high tariffs and the incumbent Grover Cleveland campaigning on the promise to reduce tariffs on imported goods. Under her married name, Florence Kelley Wischnewetzky, Florence set about to educate the American worker by publishing her translation of *Free Trade,* a speech given in Brussels by Karl Marx on January 10, 1848, together with her translation of an introduction written specially by Friedrich Engels. The pamphlet was issued by the publishers Lee and Shepard, 10 Milk Street, Boston, at a cost of 25 cents. In his 1848 speech, Karl Marx said free trade "is the economic medium in which the conditions for inevitable social revolution will be soonest created." Free trade increases competition between nations and concentrates capital in fewer and fewer hands. By the use of machinery and technology, the capitalist system learns to "do entirely without the labor of men, or to reduce its price, by superseding the labor of the adult males by that of women and children. In most of the throstle mills, spinning is now entirely done by girls of sixteen and less."

In Florence Kelley's stirring translation, Karl Marx tells his audience: "You thousands of workers who are perishing, do not despair. You can die with an easy conscience.... Generally speaking, the protective system is conservative, while the free trade system works destructively. It breaks up old nationalities and carries antagonism of proletariat and bourgeoisie to the utmost point. In a word, the free trade system hastens the Social Revolution. In this revolutionary sense alone, gentleman, I am in favor of free trade."

In February 1848, Karl Marx and Friedrich Engels published *The Communist Manifesto*, setting the stage for the proletarian revolution and calling for the abolition of private property and for state ownership of factories. In addition, the *Manifesto* called for free education for all children in public schools and the end to child labor. In 1867, Karl Marx and Friedrich Engels published Volume 1 of their epic work *Capital: A Critique of Political Economy*. In one section of the book they liken child labor to slavery. "The capitalist buys children and young persons under age.... He becomes a slave dealer. The demand for children's labor often resembles in form the inquiries for negro slaves." Marx and Engels quote advertisements seen in the English press, such as: "Wanted, 12 to 20 young persons, not younger than what will pass for 13 years. Wages, 4 shillings a week." The wording of the advertisement conformed to the regulations of the Factory Act forbidding children less than 13 years working more than six hours a day. Marx and Engels saw this as a subterfuge for "the capitalist's greed for exploitation, and the sordid trafficking needs of the parents," lying about the age of the children. Both Marx and Engels identified cheap child labor as a central feature of rapacious capitalism, a concept Kelley fully accepted. The practice would disappear only when the working classes gained control of the economy and the state.

Florence Kelley eagerly absorbed these teachings and, by age twenty-seven, she had found her life-mission. She did not allow her own poverty and family chaos to interfere with her efforts to become the crusader for the rights of children. On December 29, 1887, she wrote to Engels bemoaning the "perfectly fuddled" state of the American labor movement. Of the annual conference of the American Federation of Labor, held in Baltimore, she complained that on the "prohibition of the employment of children etc. not one word can be found." Florence wrote to Engels: "I am working on the subject of Child Labor (and Compulsory Education), using statistics from State Bureaus, State Board of Education reports, census, Factory Inspectors reports etc."[10] Though she held no public or university office, in 1889 she issued *Our Toiling Children,* decrying the use of children in the labor force.

In *Our Toiling Children*—first printed in "Our Day," a Boston-based reformist magazine—Florence Kelley Wischnewetzky wrote: "The workingman's child is a drudge from its childhood." Children four years old worked in the tenement sweating system. In New

Jersey, "the labor power of children seven and eight years old was a commodity extensively consumed in the mills." In 1889, factory inspectors reported finding 9,471 children less than sixteen years of age working in the textile mills. In 1880 in Ohio, the Bureau of Labor Statistics reported 48,593 children under fifteen working for wages. Children were put to work because they were cheap labor. Children were at risk because of poor conditions of work, the risk of fire, danger from steam boiler explosions and unguarded machinery. Mill life, she wrote, "has a most demoralizing effect on children ... who have no parents in the mills to watch over them." She advocated compulsory school attendance and a nationwide ban on children working until they reached sixteen years of age. In an 1887 talk she told college alumnae that she had joined the working class in its epic battle "to end [the capitalist] system ... that is rending society to its foundations."

In *Our Toiling Children*, Kelley (signing herself Florence Kelley Wischnewetzky), declares that in America, "child labor flourishes unchecked." Using figures from the 1880 census, she reports that there are "a million toiling children [who are] sacrificing intelligence and future usefulness to the immediate needs of contributing to the support of younger brothers and sisters." Children as young as twelve to fourteen years "and even still below that age, are put to work in mills and mines for twelve hours a day." Some are forced to work by "dissolute fathers and mothers who live by the wages the children earn," or by widowed mothers without means. "But, the mass of child workers are sons and daughters of the very poor, the newly immigrated, and those engaged in branches in which wages are below the living point. These adults cannot by their own effort banish their children" to labor.

Child labor, according to Kelley, is exploitation and robs children of "the sacred leisure of boyhood and girlhood [and leads] to the destruction of health, intelligence, morals, and often life itself." Cheap child labor distorts the workplace. "Adult workers are idle," she exclaims, "because the children are underselling adults in the labor market." The ban of labor of children under fourteen, even under sixteen, can be achieved by setting up child labor bureaus, enacting factory rules, appointing inspectors of mills and mines, compulsory education, appointing truant officers and by cooperating with trade unions working for "the banishment of the competition of child labor from the labor market." In a not-too-subtle dig at her abusive husband, Dr. Lazare Wischnewetzky, she adds, there should be "vigorous enforcement of parental duty" aimed especially at "the delinquent father."

In December 1891, Florence fled her marriage and New York, taking her three children to start a new life in Chicago. Dropping the name Wischnewetzky, she was now Mrs. Florence Kelley. She found a haven in Hull House, the settlement house run by Jane Addams, Julia Lathrop and other spirited humanitarian and idealistic women. "We were greeted as though we had been invited," Florence said later. Florence was given the job of advising immigrant girls looking for work. She soon discovered that Hull House was "surrounded in every direction by home-work carried on under the sweating-system." A few weeks after her arrival in Chicago she was ready to display her credentials by giving a talk on child labor at the Working People's Social Science Club at Hull House. Florence was eager to "investigate the sweating system in Chicago, with its attendant child labor." Florence and her Hull House friends drew maps charting the extent of tenement labor in Chicago, sending the data to legislators, suggesting that the Illinois Bureau of Labor investigate the sweating system in Chicago. These reports were presented in book form with the title *Hull-House*

Maps and Papers (1895). Kelley wrote the chapters on the sweating system and wage-earning children. In her report, which occupied a quarter of the book, Kelley recommended fixing fourteen years as the age at which a child could be employed. Based on her research skills, in May 1892, she was appointed the special agent of the Bureau of Labor Statistics of Illinois to investigate the conditions in the tenement needle-trades in preparation for regulation of the sweatshops.

In 1893, the year of the Chicago World's Columbian Exposition, the Illinois legislature accepted Kelley's recommendations and passed laws banning children younger than fourteen years from working in factories, shops, and stores. Children fifteen and sixteen years were allowed to work provided they had a certificate from school showing they had completed a required level of education. The law also established the Illinois State Factory Inspection Department. In July, the newly elected and progressive governor of Illinois, John Peter Altgeld, promoted the indefatigable Florence Kelley as chief factory inspector of Illinois, at a salary of $125 a month. With an office at 247 W. Polk Street, aided by a staff of eleven, and a budget of $28,000 a year, it was her responsibility to ensure compliance with the new state laws.

Five months after her appointment, she wrote to Friedrich Engels: "I find my work as inspector most interesting; and as Governor Altgeld places no restrictions whatever upon our freedom of speech ... we are not hampered by our position and three of my deputies and my assistant are outspoken socialists and active in agitation."[11] Florence was greatly influenced by Engels. She believed that machines did the work and that workers were slaves of the machines. With human power replaced by machine power, children were exploited as the cheapest form of labor and were replacing adult workers who were more expensive to hire. Philanthropy was a ploy to lessen the anger and weaken the revolutionary zeal of the workers. In short, the misery of children and the working classes comes from the capitalist system itself. Her descriptions of the terrible conditions of work in Illinois factories of the 1890s, and the toll it takes on the exploited child workers read much like her translation of Friedrich Engels' 1844 book.

Florence Kelley's revolutionary socialism mellowed after returning to America. Rather than overthrow the capitalist system, Florence Kelley, as a public servant, attempted to reform it from within. She visited factories, wrote many case studies and presented lengthy annual reports. In her first report as chief factory inspector of Illinois, Kelley noted the terrible conditions of work for the children, mostly of immigrant stock, with little English or education. Nearly 9 percent of the state's workers were children fifteen years or younger. In her third report (for the year 1895), Florence Kelley had truly found her reformer's voice. Enforcement of the laws, she claimed, helped lower the employment of underage children to less than 5 percent of all workers. Still, large numbers of children were found in 1895 working in sweatshops, Chicago's meat packers and the glassworks.

In the sweatshops of Chicago, Kelley found children less than ten years of age working long hours. She reported that "the filth and overcrowding are worse than I have seen outside of Naples and the East Side of New York." She witnessed "child labor in most cruel forms and render the tenement house manufacture of clothing a deadly danger to the whole community." In 1896, Chicago had 2,378 sweatshops, employing over 25,000 workers of whom one in ten was a child under fourteen years of age. The plethora of sweatshops in the tenements of Chicago (and in other cities) made inspections difficult. When dealing with "sweaters" and their immigrant workers who did not know English, it proved difficult to keep little children out of the shops. In the sweatshops Kelley and her inspectors found "boys whose backs have been made crooked for life by continuous work at heavy machines and boys and girls unable to speak English, and equally unable to read or write in any language." One sweatshop required that children work for free for the first six months, with a promise of $1 a week afterwards. So desperate were the immigrant parents for income and so willing were the sweaters to take advantage, that there were at least 1,000 little girls and 128 little boys working in the Chicago sweatshops, even after four years of determined effort by Florence Kelley and her staff of factory inspectors. The sweaters, Florence Kelley reported in 1897, "are so irresponsible, so shifting, so numerous that no small body of inspectors can adequately follow them up." Florence's first efforts to prosecute offending sweaters were met with indifference by the district attorneys. She took matters in her own hands by registering at Northwestern University for a law degree, graduating in June 1894, one of first female lawyers in the United States.

Florence Kelley also reported on the wretched lives of Chicago's children, working as newsboys and bootblacks, in the department stores and the candy factories. Her reports on the Illinois glassworks provoked howls of protest. The factory owners claimed that "the work of young children was absolutely indispensable to the manufacture of bottles," and if the law was enforced the glass companies would have to leave the state. In May 1895, with pressure from the Illinois Association of Manufacturers, the Illinois Supreme Court pronounced the law unconstitutional. From 1893 to 1897, America was in an economic recession with the bankruptcy of hundreds of railroads, and thousands of businesses. The year 1894 saw the Pullman strike with 5,000 federal troops sent in to keep order. In 1896, Florence Kelley and her band of factory inspectors, issued 769 fines for violations of the Illinois child labor laws.

With thousands out of work, Kelley's enforcement of the laws against child labor was unpopular both with the factory owners and the immigrants. The immigrants needed the money while the owners complained they could not be competitive without cheap child labor. True, the work was hard, even dangerous, it did not pay well, but it put bread on the table, In 1896, John Peter Altgeld was defeated and Florence Kelley was out of a job. No longer with the power to enforce the laws, she tried to influence opinion through her writings. The way forward, Kelley wrote in 1897, is to have "compulsory education of all school children under sixteen years of age throughout the entire year." The health of a society rests on the "carefully-nourished childhood of all future citizens."

Under the influence of Jane Addams and Julia Lathrop at Hull House, Florence Kelley came to accept steady and incremental change through social pressure and legislation rather than preaching revolution. After losing her state job, Kelley briefly returned to a more militant form of socialistic ideology. In 1899, she published her translation of a speech given in German in 1870 by Johan Jacoby, the courageous voice of the German Social Democratic Party who opposed the policies of Otto von Bismarck. In her lengthy introduction, Florence voiced her support for the American Labor Party and called for the nationalization of the land and of all means of production. American power and capital, she wrote, are in the hands of "a comparatively small class of capitalists" who control the government, which is "a far-too-humble servant of its plutocratic owners." The American working class, she wrote, should not be satisfied with small wages and a tiny share of the profits, but should fight for "the whole of the profits." Preventing child labor, she complained is "generally evaded for want of adequate inspection." Kelley encouraged American workers to read "the fundamental works upon Socialism, Marx's *Capital* and Engels' *Condition of the English Working Class*, [which] have been made accessible in translation to English-reading workers." A powerful and knowledgeable American labor movement, Florence Kelley believed, would allow for a "more peaceful change ... with the Revolution diminished in bloodshed, revenge and savagery." Sympathy and persuasion were not sufficient, charity and philanthropy mere salves for the conscience of the wealthy. Real change could only come from political action.

National Consumers League

Josephine Shaw Lowell (1843–1905), born in West Roxbury, Massachusetts, was sister to Robert Gould Shaw, who, during the Civil War, was appointed colonel of the 54th Massachusetts Regiment, made up of black troops. He led them bravely in the second Battle of Fort Wayne, near Charleston, South Carolina, where he and many of his troops were killed. Josephine, known to her family as Effie, was married in 1863 to Charles Russell Lowell, of the Lowell dynasty. On his father's side his great uncle was Francis Cabot Lowell, and on his mother's side his grandfather was Patrick Tracy Jackson; these were the two men most responsible for bringing the industrial revolution to America, and later, for the establishment of Lowell as America's first industrial city. Effie was twenty years old and Charles twenty-seven when they married. Appointed a general in the Union Army, in 1864, Charles was killed at the Battle of Cedar Creek, leaving Effie eight months pregnant.

Josephine moved to New York City where she became active in charity work, especially helping impoverished workingwomen. In 1878, she was appointed commissioner of the New York State Board of Charities. In 1890 Josephine Lowell established the New York Consumers' League, which spawned sister organizations in Boston, Philadelphia, Chicago and other cities.

Now without steady employment, Florence Kelley learned that Governor Theodore Roosevelt of New York was planning to add factory inspectors. She wrote to him from Chicago asking to be appointed chief factory inspector, since there was no one "else in the field who would work so effectively against the sweating-system as I could."[12] Noting her Illinois address, the governor responded that she would not be eligible for a New York government job. In January 1899, Florence Kelley was offered the job as executive secretary of the newly formed National Consumers League (NCL). Despite her firm socialist ideology, and her disdain for organizations dependent on charity, she accepted the position at NCL at an annual salary of fifteen hundred dollars plus expenses. During May 1899, Florence left Hull House in Chicago for New York, where she would continue her spirited campaign against child labor. Befriending Lillian Wald, she moved with her children into the Henry Street settlement house in the Lower East Side and remained there for two decades. Kelley vigorously moved the NCL to battle against child labor, night work, sweatshop-made clothing and against excessive hours of work. Buying clothes made in sweatshops was tantamount to supporting the oppression of women and children workers. Under Kelley's leadership the NCL inspected clothing factories and issued its famous White Label attached to goods meeting fair labor standards and advocated a boycott of goods lacking the NCL stamp of approval.

To spread her message she traveled across the nation addressing, in 1903 alone, one hundred and one meetings. At colleges and meeting halls, Florence inspired many young women to join the cause and fight for the rights of children, women and workers. Among them were Frances Perkins, a graduate of Mt. Holyoke College, and Florence L. Sanville of Bryn Mawr College, who were to play key roles in advancing Kelley's ideas. Another of her protégées was Mary Williams Dewson, known as Molly. A graduate of Wellesley College, Molly headed the New York Consumers' League and later joined with President Franklin D. Roosevelt to ensure passage of his New Deal legislation.

Florence Kelley remained with the National Consumers League for thirty-three years. Through her efforts, the NCL had thirty local branches by 1901, sixty-three by 1906, and over 30,000 members by 1913. The NCL became one of the leading organizations of the Progressive Era. Florence linked the NCL with the National Child Labor Committee and other like-minded organizations to increase its influence. Louis Brandeis served as legal counsel to NCL until he was selected in 1916 for the Supreme Court, after which Felix Frankfurter then professor of law at Harvard, filled the position at NCL.

In Chicago, Florence Kelley was "the toughest customer in the reform riot," wrote Jane Addams, "the finest rough-and-tumble fighter for the good of others.... Any weapon was a good weapon in her hand — evidence, argument, irony or invective." In New York, Kelley

Factory inspectors meet at a conference in New Orleans, March 1914. From left to right, they are Ella Haas, Dayton, Ohio; Mary Malone, Delaware; Florence Kelley, who served as chief factory inspector of Illinois from 1893 to 1897; Jean Gordon, New Orleans, Madge Nave, Louisville, Kentucky; and Martha D. Gould, New Orleans.

found an ally in Lillian Wald, a nurse, who had established the Henry Street Settlement House. The idea of a federal children's bureau, propagated by Kelley and Wald, gained the support of President Theodore Roosevelt, but it took longer to convince the House of Representatives. The Triangle Shirtwaist Company fire of 1911 and the Bread and Roses strike of the mill workers of Lawrence, Massachusetts, in 1912, focused public attention on child labor and the dangers of factory work. On April 9, 1912, a federal Children's Bureau, under the Department of Labor, was signed into law by President Taft with the mandate to investigate "all matters pertaining to the welfare of children and child life among all classes of our people." Selected as first chief of the Children's Bureau was Julia Lathrop, friend of Florence Kelley and yet another of the determined band of social reformers coming out of Chicago's Hull House.

Edmond Kelly (1851–1909) gained his undergraduate degree in 1875 from Cambridge University before moving to New York to take his law degree at Columbia University in 1877. After practicing law in New York for a number of years he wrote a series of books — now forgotten — on religion and politics and the plight of the unemployed. He came to the conclusion that capitalism was inherently flawed and should be replaced by benign socialism. In his 1906 book, *A Practical Programme for Working Men*, he wrote: "Philanthropy is not Charity, but Justice," and the capitalist system "sets every man fighting his neighbor and creates an environment of hate that can, by substituting co-operation for competition, create an environment of mutual happiness and love."

Around 1908, Edmond Kelly set about to write *Twentieth Century Socialism: What It Is Not, What It Is, How It May Come.* He was able only to complete the first draft before he died in 1909, having earlier entrusted the "considerable editorial work to Mrs. Florence Kelley." With its interest in tenements and the evils of capitalism, the final book holds much of Florence Kelley's pungent style and interest. The Kelly–Kelley book states that capitalism "is stupid," causing overproduction, unemployment, strikes and waste. Out of "every one hundred men who start a new business, ninety become insolvent." Even the capitalist distribution system is inefficient. Each company sells its own eggs, bread, milk, vegetables, fish and meat instead of forming a single delivery system. Kelly–Kelley hailed the government-operated post office, which collects the mail, sorts it out and delivers it to the homes and places of work. A planned, non-competitive but co-operative economy, held the authors, is more efficient and more just, than cutthroat capitalism, with its stockbrokers and Wall Street, gambling on stocks and shares.

"In a Socialistic society," claim Kelly and Kelley, "the woman and the child are provided for, being all members and all sharing in its income." Socialism is not communism and will not suppress competition, suspend liberties, abolish property rights or suppress competition.

Personality of Florence Kelley

Florence endured many disappointments and losses in her life. The most tragic of these occurred in 1905 when she received a telegram from Smith College informing her that her teenage daughter, Margaret, had suddenly died. Florence aged with her daughter's death, but still she continued to fight the battles on behalf of children and women.

In *The House on Henry Street* (1915), Lillian Wald wrote about the profound influence of "Mrs. Florence Kelley, now and many years a member of the settlement family. She has long consecrated her energies to securing protective legislation throughout the country for children compelled to labor." By her own admission, Florence was a woman of intense feelings. She was "a raging furnace, so consumed with burning indignation against everything that I saw, and smelt, and breathed, and loathed."[13] At age forty, when she came to New York to run the National Consumers League, Florence Kelley was already a heavy-set woman who showed little interest in fashion and wore her beautiful dark hair in braids. According to her protégée Josephine Goldmark, Florence's face expressed her every mood; her jowls quivered when she was angry and her eyes sparkled when she was amused. As a speaker she was unrivaled, mixing statistics with humor, denunciation with approval, emotion with objectivity, all to serve her purpose of improving the lives of working people and allowing children the gift of their childhood. "No other man or woman I have ever heard," continued Goldmark, "so blended knowledge of facts, with satire, burning indignation, prophetic denunciation and all poured out at white heat in a voice varying from flute-like tones to deep organ tones." Another protégée, Frances Perkins, added that Kelley "had the voice and presence of a great actress, although she was far from theatrical in her intentions." She was "explosive, hot tempered, determined, she was no gentle saint.... She was a smoking volcano that at any moment would burst into flames." Elsewhere, Frances Perkins said of Kelley, "She knew no discouragement and no despair, and when the rest of us were willing to give up ... it was to her but a signal to begin again." Injustice sent Kelley into action. Distressed by the persecution of people for their political beliefs, in 1920 she joined Jane Addams, Lillian Wald, Felix Frankfurter, Upton Sinclair, Clarence Darrow and others to form the American Civil Liberties Union.

Florence Kelley energized the next generation of women — especially graduates of the Seven Sisters female colleges — to join the fight for women and children's rights and a square deal for workers. Florence Kelley was tenacious. "She made her generation think," was the assessment of Lillian Wald. "She was not afraid of truth, she was not afraid of life, she was not afraid of death, she was not afraid of enemies."

Florence Kelley opposed the entry of the United States in World War I. For this act she was branded unpatriotic and anti–American. In 1918, Florence was elected president of the Inter-Collegiate Socialist Society, headquartered at 70 Fifth Avenue, New York. Her son Nicholas, a graduate of Harvard College, was a member of the executive committee. With the gathering forces of reaction and the Red scare in the 1920s, Florence was labeled by Senator Thomas F. Bayard of Delaware an agent of international communism and, based on her translation of the works of Friedrich Engels, as "the chief promoter of communism in the United States." Bayard asserted that Engels had instructed Kelley "how to introduce socialism into the flesh and blood of Americans," and that she was now acting under direct orders from Moscow. In 1927, Lieutenant Colonel Lee Alexander Stone, addressing the Illinois Democratic Women's Club, criticized the child labor amendment and called Florence Kelley "a Leninist." Kelley considered a libel suit against the Daughters of the American Revolution for defaming her in a pamphlet, *The Common Enemy*. In 1931, toward the close of her life, Florence was still responding to critics who labeled her "a Russian and one of the country's leading Communists." She reminded her accusers that her American roots ran deep. Her father, William D. Kelley, represented the Fourth Congressional District of Pennsylvania from 1861 to 1890. "I have never been a communist and am not one now, quite the contrary."[14]

Florence Kelley's unflagging energy to improve the lot of children came from various sources. She believed that girls and boys were entitled to a good education before they went out to work. From her childhood onwards she was moved by the plight of little boys working in the glass factories. With her political ideology set solidly on the writings of Karl Marx and Friedrich Engels, she believed that children were employed as cheap labor, thus putting adults out of work or depressing their wages. Only by embracing education and banning child labor could adult workers get a fair wage.

Jane Addams compared the personality styles of her great friends Julia Lathrop and Florence Kelley—"these two tremendously useful women." Julia "the diplomat, reasoned and cajoled," while Florence was "the fighter, who believed in the direct assault ... she gave of herself so unsparingly that sometimes it seemed as if her life was too hard." In 1932, American women were polled on whom they regarded as the twelve greatest of their sex during the previous one hundred years. Jane Addams of Hull House and 1931 Nobel Peace Prize winner, was included in the list along with Harriett Beecher Stowe, Susan B. Anthony, Helen Keller and eight others.[15] Asked for her comment, the modest Jane Addams said she would leave off her own name and several others from the list in preference for her great friends, Julia C. Lathrop and Florence Kelley.[16]

When Florence Kelley took ill the executive board of the Consumers' League chose Molly Dewson to fill her place until a permanent head was appointed. Florence Kelley died on February 17, 1932. Frances Perkins lauded her as "that mother of us all" and as "the head of the family in this enterprise which binds us all together." Her son, Nicholas Kelley, was born in Zurich and came to the United States as a little boy. A graduate of Harvard College and Harvard Law School, he served as assistant secretary of the treasury in two administrations. Nicholas became a prominent New York corporate lawyer while still sharing his mother's social values. In the 1930s he settled an automobile company strike and was appointed to serve as a director of the Chrysler Corporation. His daughter, named Florence after her grandmother, served as a judge of the New York family court and followed the family heritage to serve the poor.

4

Settlement Houses — Jane Addams, Julia Lathrop and Lillian Wald

Child Labor, of course, is a menace not only to the young people but to all workers. —Eleanor Roosevelt, *Collier's,* June 15, 1940

At the start of the nineteenth century, New York City had 60,575 people. Seventy years later its population topped one million and in 1900, America's first city was home to 3,437,202. Chicago's expansion was similarly astonishing. In 1833, it had only 360 people but sixty-seven years later it was America's second city with a population of 1,698,575. By 1870, the population of the United States was 38,566,000, made up mostly of native-born Americans. The wealth of the nation was still concentrated in the Northeast, especially New York, Massachusetts and Pennsylvania. Even before the great wave of European immigrants, American cities attracted large numbers of foreign-born settlers. Thirty million European immigrants arrived on America's shores between 1880 and 1910, and crowded ever more into its cities.

The tenement buildings of the Lower East Side in New York City were originally built as five- or six-story walk-ups with four comfortable family-sized apartments on each floor. Speculators bought these buildings, cut them into smaller units and rented them to immigrant families, stuffed to the rafters with six to eight people to a room. Here they lived, and here they worked. Soon after the Civil War came to an end, the tenement districts of New York, Chicago, Boston, Philadelphia and other American cities became the great centers for labor-intensive industries. "The moment one enters the hall-door his nostrils are saturated with the intolerable odor of moldy tobacco…. From ceiling to attic the business carried on is the stripping of tobacco or manufacture of cigars, women as well as men, girls as well as boys, toiling for dear life in an atmosphere foggy with tobacco dust and reeking with odors too foul to describe."[1] After paying the rent, use and repair of the tools of the trade, "the poor worker has scarcely enough left to pay the clamorous grocer. While the families are tied down to a servitude worse than death." By 1882, an estimated 40,000 persons were working in New York's tenement tobacco factories, 100,000 in its sweatshops, and thousands more in other tenement-factories.

One irate observer complained of the "barbarism of huddling working people like cattle and working the life out of them, men, women and children."[2] Another New York commentator wrote passionately about the children of the poor: "Their passage from cradle to workbench is a short one…. Passing through any of the leading streets or avenues in the early morning, hundreds of these children may be seen walking in hurried steps to store or shop or factory to work through the long hours of the day until the dusk of the evening sets them free to return to their squalid homes in crowded tenements."[3] In his provocative 1890 book *How the Other Half Lives,* Jacob Riis described the gutter life of New York's poor and downtrodden. In one sweatshop on Ludlow Street, Riis found "five men and a woman, two young girls, not yet fifteen, and a boy, who says unasked that he is fifteen, and lies in saying it, in a small room sewing knickerbockers.... The faces, hands and arms to the elbows of everyone in the room is black with the color of the cloth on which they are working." The children were paid a pittance for their long hours of work. After the fire of 1871, Chicago, to accommodate the flood of immigrants, was festooned with squalid homes stretching from the Old Town to the North Side, the West Side and around the stockyards.

The immigrants, huddled in the inner-city slums, were invisible to the middle- and upper classes that rarely crossed to the other side of the tracks. There were but a few noble people who cared enough to move out of their comfortable homes and neighborhoods and to live among the immigrants and help them integrate into American life. Florence Kelley and three other women stand center stage among these remarkable people—well educated, well off, well organized, responsible and compassionate. The others were Jane Addams, Julia Lathrop and Lillian Wald. Their upper-middle-class values had served them well and now they wanted to impose these values on the teeming immigrant masses.

Jane Addams, one of America's most remarkable women, was born in 1860 in Cedarville, Illinois, the eighth of nine children. Her mother died when Jane was two years old and she was raised by her father, a wealthy miller, and by her older sister. In 1881, Jane graduated from the Rockford Female Seminary, where her classmate was Julia Lathrop. The next six years were spent touring Europe and seeking a mission for her life. This she found in 1887 while visiting Toynbee Hall, a community of educated men dedicated to serving the poor in London's East End. With her friend Ellen Gates Starr, Jane Addams was determined to establish a settlement house in Chicago. In 1889, three years after the Haymarket riot, the two women moved into Hull House, at 800 S. Halsted in Chicago's Near West Side, which became a remarkable "community of university women" (and at least one man, Robert Hunter) eager to help the deracinated immigrants crowding in the surrounding tenements. Jane Addams and her friends used their own money to keep Hull House afloat, with help from a number of immensely wealthy yet progressive-minded Chicago residents such as Anita McCormick Blaine, daughter of Cyrus McCormick, the maker of the mechanical reaper, and daughter-in-law of James G. Blaine, twice United States secretary of state.[4]

Addams and her team of idealistic, American-born young women learned quickly how harsh life was for the newcomers. "Our very first Christmas at Hull House, when we as yet knew nothing of child labor," she wrote, was a shock when a group of little girls refused the gift of candies, because "they worked in a candy factory and could not bear the sight of it." Addams met children who worked "from seven o'clock in the morning until nine at night," making clothing in the sweatshops. That winter she saw three boys with serious injuries from machinery. The parents were bribed by the factory owners to sign documents saying they would make no claims because the injuries were the result of carelessness. "The visits we made in the neighborhood constantly discovered women sewing upon sweatshop work, and often they were assisted by incredibly small children. I remember a little girl of four who pulled out basting threads hour after hour ... a little bunch of human misery."

Jane Addams, known as "the mother of social science," was a pacifist and was elected chairperson of the Woman's International League for Peace and Freedom. Lillian Wald (center top) and Jane Addams hold a press conference in Washington 1916. Male reporters lean forward to catch what Ms. Addams is saying.

Not only did children help their parents, but also many worked while the parents were idle. "We learned to know many families in which the working children contributed to the support of their parents, not only because they spoke English better than the older immigrants and were willing to take lower wages, but because their parents gradually found it easy to live upon their earnings." The children, lamented Addams, were forced "prematurely to bear the weight of life."

In 1896, Jane Addams traveled to Russia to visit her spiritual hero, Leo Tolstoy. She was but one of thousands of visitors eager to see, touch and hopefully, speak to the great writer, pacifist and champion of the poor. To Jane Addams the visit to Tolstoy's home inspired her to continue to live among and assist the immigrants in the tenements close to Hull House. She established a public kitchen, kindergarten, club for older girls, vocational counseling, an art studio, music room, drama club, and a library. In her autobiography, published in 1911, she described Hull House as a place where immigrant children "are taught the things which will make life in America more possible."

Based on Marxist ideology, Florence Kelley regarded child workers as a capitalist trick to increase profits by the use of the cheapest forms of labor. Jane Addams came from a humanistic perspective, guided by religion and Tolstoy based on the belief that people must learn to do well to each other. American industry, she wrote, was built by self-made men who came up the hard way, and believe that work teaches children responsibility and gave them the drive to improve themselves. "The Southern employers say," wrote Addams in 1902, "that these children are brought in from the farms and mountains where people are very poor, and there are no schools, and that it is better for them to come to the mill villages where there are schools and churches." Jane Addams viewed child labor as evidence of a nation's low moral and social development. By its elimination, the United States and other nations will rise to a higher moral level, making peace between them much more likely.[5]

Among her many causes—women's rights, a world without wars, sanitation, housing, fighting corruption and greed—Jane Addams remained a strong advocate for the right of children to a good education and protection from early labor and work at night. She accepted the capitalist system so long as the bosses were fair and reasonable. Jane Addams attended meetings of the National Child Labor Committee and joined its board of trustees in 1911. Speaking at the second conference of the NCLC, in 1905, Jane Addams made clear her goal of an educated proletariat. In no way, she said, did she "advocate a life of idleness or of meaningless activity." The children of the immigrants were destined for factory work, "which makes no demands upon originality," but is a monotonous, thoughtless grind. By staying in school until age fourteen and beyond these children could be educated so "that their minds may finally take possession of the machines, which they guide and feed." She wanted child labor legislation "which increases the free and full development of the individual because he thereby becomes a more valuable provider." She supported the efforts of her friends Lillian Wald and Florence Kelley for a federal children's bureau to ensure that "children are properly protected up to the time they may go to work without injury to themselves and without injury to the nation." Addams, who was called the mother of social service, wanted "to have the labor of children protected and regulated through legislation [and spared from] premature toil, because our commercial and industrial life has been so ruthless and so self-centered that it has never given them a thought." In 1908, she advocated an apprenticeship system to train the young worker "to master the machine with his mind, and to supplement the daily grind of the factory with some spiritual power, which will humanize and lift the workman above its demeaning effects."

The pioneering work done at Hull House attracted other university-educated, well-off and high-minded women "of old American stock." Julia Lathrop was born in 1858 in Rockford, Illinois, where her father was a prominent lawyer. She attended Rockford Female Seminary. After graduating from Vassar College in Poughkeepsie, New York, she returned to Rockford to work in her father's office. In 1890 she moved to Hull House to join her Rockland Seminary classmate, Jane Addams. Julia's first educational activity for the impoverished tenement residents was her highbrow Sunday afternoon Plato Club, using the Benjamin Jowett translation from the Greek into English of the *Dialogues*.

During the smallpox epidemic that hit Chicago at the time of the 1893 World's Columbian Exposition, Julia Lathrop worked closely with Florence Kelley, fearlessly going into the infected tenements and, armed with court orders, confiscating and destroying contaminated clothing, and saving "hundreds, perhaps thousands of lives." Kelley and Lathrop were close in age, both were daughters of lawyers and both trained in the law themselves, but they were far apart in temperament. Lathrop was the diplomat, reasoned and calm, while Kelley was the fighter, given to hyperbole and anger. Lathrop worked comfortably within the legal system, and was able, according to Northwestern University law professor

A. A. Bruce, to "sympathize with the problems of the employer as well as those of the employee and the unemployed." Kelley, by contrast, solidly backed the poor and down-trodden, and agitated for a workers' revolution, peaceful if possible. Together, they were a forceful partnership for progress.

In 1893, Illinois governor John Altgeld appointed Kelley as chief factory inspector and appointed Lathrop to serve on the State Board of Charities. In this capacity Julia visited the state jails and poorhouses and witnessed firsthand the neglect of children. In the Cook County poorhouse, Julia wrote, "there are usually from fifty to seventy-five children of whom a large proportion are young children with their mothers." There were also abandoned "children whom no one cares to adopt because they are unattractive, scarred or sickly." These children remained in the institution for years, were dressed in ugly clothes and jeered at while attending local schools. Julia fought to improve the care of the mentally insane, housed far from the cities in huge mental asylums. In 1898, she visited Europe to study the "boarding-out" system and the care of the mentally ill in small communities.

From the beginning of her residence at Hull House, Julia Lathrop showed a special interest in the children. One young resident remembered Julia's "brown eyes, so sincere but with a sparkle lurking in them, her slow redolent voice, her flavor of Illinois." In her 1935 book *My Friend, Julia Lathrop*, Jane Addams recalled, "Lathrop's profound compassion for her helpless fellow men, and her sense of responsibility for basic human needs." On learning that delinquent children appeared in the police courts and were placed in jail with hardened criminals, Julia Lathrop in 1899 joined forces with wealthy Chicago women to guide the Illinois Juvenile Court Act into law, and set up a separate system to care for young offend-ers — the nation's first juvenile court system. The juvenile courthouse was built on South Halsted Street diagonally across from Hull-House. Instead of police custody, troubled chil-dren were placed under the care of probation officers.

In 1903, Lathrop was elected president of the new Juvenile Court Committee, with the task of caring for troubled children before their cases reached the juvenile courts. In addition she ran a detention center, and raised funds to expand the probation system. Many of the children appearing before the court suffered from mental illness. Lathrop persuaded the wealthy Mrs. Ethel Dummer, wife of the banker William F. Dummer, to provide the funds to set up a children's mental health clinic. This clinic evolved into the Illinois Institute for Juvenile Research. Ethel Dummer maintained her interest in child welfare and in 1905 joined the National Child Labor Committee.

Julia Lathrop helped establish the Chicago School of Civics and Philanthropy, the Chicago Women's Club and the Immigrants Protective League. In 1909, she joined the New York-based National Committee for Mental Hygiene dedicated to improving mental hos-pitals, conducting research into mental illness and training staff. In 1910, in the company of her widowed sister, Anna Lathrop Case, she went on a journey around the world. She was deeply moved by the plight of the child-widows of India, the grinding poverty through-out Asia, and even poverty in the East End of London. The long journey gave her a world-wide perspective of poverty and the suffering of children. When she returned to Chicago as a resident of Hull-House, Julia Lathrop had a nationwide reputation as an ardent protector of the under-privileged. She did not remain long in Chicago; in 1912 she moved to Wash-ington upon accepting the appointment by President Taft as chief of the newly formed federal Children's Bureau.

Julia Lathrop (1858–1932) graduated Vassar College. In 1890 she moved to Chicago to join Jane Addams and later, Florence Kelley, in the Hull-House Settlement. In 1912, President William Taft appointed Lathrop as the first chief of the U.S. Children's Bureau. She is shown at her desk in Washington, 1913.

In 1915, Julia Lathrop issued a comprehensive state-by-state account of the *Child Labor Legislation in the United States*. There were still wide discrepancies, but the states were working toward a national standard of the laws governing minimal age of employment, hours of work, night work and compulsory school attendance.

Robert Hunter (1874–1942) was born in Terre Haute, Indiana, where his father manufactured horse-drawn carriages and buggies. After graduating from the University of Indiana he came to Chicago to work as organizing secretary of the city's Board of Charities. In this capacity he met Jane Addams, Julia Lathrop and Florence Kelley and was one of few men to take up residence at Hull-House to join the women in their pioneering work. Under Addams' leadership, Robert Hunter conducted a survey on the *Tenement Conditions in Chicago* (1901). The damning report claimed that landlords "cover every inch of the ground space with large tenements without sufficient provision for light and ventilation," making a large swath of Chicago as crowded as Calcutta and New York's Lower East Side. The poor people who live in the small apartments "try to reduce their rents by overcrowding a few rooms." The streets were filthy and the children had no place to play.

In 1899 Hunter traveled to England where he lived at Toynbee House and came under the influence of the socialist leader Keir Hardie. Returning to the United States, he settled in New York as manager of the University Settlement House at 184 Eldridge Street. There he met J. Graham Phelps Stokes, the son of a wealthy New York banking family and, through him, his sister Caroline Stokes. Both Graham and Caroline renounced their lives of privilege, joined the Socialist Party, and moved to the Lower East Side.

The demand for labor and the need for cash in New York City was so great that by 1901, an estimated 400,000 children between five and eighteen years were absent from school, and at work. In 1902, Florence Kelley, now settled in New York as leader of the National Consumers League, joined forces with Hunter (as they had done a decade earlier in Chicago) and with Lillian Wald set up a committee to investigate child labor in New York. Robert Hunter was elected chairman of the committee seeking legislation to abolish child labor. One bill proposed that children under the age of ten years be prevented from selling newspapers on the streets "because the lives of the little ones are physically, mentally and morally damaged by this sort of street work." The zealous Hunter claimed that one-third of these children "will become inmates of our penal institutions" and 70 to 90 percent will have "the most loathsome of all diseases by the time they are fifteen years of age." Through the New York Child Labor Committee, Florence Kelley sought legislation to ensure that the age of the child given by its parents was correct and to prevent under age children from going to work. The New York Child Labor Committee had offices at 105 East Twenty-second Street, with prominent New Yorkers on its board including Professor Felix Adler, Mornay Williams, V. Everit Macy (who inherited twenty million dollars when a boy of only five), George Alger, lawyer, and Jacob Schiff and Paul M. Warburg, the prominent bankers.

In 1904 Robert Hunter married Caroline Stokes and that year he published his book *Poverty*, an indictment on child labor. During the eighteenth century, when children helped their parents on the farm, child labor "was a great thing," but the industrialization of the nineteenth century rendered child labor an evil. "Child labor," wrote Robert Hunter, "must be counted as one of the important causes of unemployment among adults.... Child labor has been synonymous with child slavery.... Employers, in the parasitic industries, who go to our legislative halls in order to defeat child-labor laws, using the argument that only by the toil of infants are they able to make profits." Echoing Florence Kelley, Robert Hunter asserted that jobs go to the cheapest labor. "The child-labor laws, which have been won in the Northern states by years of vigorous agitation gave an advantage to the parasitic industries of the South. It is even likely that the textile industries may move to the South ... in order to have the privilege of employing little people." In 1905, the impetuous Hunter caused a ruckus by accusing the New York Commissioner of Labor of failure to enforce child labor laws and permitting child slavery to flourish.[6]

The conservative men who took control of the New York Child Labor Committee believed that improvement would come gradually from within, forcing the restless socialist members such as Robert Hunter, Florence Kelley and William English Walling to resign.

Robert Hunter ran unsuccessfully for the United States Senate on a socialist platform but his zeal burned out during World War I when his politics became more conservative. He moved to California and became a designer of fashionable golf courses.

Mrs. Florence Kelley was a resident at Hull-House, Chicago, for nine years and after moving to New York she joined Lillian Wald at the Henry Street Settlement House, in the Lower East Side. Lillian Wald was cut from the same cloth as Jane Addams, Julia Lathrop and Florence Kelley, only younger. She was born in Cincinnati in 1867, to a well-to-do

German–Jewish family. Her father was in the optical business and in 1878 he moved the family to Rochester, New York. At age twenty-two Lillian came to New York City to attend nursing school. In the course of her training she saw the poverty of the immigrants. The Lower East Side, she wrote, "was a vast crowded area. A foreign city within our own." The area was dirty with "odorous fish-stands" and uncovered garbage cans, with tenements converted into cigar factories. Hester Street and Essex Street were choked with pushcarts, many with child vendors, selling vegetables, fruits, meats and fish. With a friend, Lillian resolved "to move into the neighborhood as nurses, identify ourselves with it socially," and to serve the poor. "They were all immigrants, Jews from Russia and Roumania." With the financial support of the banker Jacob Schiff, Lillian opened in 1895 a settlement house at 265 Henry Street. By 1902, the settlement house had expanded to 299, 301 and 303 Henry Street, adding a playground and a gymnasium. At its peak the Henry Street Settlement Home had ninety-two nurses on its staff, making 200,000 home visits a year in Manhattan. Under the influence of Florence Kelley, Lillian was moved by the plight of the working child in the tenements, kept out of school to earn money for the family. So poor were the people and so low their wages they sent their children to work.

Lillian Wald said categorically that "tenement house work should be abolished." Appearing on June 4, 1914, before the Commission on Industrial Relations, created in 1912 by an act of Congress, she said: "Children suffering from chicken pox, measles, scarlet fever or women in advanced stages of tuberculosis were working upon garments which would later be taken home and worn by children.... We dislike home work, particularly for children." Tenement industry was bad "because it means many hours of work; work after school, work in the early morning, promotes truancy."

Hull-House in Chicago, and Henry Street and University Settlement in New York were the pioneers of the American settlement movement. By 1900, there were over a hundred settlement houses in American cities and by the start of the First World War over four hundred, close to the tenements. Here progressive-minded Americans chose to live and help the hordes of new immigrants living in the slums and tenements of America's cities. The tenement industries included clothing of all types, paper boxes, toys, artificial flowers, embroidery, nut picking, glove stitching, making lampshades, sewing fancy feathers, making suspenders, brushes, garters, rolling cigars and many other goods. Parents with their children of all ages sat together and made things in the kitchen, living room or bedroom, out of sight of the inspectors. Desperate for money, the little children were put to work, morning, noon and night, alongside their parents.

Florence Kelley, Jane Addams, Julia Lathrop and Lillian Wald were the leaders in the battle to end child labor. Before and during their time there were others with similar goals. Some adopted the scientific approach of research and analysis, while others used muckraking techniques to expose how children were exploited in the workforce.

5

Reformers and Muckrakers

To the children of the wealthy, or of those in moderately comfortable circumstances, the years of childhood are free from care and toil.... To the children of the poor, their passage from the cradle to the workbench is a short one.... Passing through any of the leading streets or avenues in the early morning, hundreds of these children may be seen walking with hurried steps to store or shop or factory to work through the long hours of the day until the dusk of the evening sets them free to return to their squalid homes in crowded tenements.
— *New York Times*, December 26, 1882

Q: Have you any laws in Mississippi regarding the hours of labor, or ages at which children should be employed?
A: No, Sir.
Q: Have you compulsory school laws?
A: No, Sir.

— United States Industrial Commission,
*Report of the Industrial Commission on
Agriculture and Agricultural Labor*, 1901

The Great Exhibition held at Crystal Palace, London, in 1851 displayed Britain's industrial prowess. Among the fair's fourteen thousand exhibits were five hundred from the United States. Queen Victoria was unimpressed by the range and quality of American made goods. True that John Chickering's pianos and Cyrus McCormick's mechanical harvesting machines were world-class, but most other products in the American section fell well below European standards. The 1876 Centennial Exposition held in Philadelphia showed how rapidly manufacturing had advanced in the United States with its power looms, agricultural machinery, shoes, textiles, the gigantic Corliss steam engine, locomotives, newspaper presses, sewing machines, kitchen ranges and its abundant agricultural output. This was the age of the tycoon and robber baron. The wealth of the nation — in manufacturing, railroads, agriculture and mining — was concentrated in the hands of a few men such as Andrew Carnegie, J. P. Morgan, John D. Rockefeller and Cornelius Vanderbilt with their yachts, Newport cottages and New York mansions. As the historian Michael McGerr notes, these men believed that their achievements came from their individual and exceptional skills. The foresight, determination and skills of the few distinguished them from the masses stuck in their humdrum lives and repetitive jobs, living in tenements and eking out a subsistence living. Immigrants, largely from southern and eastern Europe, were further handicapped by their poverty, lack of English and their old-world habits and dress. They congregated in the slums of the booming cities, taking whatever jobs they could find. Separating the robber barons and the vast working class was the small but comfortable middle class of professionals and managers. As the United States expanded to the West and the South its appetite for cheap labor, including the labor of children, grew exponentially.

Decades before Florence Kelley, Julia Lathrop, Jane Addams and Lillian Wald began their reformist work, a few American voices had agitated for little children to remain in school rather than go to work. Catharine Esther Beecher was among the first in America to advocate that all children, even of the poor, deserved a decent education. In 1846, she published a book on *The Evils Suffered by American Women and American Children: The Causes and the Remedies*. In America there were "more than two million children utterly illiterate and entirely without schools." Her plan was to employ the educated women of America as teachers "to educate destitute American children."

In 1858, the thoroughly modern 20-year-old Julia Archibald Holmes climbed Pike's Peak, wear-

In 1858, Julia Archibald Holmes was the first woman to climb the 14,115 foot Pike's Peak. She was among the first in America to examine the world of working children. As early as the 1870s, the Lower East Side of New York had an estimated 100,000 children engaged in tenement work, such as making ink, paper collars, cigars, artificial flowers, and envelopes. This illustration from Holmes' article on *Children Who Work* shows a little girl cutting tobacco leaves (*Scribner's Monthly* 1, 1871, pp. 607–615).

ing bloomers, the first woman to scale that mountain. She later developed an interest in child labor. Inner city and tenement industries had their start soon after the Civil War came to an end. In 1871, Julia A. Holmes wrote *Children who Work,* one of the earliest studies of child labor in America, authorized by the U.S. Commissioner of Education. "How few residents of Manhattan Island," she wrote, "realize that within its confines are at least one hundred thousand children ... to whom the morning light on six days of the week brings only toil. For these children there are no schools, no outings in the woods, no bright walks in Central Park." The children going to work were orphans, runaways or from poor families, native-born and immigrant alike. Julia Holmes visited factories along Walker Street and Broadway in lower Manhattan with many child laborers. There were a "vast number of occupations in which boys and girls under the age of fifteen years are made to earn from fifty cents to five dollars per week." Children were put to work making ink, tin boxes, whips, paper collars, bags, beads, artificial flowers, envelopes and brushes. Children worked long hours as domestic servants, running errands or cutting tobacco. In the America of 1871, surmised Julia Holmes, "Man is not his brother's keeper, and he is not bound to look after other people's children."[1]

The notion that child labor was an evil that permanently damaged the bodies and souls of children dates back to the early 1870s. In 1871, the *New York Times* lamented: "A great class of youth is growing up in this City enfeebled in body and only partially educated. " These poor working children will "swell the great mass of ignorant voters who now threaten the very structure of our society." Massachusetts, Rhode Island and Connecticut had long since passed laws "to control the evil" of child labor. The injustice persisted in New York where working children are "pale and worn and grown old before their time." The children "of the comfortable classes are in nurseries and schools, while those unfortunate children are obliged to contribute to the support of their families by severe and premature labors."

It was time, the writer concluded, for New York "to restrain by law the employment of very young children in the factories and workshops of the State."

The New York Times on October 8, 1871, called for legislation "for the protection of the large numbers of children of tender years employed in the factories and workshops of the State.... In the City and in many towns and villages, it often happens that children between the ages of ten and sixteen can and do by their labor keep the widowed mother and the family from the almshouse or from begging." Legislation, continued the *Times*, was needed "to cut off at once the cruel employment of considerable numbers of children as young as eight years, in our tobacco factories." With 100,000 children working in New York City, the Children's Aid Society led the battle to end this exploitation, but "each year the selfish manufacturing interest has defeated the proposed humane law."

Change came in 1876 when

Second drawing illustrating Julia Holmes' story of 1871, showing two girls in a tenement sorting feathers. Child labor in the tenements of the Lower East Side started years before the large immigration of central and eastern European (*Scribner's Magazine* 1, 1871, pp. 607–615).

New York passed laws mandating that children receive "at least fourteen weeks of schooling each year" and prohibiting children under fourteen years from working. In the 1883 the New York State Bureau of Labor Statistics was formed with Charles F. Peck as commissioner. One of his first tasks was an "investigation of the subject of employment of children in manufacturing and mercantile establishments." Peck focused largely on the tenement-house tobacco and cigar industry, where one worker in ten was a child below fourteen years of age. He sought evidence from tobacco company owners and workers. One exchange went as follows:

Q: Does child labor help to swell the earnings of the family?
A: From the economical point of view I think child labor is not an assistant in increasing the family earnings; I think it rather detracts by reason of its throwing too frequently, the father out of employment.
Q: Do you consider child labor a benefit or an evil to society?
A: Emphatically an evil below a reasonable age.
Q: Why an evil?
A: A child who is deprived at a tender age of the privilege of going to school has been robbed of his opportunities for an education.... It is highly immoral to send a child to a factory.

Another witness blamed the "manufacturers who use children in order to swell their own pockets out of the work of two children in place of one man, they receive more work than they would get out of an adult and get the work for less pay." In the tobacco and cigar factories children earned $1.50 to $3 for a sixty-hour workweek.

Based on the findings of his child labor committee, Commissioner Peck recommended compulsory education of all children until age fourteen, the passage of a factory and work-shop inspection act along the lines of Massachusetts and penalties against companies that broke the laws. The tobacco lobby fought the bill claiming that it would deprive needy families of the child's income and it would force the industry out of the state. The laws were passed by the state legislature but declared unconstitutional by the New York Court of Appeals, arguing that they interfered with personal choice and private property.

Commissioner Charles F. Peck was a close friend of Lieutenant Governor David B. Hill. His political appointment gave him a cushy $3,000 a year job with trips to Europe "to examine labor conditions abroad." He presented himself as a friend of labor but lacked the commitment of a Florence Kelley to fight relentlessly for the rights of children. When Hill was elected governor of New York, his lackey Charles Peck was appointed commissioner of labor. In 1892 Peck submitted a report that struck his opponents as false. When asked to show the evidence to back his report, Peck burned the papers and was arrested for destroying public property. He was released from prison on a $100 bond but in 1893, Charles Peck fled the country.[2]

Child labor continued even in New England despite long-enacted laws to prevent it. In 1876, George E. McNeill published his findings on *Factory Children*, claiming there were sixty thousand children in Massachusetts "of school age who are growing up in ignorance." These children dropped out of school in order to go to work. "Poverty is the motive force that takes the child to the factory."

The reformers were especially active from 1890 to 1920, a period of great immigration, growth of cities and the ascendance of the United States as a world power. Their aims were to shame the elite and to use legislation, rather than revolution, to spread America's wealth down to the poor. To correct the great imbalances in the American body politic, these reformers campaigned for women's suffrage, the rights of workers (minimum wage, eight-hour work day, pensions, sick leave, disability insurance, pensions), a ban on child labor and the right of children to remain at school.

Henry George (1839–1897) was an adventurous lad who went to sea at age fifteen as a foremast boy on the 586-ton *Hindoo*, with a crew of twenty, bound for Melbourne and Calcutta. His less than delighted father asked the captain "not to make the boy's berth too comfortable but to let him see and feel the rigors of the sailor's life so that, by a single voyage, the desire for roving should be destroyed." Young Henry was away 575 days before he returned home to Philadelphia to serve as apprentice typesetter. In adult life he made his way to San Francisco where he worked on his book *Progress and Poverty*, published in 1879. Land speculation and the railroads, he observed, were concentrating wealth in fewer and fewer hands while the mass of the people were impoverished. Henry George regarded land a common inheritance and advocated a tax on raw land.

Progress and Poverty hit a nerve, was republished many times, translated into many languages and sold over three million copies, making Henry George a celebrity. One of his great admirers was the writer Leo Tolstoy, who wrote the introduction to the Russian language edition. Tolstoy himself gave away most of his land, believing that the land belonged to the farmers — the crushed and voiceless masses — who worked it, not to the ruling classes. Land is the common property of all; the money from taxes on land speculation should be distributed to the poor but their labor should not be taxed.

Henry George observed the great western migration of families looking for land to farm. Owning little money these families traveled wearily past fallow land they could not afford until they finally reached a place where land was cheap. Here they settled down, cleared the land and built a shelter. The husband and wife and even the children worked. They "work like horses and live in the harshest manner — Such a man deserves encouragement, and should not be taxed." George moved from California to New York City where he advanced his theories on wealth and poverty. Despite working long hours a laborer did not earn enough to support his family. In the effort to make enough money, he put his wife and children to work, observed George, only to find that excess production brought down wages, leaving the family exhausted but no better off. In an open letter to Pope Leo XIII, Henry George wrote that the parents were largely to blame for sending their under-aged children to work. These parents, "prompted by poverty, misrepresent the age of their children even to the masters, and teach them to misrepresent." The parents are aware that their children "ought to play," but what drives them to work is "the sting of poverty."[3] Henry George suffered a stroke in 1890 that left him weakened. He died in 1897.

The Order of the Knights of Labor was established in Philadelphia in 1869 with the aim to form a nation-wide trade union for all workers in America. By 1880, it was the nation's largest workers' organization. The Knights called for an eight-hour workday, ending convict labor, and securing for the workers "the full enjoyment of the wealth they create." Following Henry George, the Knights believed that unoccupied land "was the heritage of all the people," and should be subject to tax. Noting that child work kept down workers' wages, the Knights of Labor were among the first of the labor organizations to campaign against child labor. Their charter in the 1870s called for "the prohibition by law of the employment of children under fifteen years of age, the compulsory attendance at school for at least ten months in the year of all children between seven and fifteen years, and the furnishing at the expense of the State of free text books." The Knights of Labor reached its peak in the early 1880s with 700,000 members. Its popularity and influence fell precipitously after the Haymarket Riot of May 1886.

Samuel Gompers was born in London in 1850, the son of a cigar maker. The family moved to New York City in 1864, where young Samuel joined the cigar makers' union. In 1881, he joined the newly formed Federation of Trade and Labor Unions and served as its vice president. The federation campaigned for a ban on employment for children under fifteen years, only to see its efforts fought back by powerful industrialists. In 1886, the federation formed itself into the American Federation of Labor (AFL), with Samuel Gompers as president, a position he held for almost forty years. AFL took up the fight against child labor. At its 1888 convention in St. Louis, Gompers railed against "the exploitation of the tender and young, drawn into the factory, into the shop, into the mill, into the mine and the stores by the drag-net of modern capitalism, frequently supplant[ing] the labor of their parents; robbed in their infancy of the means of an education, dwarfed both in mind and body." He called on his fellow members to support laws "absolutely prohibiting the employment of any child in any occupation" who was younger than fourteen. On another occasion Gompers thundered, "There is no greater crime under the heavens than the employment of children in factories."[4] At its 22nd annual meeting, held in 1902, the American Federation of Labor noted, "Child labor prevails to a greater or lesser degree in the states of North and South Carolina, Georgia, Florida, Alabama and Mississippi ... breeding ignorance and poverty; threatening the very foundation of society ... the American Federation of Labor [is] in support of legislative action abolishing child labor."[5]

Gompers invited Senator Robert La Follette to address the AFL convention, held in Cincinnati, Ohio, in July 1922. La Follette spoke on the topic of "Child Labor and the Federal Courts." The Child Law passed the House in September 1916 with a convincing 337 votes in favor and only 46 votes again. In the Senate the vote was equally convincing with 52 in favor and 12 against. In La Follette's assessment putting children to work deprived them of a healthy childhood of play and study, which resulted in "race deterioration." The "enlightened and humane child labor laws," passed by Congress, protected the nation from "the goods turned out by cheap and underpaid child labor."

The decision of the Supreme Court to declare the Child Labor Laws unconstitutional was yet another example of unbridled power, wrote La Follette, that: "Today the actual ruler of the American people is the Supreme Court of the United States. The law is what they say it is and not what the people through the Congress enacted." La Follette regarded a number of the federal judges as "petty tyrants and arrogant despots." He decried the "usurpation of power" by the court. It was "a Frankenstein which must be destroyed or else it will destroy us."

Now, the remedy. "The Federal judiciary," wrote Senator La Follette, "must be made, to some extent at least, subject to the will of the people." He called for an amendment to the Constitution to allow Congress the power to override the "usurped" judicial veto.[6] In the 1924 presidential election, La Follette ran on the Progressive Party ticket and carried 17 percent of the national popular vote.

The World's Columbian Exposition, held in Chicago in 1893, dazzled the nation with the brilliance of its architecture and the dizzying array of consumer products. American factories produced watches, bicycles, typewriters, canned foods, furnaces as well as horse-drawn farm equipment, horse carriages and, now, electric light. After the recession of 1893 to 1896, the nation entered a period of dramatic growth and profound social change. Women's suffrage, scientific advancement, cleaner government, freedom of speech, the avarice of the Robber Barons, and the wretched conditions of the working poor were the great issues hotly debated. The Progressive Era brought to the fore a cadre of well-off, educated and largely American-born men and women who identified not with their own class, but with the sufferings of the poor, the immigrants and, especially the children who were sent off early in their lives to work. They were determined to bring about change.

After graduating from Columbia College, Richard Theodore Ely traveled to Germany to study in various universities. He received his Ph.D. from the University of Heidelberg and returned to the United States a convinced socialist. In his *Introduction to Political Economy*, published in 1884, Richard T. Ely wrote, "Child labor is one of the most serious evils of our day, and it is increasing with alarming rapidity in the United States, growing far more rapidly than population." Child labor lowers wages; "it is, essentially, cheap labor." In Minnesota this "meant the taking of more children from school and placing them in factories at an immature age, thereby cutting off their chances of physical and mental development." Reports in the late 1880s from factory inspectors in New York and elsewhere made note of the increase of accidents among children working with machinery. Ely wrote: "As long as one manufacturer employs child labor others may feel obliged to do so to hold their own in competition. The way forward was through social reform, not revolution. By legislating against the practice such evils as the sweatshops should be abolished."[7]

In 1888 the *American Economic Association* offered a prize for the best article on the subject of child labor. The prize money was given by Amelie Louise Rives, recently married to John Armstrong Chanler, a scion of one of the leading families in New York City. The marriage lasted only seven years, after which John Chanler moved to North Carolina and opened a textile mill. He insisted that the child workers be educated at the company's expense. John was showing paranoia and his family had him committed to a New York psychiatric institute. Using his vast inherited wealth he fought his family and the psychiatric establishment in a long, legal battle to prove that he was sane.

The sober statistician William Franklin Willoughby and the passionate crusader Mary Clare de Graffenried shared the Chanler prize. Willoughby commented that in Britain, Parliament enacts laws for the whole nation, while in the United States the duty to regulate factories and labor "falls on the different State legislatures." In New York, he reported, "child labor exists in the State in its worst form." Inspectors in Ohio in 1887 noted "the alarming growth of women and child labor in gainful employment." From New Jersey came complaints that thousands of children move "from the workshop to bed and from the bed to the workshop." Despite these concerns, only eleven states in 1890 had laws regulating the employment of children. Even among this small number, some still allowed children as young as ten years to work. Willoughby believed child labor increased with the expansion of the factory system. Quoting figures from the 1870 census he showed that one worker in seventeen was a child fifteen years or younger. Ten years later one out of every sixteenth worker was a child aged fifteen or younger. New Jersey had 15,000 children in the workforce; 24,000 out of 87,000 coal miners in Pennsylvania were children below age sixteen. In every industry there were children working. Among the worst offenders were the tenement industries where little children "labor as slaves to their parents."

Many of the social activists who led the American Reformist Era from 1890 to the 1920s came from privileged backgrounds. They included philanthropists and communists, religious leaders and atheists. Among them was a small group of declared socialists who formed, in December 1904, the Intercollegiate Socialist Society. The aim of the society was "to promote an intelligent interest in Socialism among college men and women." The leading light was Upton Sinclair whose book *The Jungle* was a searing indictment of the labor practices in the meat cutting business. Other early members included the lawyer Clarence Darrow, Graham Philip Stokes and Robert Hunter of the University Settlement House in New York, the Reverend Owen Lovejoy, the author John Spargo and Florence Kelley.

Writing for *McClure, Collier's, Harper's, Cosmopolitan* and *Century* magazines, muckraking journalists exposed the greed and power of the factory owners and the suffering of the masses. Mary Clare de Graffenried (1849–1921) told the story with flair and drama. She was a descendant of Baron Christopher de Graffenried, the Swiss-born founder of New Bern, North Carolina. Mary Clare grew up in Georgia, graduating with distinction from a women's college at the early age of sixteen. Later, she moved to Washington and found work as a special investigator in the newly established Department of Labor. Her 1891 scathing article in *Century Magazine*, titled "The Georgia Cracker in the Cotton Mills," provoked strong emotions. Some accused her of failing to appreciate how the cotton mills helped the impoverished whites, while others applauded her criticism of the risks of factory work to children. The workplace with its unkempt, foul-mouthed people was hostile ground for the innocent. Here children witnessed "degrading acts and ugly passions." Children "are taught the alphabet of sin." They learn to cheat, deceive, lie and swear. Work at a tender age is morally corrupting, stunting their character. The solution is compulsory education. Countering the argument that children had to work to assist the family, de Graffenried suggested that the state "pay destitute parents an equivalent of the services of the child while educating it." Clare de Graffenried continued for years her campaign for stricter child labor laws, compulsory education, improved factory inspection and industrial safety.

In 1880, the states with the largest number of industrial workers (New York, Pennsylvania, Illinois, Massachusetts and Ohio) reported 2 to 3 percent of their factory labor force was younger than fifteen years of age. Twenty years later, with strict laws in place, these states saw a fall in child labor in factories, to 1 to 2 percent. There was no cause for celebration as the children shifted their work to less regulated industries. Of the 1,569,633 school age children in New York State in 1900, 450,085 were not attending school and "must have been working at home, in stores, in household services, etc." However in the rapidly industrialized South, the percentage of children under fifteen years working in factories increased from 7 percent in 1880 to 14 percent in 1900.[8]

Edwin Markham (1852–1940) was born in Oregon City, Oregon, the youngest of six children. As a boy of twelve he was compelled by his mother to work on the family farm but later acquired an education and taught school. The workingman, he wrote, was a "slave of the wheel of labor." His 1898 poem "The Man with the Hoe," a protest against oppression and drudgery, brought him fame and fortune. It begins:

> Bowed by the weight of centuries he leans
> Upon his hoe and gazes on the ground;
> The emptiness of ages in his face,
> And on his back the burden of the world.

Markham settled in New York in 1901 and extended his literary interest in the workingman to the plight of the laboring child. He was appointed poet laureate of the labor movement and was known as "the poet of the muckrakers." From 1906 to 1907 he wrote a series of articles in *Cosmopolitan Magazine*, based on the findings of the National Child Labor Committee, telling the heart-wrenching stories of children in the textile mills, the glass factories and working in the mines. Markham and *Cosmopolitan* were on a crusade against the "slavery of children." American children were being "crushed by slavery and mental and moral oblivion."

His October 1906 article in the *Cosmopolitan Magazine* declared:

Two and a half millions of children under fifteen years of age are now at long and exhausting work in the offices, shops, mills and mines of our moral republic. In Pennsylvania alone there are at least one hundred different kinds of work at which children are employed, and, unhappily, it is into the cheap and dangerous work that the children always swarm. They are doubled over coal-breakers, breathing black coal-dust; they are racked in the cotton mills, breathing damp lint; they are strained in furniture-factories, breathing sawdust; they are parceled in glass-factories, breathing dust of glass; they are crowded in soap-factories, breathing dust of alkali; they are headed into felt-factories, breathing dust of fur; they are twisted in tobacco-factories, inhaling the deadly nicotine; they are bent over dye-rooms, absorbing noxious fumes; they are stifled in rubber-factories, where they are paralyzed with naphtha; they are chocked in match-factories, where they are gangrene with phosphorus; they are huddled in type-foundries where they are cramped with poison of lead.[9]

The rapacious factory owners were not the only group to blame, Edwin Markham explained. In his 1906 *Cosmopolitan Magazine* article, he railed against the parents who put their own children to work "under the protection of perjured certificates — documents that falsely represent them to be of legal age for men's work." In Philadelphia, tenement tobacco factories were known as kindergartens "on account of the extreme youth of the child workers."[10]

Edwin Markham was elected president of the Child Labor Federation, 1789 Broadway, New York, to fight the powerful manufacturers who had thus far "succeeded in defeating effective child-labor legislation." Markham became the literary spokesman for the National Child Labor Committee, putting passion into cold scientific reports. In 1911, he wrote *Children of Bondage* "to secure public recognition of child labor as a *fundamental* [his emphasis] evil." He railed against "those ruthless employers who drag babies from their beds to labor in the shucking sheds and feed their flesh to the acid of the shrimps.... Child labor, no less than the tariff, the trusts and monopoly, is a foundation stone of the towering structure of Big Business." In the cotton mills of the South there were "an array of unprotected, unregarded little ones who do some one monotonous thing — abusing the eyes in watching the rushing threads; dwarfing their muscles in an eternity of petty movements; befuddling their lungs in breathing flecks of flying cotton." Getting into his stride and revealing his own bigotry, Markham wrote further: "And these are not the children of recent immigrants, hardened of the effete conditions of foreign servitude. Nor are they negro children who have shifted from field to mill. They are white children of old and pure colonial stock.... These white children often begin work in the mill with no fragment of education."

Edwin Markham in 1922 wrote the poem "Lincoln — The Man of the People" that was chosen for presentation at the dedication of the Lincoln Memorial. From 1923 to 1931 he was poet laureate of Oregon. A popular after-dinner speaker, he once addressed a druggist convention by reciting his poem "Slaves of the Drug" on drug addiction. Markham died at the age of eighty-eight.

Cornelius van Vorst settled early in the eighteenth-century along the banks of the Hudson River. Together with the Roosevelt and Rensselaer families, the van Vorsts were among the prominent Dutch families in New York. Judge Hopper Cornelius van Vorst, who died in 1889, was president of the Holland Society and served on the United States Circuit Court. His son John married Bessie, who proudly went about New York City as Mrs. John van Vorst. After John died she took up writing, signing her work as Mrs. John van Vorst. In her studies of child and women labor she collaborated with her sister-in-law Marie. In 1902, the two ladies posed as workers to start jobs in the shoe factories of Lynn, Massachusetts. Bessie was known as Esther Kelly and Marie as Bell Ballard. Their depiction of the harsh conditions in the shoe trade was published in 1903 as *The Woman Who Toils*, with an introduction by Theodore Roosevelt. In 1908, Bessie followed with *The Cry of the Children: A Study of Child-Labor*.

With her nose in the air, the New York sophisticate Bessie van Vorst traveled down to the South to report on child labor. In Alabama City she visited the Dwight Manufacturing Company, opened in 1895 by the long-established Chicopee, Massachusetts, firm of the same name. In Lindale, Georgia, she toured the Massachusetts Cotton Mill, founded 1896, and in Huntsville, she visited the Merrimack Manufacturing Company — both subsidiaries of venerable but aging Lowell, Massachusetts, companies. As she traveled on the railroads she saw the monotony of the mill towns, each owned by the textile companies, with rows of workers' small wooden cottages, a church or two, the company store and the large mill belching coal dust. Everywhere, she found children twelve years or younger working as doffers or sweepers, earning twenty to fifty cents for a twelve-hour work day, often on the night shift. The families were charged $1.50 a week to rent a cottage, requiring as many hands as possible — children and parents — to earn enough for rent, food and clothing. Everywhere in the South she found little children — homespun, impoverished and newly off the land — working in the mills. To help their families, these children chose work over school.

Bessie van Vorst found a different story in New England — the home of the American textile industry. "Side by side with the church-spire and the native New Englander, one finds the towering mill-chimney and the scum of Europe's population." The American-born had long since abandoned work in the mills, leaving the jobs to eager European and French-Canadian immigrants seeking a toehold to American life. Despite stringent labor laws, under-aged children still worked in the Northern mills by lying about their age.

More a muckraking journalist than reformer, Bessie van Vorst soon abandoned her mission to expose the abuses of women and children in the workplace. She settled in Paris and, in 1914, mingled with the expatriate American community, including Gertrude Stein, and married Hughes Robert Charles Henri Le Roux, explorer, collector of animal trophies, writer and an editor of *Le Matin*. Her sister-in-law and companion journalist, Marie van Vorst, also settled in Paris where she married Count Gaetano Cagiati. During World War I, Marie was active in the American Ambulance Corps and later published her *War Letters of an American Woman*.[11]

One of the most tenacious of the reformers was Florence L. Sanville. In 1903 the recent graduate from Bryn Mawr College heard Florence Kelley speak in Philadelphia. Sanville later wrote that Kelley, "with her usual eloquence pictured the lives of children she had met in sweatshops in the cities, and in the factories." This encounter converted the young Florence Sanville to a disciple, devoted to keeping children longer in school and out of the factory. Sanville was appointed executive secretary of the Consumers League of Philadelphia. In 1909, she went undercover for several months visiting sixteen silk mill towns and getting a job in a silk mill in Scranton, with the hope "to become more naturally and closely acquainted with the girls and children whose daily lives took them into the mills." A member of a prominent Philadelphia family, Sanville was shocked by the vulgar talk and earthiness of the girls from the mining towns. They worked long hours in the mills doing repetitive tasks "with little or no opportunity for improvement." The only escape from the life dulled by early labor was to marry and produce the next generation of breaker boys and mill girls.

Based on her experiences in the mills, Florence Sanville wrote a series of articles for influential magazines. Her "Child Labor in Textile Factories," "Home Life of the Silk Mill Workers," and "A Woman in the Pennsylvania Silk Mills" were widely read.[12] In a piece titled "Disguised as Factory Girls," the *New York Times* in 1909 reported on the sleuthing done by Sanville on behalf of the Consumers League. Not only did Sanville work alongside the mill girls, she went home with them to get "glimpses into their life and the influences that surround them."[13] Since girls were not permitted to work in the coal mines, Sanville wrote, the silk mills were built nearby, "due to the cheap labor obtained."

In his December 5, 1905, speech before the fifty-ninth Congress, President Theodore Roosevelt announced he had ordered the Department of Commerce and Labor to pay special interest "to the conditions of child labor and child-labor legislation in several States," with the intention of setting up nation-wide rules regarding the use of child labor. Florence Sanville's article "Children and Textiles" appeared in 1909 in the prestigious *North American Review* and was read by Theodore Roosevelt. So impressed was Roosevelt that, at the close of his presidency, he motored to Scranton to meet with Florence Sanville, who took him on a tour "of a typical silk mill and a coal breaker." The outcry of Sanville's expose led to the drafting in Pennsylvania of more stringent child labor legislation, including closer checks on the child's age.

In 1911, Roosevelt addressed the National Child Labor Committee at its 7th annual conference held in Birmingham, Alabama. Displaying his progressive ideas, Roosevelt spoke in favor of setting a national standard for "the age under which children shall not be allowed to work [and] prohibit by law working them at night." Childhood, he said, should be reserved to give children "a chance to be educated," not to have to go to work.[14] Florence Sanville continued for many years to advocate for the rights of children and women.

Yet another female activist who wrote extensively about the plight of women and children was Rheta Childe Dorr, born in Omaha, Nebraska, in 1868. With Jane Addams and Florence Kelley, Dorr was also active in the suffrage movement. In 1913 she was appointed editor of *The Suffragist*, a weekly magazine fighting for an amendment to the U.S. Constitution granting equal rights. As a columnist for *Hampton's Magazine*, she wrote a series of reports on child labor, such as "The Child Who Toils at Home" in April 1912. Dorr placed some of the blame on the father who "rent[s] out the services of his under-age children [and] claim[s] the services of his children from the day their baby hands are capable of performing a task. He may work them until they drop asleep from exhaustion. He may put them at work injurious to health in surroundings actually conducive to physical and mental destruction; provided the work is done at home." In the tenements of the Lower East Side, parents put their own children to work for long hours making clothing, artificial flowers and cigars.

Rheta Childe Dorr was one of the first women reporters to serve on a newspaper as its foreign correspondent, writing about the Russian Revolution. She declared herself a socialist, advocating the "common ownership of the principal means of production." Like Florence Kelley, she believed that education of children was the key "to create in the coming generation a thinking working-class, one which will accept responsibility as well as demand power."[15]

Katharine DuPre Lumpkin was born 1897 in Macon, Georgia, to a family steeped in the delusion of white supremacy. Attending college in New York, Wisconsin and Massachusetts her beliefs changed and she became an ardent supporter of civil rights. In 1937, with Dorothy V. Douglas, she published *Child Workers in America*. Lumpkin believed that "no children had to begin work at 14 or even 15." Yet, as late as the 1930s there were still 250,000 American children aged eleven to thirteen and over 400,000 aged fourteen or fifteen employed by companies, not counting the many thousands more selling newspapers, doing housework or working on farms. Since 1900, regulations affecting the textile and mining industries had markedly reduced child labor in these industries but the problem had popped up in less regulated industries. Child labor had decreased in the Northern states but increased in the South. Black children, Lumpkin wrote, "are proportionately far more likely than white found at work. Negro children are not welcomed in most factories and store occupations, the only ones regulated." As the children of sharecropping families, young black children joined their parents to provide the hands to pick cotton, strawberries, peaches and melons.

Whether picking cotton, shining shoes, shucking oysters, cleaning shrimp, picking strawberries, or doing domestic service, few of these children benefited from any vocational training or apprenticeship. Rather "nine-tenths went into the labor market for any work they could get." Some of these children were made to work longer than the regulated fifty hours a week. These jobs were "routine and non-educative," dead-end jobs that dulled the mind. Furthermore, claimed Lumpkin, the children were accident prone, especially the bicycle-riding messenger boys.[16]

By the start of the twentieth-century the anti-child labor movement was finding support inside academia and government. In March 1906 the American Academy of Political and Social Science published a symposium on *Child Labor: A Menace to Industry, Education and Good Citizenship*, highlighting the harm done to the physical and mental well-being of children. The lead speaker at the symposium was Charles Patrick Neill, U.S. commissioner of labor in the administration of President Theodore Roosevelt. Charles P. Neill was born in 1865 in Rock Island, Illinois. He worked his way from newsboy and clerk and living in a settlement house at the Chicago stockyards. After graduating summa cum laude from Georgetown University, he joined the faculty and rose to professor of economic history. In his *Child Labor in the National Capital*, Neill described the District of Columbia as "preeminently a residence and not an industrial center, and the opportunity to make use of child labor is consequently limited." Yet, the 1900 census showed that "over 2000 children under 15 years of age engaged in gainful employment."

In his perambulations around Washington, Commissioner Neill found children as young as twelve years working in laundries, as bellboys in the leading hotels, newsboys, candy sellers, shoeshine boys and messenger boys. These boys carried messages from prostitutes and drug dealers to their clients. Neill believed that street trades were "particularly dangerous to the morals of children," leading to delinquency and crime. He opposed night schools that "have merely temporized with the evil," but called for a "model child labor law," that banned the practice nationwide and demanded compulsory education for all children up to the intermediate level.[17] Neill later served as commissioner of labor statistics.

Royal Meeker (1873–1953), professor of economics at Princeton University, was alarmed by the high dropout rate of children from school. In April 1913 Meeker published his provocative views on child labor and education. "Every normal child," he wrote, "can, and must, finish the intermediate grades of public school. Systematic loafing in the streets, in saloons and elsewhere, as well as blind plunging into occupations ending nowhere, should be made impossible." Instead of allowing children to leave school early, the federal government should set up a nationwide civic service to teach trades or prepare children for college. The length of service to the state should be two years. There would be life-long consequences for those who failed. "Only those men and women," emphasized Meeker, "who have completed the period of civic service should be admitted to full citizenship with the privilege of the franchise and the right to hold public office." Four months after Meeker published his authoritarian views on education, President Woodrow Wilson appointed him to replace Charles P. Neill as commissioner of labor statistics.[18]

6

Tenements

For many years the system of tenement-house cigar manufacturing has formed one of the most dreadful, cancerous sores in our city.
— Samuel Gompers, October 1881

Tenement Sweat Shops

Elias Howe Jr. was born in Spencer, Massachusetts, in 1819, one of eight children of a poor father. In delicate health, Elias was not suited to farm work and at age sixteen set out for the magical industrial city of Lowell, where he found work in one of the textile mills. During the financial panic of 1837, he lost his job and moved to Cambridge to find work in a machine shop. He married, had three children and lived from hand to mouth. Elias's despair lifted when a friend talked to him about the need for a machine to sew. Hand sewing was a slow and laborious process, a sewing machine would work more quickly. "He who invents a sewing machine," Elias was told, "would soon become very rich."

Elias watched as his wife did her sewing and used his mechanical skills to build a machine "which should do what she was doing." It took him two years of intense work to design and build a sewing machine. Other tinkerers heard about the Howe machine and built their own models. Between 1850 and 1900, over two hundred and fifty sewing machine companies sprang up across America. The most successful of Howe's competitors was Isaac Merritt Singer, whose name became synonymous with sewing machines. Millions of Singer sewing machines were sold and in millions of homes women and their daughters used this convenient hand- and foot-operated machine to sew clothing for the family. The American sewing machine and the great abundance of American-made cloth gave rise to a massive industry of ill repute — the sweatshop.

Contractors bought bolts of cloth from the wholesalers, cut them up and sub-contracted the sewing work to the thousands of tenement sweatshops located in the shabbier neighborhoods of New York and other large cities. The great flow of immigrants, many with large families, provided a ready source of cheap labor. Often whole families, father, mother and children went to work sewing clothing in the sweatshops. The owner, known as a sweater, set up his sewing workshop in his own tenement apartment. "With $2,500 and a few customers," a newspaper column declared, "and a colossal amount of nerve, almost anyone can go into the dress business." Small-time entrepreneurs leased a few sewing machines, bought cloth on credit and set up small sweatshops in the living rooms of their crowded apartments. New York City's Lower East Side became the center of the American clothing industry followed by Chicago, Philadelphia, Baltimore and Boston. Working in cramped, smelly and dirty conditions, immigrant workers slaved away at their machines twelve or more hours daily. In 1891, Massachusetts promulgated the first law in the nation regulating the making of clothing in tenements by categorizing these new businesses under its factory laws, requiring licensure and regular inspection. Other states soon followed in an effort to regulate the "sweating business" dominated by Jewish and Italian immigrants. These small sweatshops — sewing dresses, skirts, shirts, jackets, trousers and men's suits — hired cheap child labor because their profit margins were so slim.

On March 17, 1892, the Committee on Manufacturers of the United States House of Representatives, under chairman J. De Witt Warner, met to consider this new facet of American industrialization. Warner, a Cornell graduate and lawyer, was a congressman from New York City. Tenement industries began soon after the Civil War came to an end, expanding rapidly after 1880 with mass immigration of poor families from central and southern Europe. Children worked alongside their parents, each working seventy or more hours a week and earning a subsistence wage. A typical sweatshop, the committee learned, was a room ten by forty feet, holding the machines, forty women, ten men and twelve children. Men earned $6 to $10 a week, women $5.40 and the children only $2 a week.

One witness reported to the committee that he found children working in half of the sweatshops he examined.

Q. Of what age were they?
A. All the way from 9 to 13.
Q. What sex?
A. All girls.

In another exchange:

Q. How about child labor?
A. That is carried out extensively, especially in the clothing industry.
Q. How extensively.
A. Well, about as soon as they can work they have to work in the sweatshop.... As soon as they are able to go out to work they are sent out to work in those sweatshops amongst those sweaters and their families.

Known as the "boy agitator of the East Side," Harry Gladstone, as a fifteen-year-old immigrant, organized his fellow child workers in the sweatshop industry. In a rousing speech to the members of his machine tenders union on August 13, 1898, held at 78 Essex Street, young Harry said:

Fellow workmen, I tell you to stick together. Think of your poor fathers and mothers who you have got to support. Think of the schools and how you can't go there to get your education, but must spend from 14 to 15 hours a day in a pest-hole, pulling bastings, turning collars and sleeves and running around as if you were crazy.

If you don't look out for yourselves, who will? You have not had time to grow up, to get strength for work, when you must spend your dearest days in a sweatshop. Think of the way your mothers kiss you, how they love you, and now they shed tears over you, because they see their dear boys treated like slaves.... The only way to get the bosses to pay us good wages is to stick together, so let us be true to our union.[1]

The Independent Magazine in 1902 told the story of Sadie Frowne, her work in a New York sweatshop, and her gutsy adaptation to American life. Sadie grew up in a village in

Poland where her mother ran a small grocery shop and her father worked the land. "By the time I was six," recounted Sadie, "I was able to wash dishes and scrub floors, and by the time I was eight I attended the shop when my mother was out driving her wagon or working in the fields with my father." Sadie's father died when she was ten, leaving her in dire straits. Sadie's mother wrote to her sister in America, who advised them to come to New York to start a fresh life.

Sadie and her mother traveled steerage "in a very dark place that smelt dreadfully. There were hundreds of other people packed in with us." On reaching New York, Sadie found work as a domestic servant while her mother worked in a sweatshop making women's clothing. Soon after arrival, her mother died, leaving Sadie an orphan at age thirteen. "So I went to work on Allen Street [Manhattan] in what they call a sweatshop, making skirts by machine. I was new to the work and the foreman scolded me a great deal."

"Now then," he would say, "this place is not for you to be looking around in. Attend to your work. That is what you have to do." Because she made mistakes, she was called "a stupid animal." But, soon Sadie got used to the work and was making $4 by working sixty hours a week. She shared a room with a fellow worker, paying $1.50 a week. Food was 50 cents; she spent $1 a week on clothes and pleasure and saved $1.

With increasing confidence, Sadie found another job, paying 50 cents a week more. The factory was on the third floor of a building. It was a room measuring twenty by fourteen feet holding fourteen sewing machines and twenty people. There she met Henry, two years older than herself. They liked each other and after work often went to Coney Island, to see a play or go dancing. Henry was ambitious and was saving money to open a real estate office.

Tenement industries. Children of the Catarella family, including the son, busy crocheting, in the back yard of their home in Somerville, Massachusetts. 1909. New York, Chicago, Philadelphia and Boston all had tenement districts that attracted immigrant families, working together.

The work in the sweatshop started at seven in the morning when the supervisor "brought each of us a pile of work." The workday continued until six in the evening, but longer if the work was not finished. "The machines go like mad all day," Sadie continued, "because the faster you work the more money you make. Sometimes in my haste I get my finger caught and the needle goes right through it. It goes so quick, tho' that it does not hurt much. I bind the finger up with a piece of cotton and go on working.... Sometimes the finger has to come off. Generally, tho' one can cure it by a salve." The sewing machines ran on foot power, "and at the end of the day one feels so weak that there is a great temptation to lie right down and sleep. But you must go out and get air and have some pleasure."

Despite the long hours and pressure of work, young Sadie Frowne found the strength to attend Public School 84 on Glenmore Avenue and learned to read and write in English, follow the newspapers and read novels written in English. She joined the United Brotherhood of Garment Workers (25 cents a month) and went on strike for shorter hours. The union won and Sadie worked only nine and a half hours a day. "So the Union does good after all," she concluded.[2]

Despite attempts by the various states to control tenement sweatshops, the industry continued to grow. On March 8, 1908, thousands of women marched through the Lower East Side protesting the conditions in the workshops and the use of child labor. As part of the demonstration girls working in the sweatshops carried signs that declared "Abolish Child

Picture was taken, probably May 1, 1909, at the Labor Day parade in New York City. Girls carry the American flag and signs in English and Yiddish reading: Abolish Child Slavery (George Grantham Bain Collection, Library of Congress).

Corner of Rivington and Essex Streets, in the heart of the tenement district of New York's Lower East Side, c. 1909. Rivington runs parallel to East Houston and Delancey streets. Pushcarts selling fruit, vegetables, fish, meat and clothing filled the streets. Six-story walk-up buildings were crowded with people who lived, slept and worked in their apartments. Lillian Wald's Henry Street Settlement House was close by.

Labor" in English and Yiddish. By March 31, 1911, the State of New York had issued 13,195 tenements licenses for home work, largely clothing (women's and girls' dresses, trousers, shirts, lace, embroidery, garters) but also artificial flowers, ostrich plumes and human hair products. To earn a little money the mother, with the help of her children old enough to work, labored from early morning often until long after dark. The Lower East Side of New York was especially thick with tenement sweatshops. "One block alone, that bounded Broadway, East Houston, Crosby and Prince streets, is said to contain 77 factories, employing 40,000 workers.... This part of New York is the leading clothing making center of the world, which accounts for the number of men and women, and even little children, constantly carrying large bundles through the streets."[3] The Education Department of New York reported high levels of truancy among the children of these districts.

The Triangle Shirtwaist Company Fire

The garment industry grew out of the tenements into the high-rise buildings of the lower East Side. The Triangle Company was part of the vast sweatshop industry of ready-

Mother, using her Singer sewing machine, and her four children, working in a New York tenement apartment, making garters. 1910.

made clothing that was based on American-made cloth, cheap sewing machines and the huge influx of immigrants eager to work even for little wages. The Triangle Shirtwaist Company fire in the Asch Building, at the corner of Greene Street and Washington Place, took place on March 25, 1911. It was the deadliest industrial fire in the history of New York City. The company, the largest blouse maker in the city, employed nearly five hundred workers. They were mostly young women, largely Jewish and Italian, working for low wages, twelve hours a day, and six days a week. The fire started in a bin with scraps of flammable material around 4:30 P.M. on the eighth floor and spread to the ninth. The elevators stopped working and the door to one of the stairwells was locked. One hundred and forty-six garment workers perished in the conflagration. Thirteen were 17 years of age, eleven were 16, four were 15 and two 14 years old. Most of the dead were burned beyond recognition, and others jumped to their deaths.

Among the young victims of the Triangle fire was Bessie Viviano, age fifteen years, born in Italy and living at 352 East 54th Street. Also killed were Rosie Mehl, age fifteen, of 278 East Seventh Street; Jeannie Stellino, age sixteen, who arrived from Italy four years earlier; and Tillie Kupferschmidt, age sixteen, born in Austria, and arrived in America three years earlier. Ida Brodsky, age sixteen, arrived in America only nine months before her death in the fire. Rebecca Felbish was a seventeen-year-old with brown eyes and black hair who had arrived at Ellis Island in 1907 on the SS *Kaiser Willhelm der Grosse* from Bremen, Germany. Rebecca jumped from the 9th floor of the building, surviving only a day to die in the New York Hospital.

The bereaved families came to the morgue to examine the charred bodies in the hope of identifying their loved ones. Dominick Leone and his extended family had already identified the remains of Nicolina Nicolse and Anotonina Colletti but

the search for his brother's child was unavailing. Now they thought they had found her. The shoe on the body ... seemed like hers. Then the uncle stooped down and parted the singed and matted hair. He reached in where the tresses close to the head seemed to have been unharmed and with his penknife cut off a lock of her hair. [The family went out into the light to examine the lock of hair.] Suddenly a sister cried out. She had made up her mind that the lock of hair came from the head of the girl they were looking for. The men in the party sobbed. Their search was successful, and the toll of three out of four members of the family was successful. In a sorrowful file they went into the office while the death certificate was made out. Then unmindful of the heavy rain, they left the building.[4]

Among the survivors of the Triangle Shirtwaist fire were many girls, including Russian-born, sixteen-year-old Esther Chaitin, who bore scars on her face and arms for the rest of her life. Annie Spinsock, aged seventeen, was saved when a friend carried her out on the last trip of the elevator. Pauline Berlin, aged sixteen, worked on the 10th floor and escaped by going up to the roof and across the rooftops of other buildings.

After losing the Republican nomination, former President Theodore Roosevelt formed

The Triangle Shirtwaist Company at 23–29 Washington Place, New York, burned on March 25, 1911, killing one hundred and forty-six workers, of whom thirty were younger than eighteen. The trade union movement held a parade along Broadway to honor the dead and injured.

the Progressive Party. The party stood on the platform that "the country belongs to the people," with the promise to fight monopolies such as the sugar, steel, harvester, tobacco and oil trusts. The party called for equal suffrage, the prohibition of child labor, workmen's compensation, a minimum wage and an eight-hour workday. Little wonder that Roosevelt's Progressive Party caught the imagination of socially active women, even though they did not have the vote. Jane Addams showed her support of Roosevelt at the Progressive Party convention, held in Chicago. The nation was not ready for so radical a social agenda. In the 1912 election, Theodore Roosevelt won 27 percent of the vote, losing to the Democrat Woodrow Wilson with 42 percent.

Founded in 1900, the International Ladies Garment Workers Union (ILGWU) fought to improve the conditions of the workers. In 1913, the union called a strike and sought the support of Roosevelt. The former president had recently returned from a safari in Africa where he and his party bagged 512 big game and hundreds of smaller animals. During July, Roosevelt traveled from his home in Oyster Bay to the Lower East Side to meet with several hundred immigrant girls aged fifteen years and younger who were employed by kimono and wrapper makers. Seated in the center of a hall as the girls gathered around him, Roosevelt said, "Now young ladies, I want to know all about your lives, how you work and how you manage to be cheerful." Through interpreters, the girls told Roosevelt that they worked ten to twelve hours a day, earning a mere 4 cents for each completed kimono. Working hard

Mother at her Singer sewing machine, working with her children, making dolls' clothing. Tenement apartment on Thompson Street, lower Manhattan. 1914.

they earned at most $7 a week. Whatever the language, it was "always the same story of extreme privation, long working hours and small wages." One girl told him in Italian, "If only they would let us sing while we worked."

"The brutes," Mr. Roosevelt muttered under his breath. "This is crushing the motherhood of the country. It must be stopped. It is too horrible for words." Roosevelt promised to act on behalf of the girls working in the ladies garment industry.[5] In December 1913 Roosevelt was away on an adventure into the jungles of Brazil.

Cigars, Cigarettes and Chewing Tobacco

Virginia was the first of the American colonies to grow tobacco. As its great cash crop, Virginia used slave labor to plant, tend, harvest and prepare tobacco leaves for markets in Britain and on the European continent. At his estate at Mount Vernon George Washington grew tobacco for export. Tobacco was to Virginia what cotton was to the Deep South and sugar to the islands of the West Indies. Born in slavery, Booker T. Washington wrote, "There was no period of my life that was devoted to play. From the time I can remember anything almost every day of my life has been occupied with some type of labor.... I was occupied most of the time in cleaning yards, carrying water to the men in the fields, or going to the mill." Two-thirds of the slaves of the Chesapeake Bay worked on the tobacco fields. Slave children started working in the fields by nine years and by their teens were skilled in the various aspects of tobacco cultivation. After the Civil War, black and white alike became sharecroppers or tenant farmers, putting the children to work out of sheer economic necessity. As with the cotton fields, those working tobacco raised large families to earn enough to survive. The tobacco leaf was sent to New York and other cities to make cigars, cigarettes and chewing tobacco.

Tobacco factories in America date back to the late eighteenth century. In 1793, James Caldwell opened his factory near Albany, New York, employing "about fifty men and children." In tobacco factories the children "prepare the leaf for the cigar makers, pack chewing tobacco in its paper and tin foil wrappers, and make cigarettes.... In the packing of chewing tobacco it is not uncommon for a girl to wrap in a day in 10 hours, 22 gross in paper wrapping and 16 gross in foil." In 1882, an estimated 100,000 children in New York City were working in tenement industries. On October 17, 1884, the De Capo Cigar Factory at 38th Street and First Avenue, New York, caught fire. The factory occupied four tenements and also housed "60 families of the firm's employees." So much water was used to put out the fire that "the tobacco in the cellars was floating."

Samuel Gompers, himself once a boy cigar-maker, recorded in his diary October 31, 1881, the deplorable conditions at 90 Connors Street, New York, a five-story tenement building, housing fifteen families, with fifty-two people in all. This was the tenement tobacco factory owned by Herman Blasfoff. The families were crammed into the upstairs apartments while the cigar factory was located in the basement and one-half of a lower floor. All the families worked in the factory, paying rents of $7 to $9 a month. A family of four to six people, each of whom working twelve or more hours a day stripping tobacco leaves and rolling cigars, earned together $40 to $60 a month. The odor of tobacco was everywhere, in the food, the yard, the beds and beddings, on the clothes, but: "You get used to it." "Even in the yard where the children are still too young to be able to work — and they have to be very young not to — are playing, great piles of drying tobacco are largely about." There were hundreds of similar cigar tenement factories in New York.

Fires in the tenement tobacco factories were common. In May 1893 Buchner & Company, makers of chewing and smoking tobacco, on Mulberry Street, between Grand and Hester, was ablaze. The factory occupied three tenements employing 400 workers. The fire, fueled by the dry tobacco, was so fierce that the iron shutters across the windows "became red-hot [and] warped and curled up like paper."[6]

With mounting complaints against tenement tobacco factories, manufacturers at the close of the nineteenth century built factories to meet the safety and sanitation standards, as well as restrictions on child labor imposed by new laws. Companies like Lichtenstein Brothers employed one thousand workers in their factory but continued to employ as subcontractors "a large number of people who work outside the factory and in their tenement homes." In these settings "only the cheap grades of cigars selling for 5 and 10 cents are made in the tenements." The children were put to work by their impoverished parents. One observer in 1895, reported "seeing children at work stripping tobacco ... with feet and legs bare [they] worked with tobacco laid across the knees." Pale, undernourished, with sores on their knees and eyes inflamed, such was the fate of the children in the tenements. Little Joe Duff was "a very small boy ... [who] looked to be ten years old; his clothes were patched, but neat and clean." He was asked: "'Wouldn't you rather go to school than work?' The little fellow answered, 'My father is sixty-five years old and he can't work.'"[7]

The cigarette and cigar factories in nineteenth century America extended to New Jersey, Florida, Louisiana, and beyond. Everywhere were boys and girls, many of them puffing away at cigarettes or cigars, as they worked. Political turmoil in Cuba convinced Vincente Martinez Ybor to move his tobacco business to the United States. He established Ybor City, now a neighborhood of Tampa, Florida. Ybor City became the cigar haven for dozens of cigar factories attracting thousands of immigrants from Cuba, Spain and Italy. Old World work patterns were established and by 1900, there were two thousand children aged fourteen or younger — one quarter of the cigar workforce — toiling through eleven-hour days, six days a week, rolling cigars. In addition to the factories with German or Spanish names, there were also "buck-eye factories" where a cigar-maker brought work home at night and employed his children. In Tampa, in 1904, forty cigar companies, occupying 200 tenements in the business district, went up in flames, leaving "hundreds of families of cigar makers homeless."[8] Ybor City, now a National Historic Landmark District, has lost its cigar-making factories.

Other Tenement Industries

In New York State 8.4 percent of factory workers in 1880 were children under sixteen years of age. This percentage declined year by year and by 1900, only 2.3 percent of factory workers were children. Yet, in 1901, one-third of the 1,593,653 children younger than sixteen years were not attending school. Instead they were working in poorly regulated settings such as stores, in private households, offices, as messengers but especially in tenement industries. The largest of these were clothing and tobacco, followed by a host of other industries including artificial flowers, feathers, hats and caps, millinery, dolls' clothing, crocheting, nut picking, embroidery, suspenders and neckties. At the start of the 20th century, three-quarters of the nation's artificial flower trade was centered in lower Manhattan and the Bronx. Manufacturers circumvented the labor laws by sending out work to be done in the tenements. Whole families, including very young children, were put to work for long hours assembling artificial flowers.

The overcrowded, unsanitary and dangerous conditions of tenements, especially in New York City, gave rise to the reformist Tenement House Act of 1901. This act required that all new construction come with windows facing the street, an open courtyard, proper fire protection and water-borne sewage disposal. The law troubled the landlords who soon found a way around it by seeking exceptions. By 1912, over 13,000 tenement buildings in New York City were licensed to manufacture any of the forty-one listed articles specified in Section 100 of the Labor Act.

The overcrowded tenements with home industries and pushcarts clogging the streets created an anti-immigrant movement. Lillian Wald, however, was "very hopeful for New York's tenement house people.... Emigration every year brings in an army of new youth. [They] all need guidance, hospitality, opportunity.... They are willing to struggle to attain what they seek." The children of the tenements put in a hard day's work and then attended night school. "Extraordinary men and women," wrote Lillian Wald in 1913, "emerge from New York's tenements."[9]

7

In the Mines

Nine-year-old Ben Burton set off to work as a breaker-boy to support his
family. "But, I'll be good then he won't have to beat me," thought the
little hero. "I'll always think of my poor blind father and my mother at
home, and I won't never play with the boys at all, and then the cracker-
boss won't have to beat me like he does the others."
—Harry Prentice, *Ben Burton, The Slate Picker*, 1888

Silkstone was a coal-mining village in Yorkshire, England. On July 4, 1838, the Huskar Pit was flooded in a freak storm trapping miners underground including forty-four children working as hurriers and trappers; they were busy below ground pulling heavy loads of coal through narrow passages, or opening and closing wooden doors to let the coal cars pass through. On the surface, children were employed to sort coal by size. Many of the children escaped harm but twenty-six, between the ages of seven and seventeen, drowned in the flood. Among them were seven-year-old James Barkenshaw, eight-year-olds Sarah Jukes and Catherine Garnet and nine-year-old George Barnett. The bodies were brought in carts back to the village for burial in the cemetery. The 1842 Royal Commission reported that thousands of children, as young as five years, were working as colliers, often under awful conditions. The Mines and Colliers Act prohibited children in England under ten years from working in the mines.

The United States has vast deposits of coal stretching from the eastern states to the Rocky Mountains. Pennsylvania fields, under the towns of Scranton, Wilkes-Barre, Hazleton and Latimer, were the first to be mined. The diabolical practice in Europe of sending young children underground to dig coal and minerals was followed in the American mines. Using little boys in the mines started as early as 1795 with the discovery in Pennsylvania of anthracite coal. "It was quite customary for boys of eight, nine and ten years to be employed."[1] In 1882, there were 87,000 coal miners in Pennsylvania of whom 24,000 (27.6 percent) were boys fifteen years old or younger. In 1905, it was estimated that 12,800 of a total of 153,000 coal miners in Pennsylvania were children under the age of fourteen (8 percent). One expert observed in 1911 that "there are still a great many children of eight years in the coal breakers of Pennsylvania, and a large number of children of ten years employed inside the mines." No one checked when the parents gave the child's age as fifteen. Early in the twentieth century in West Virginia, boys as young as twelve years could legally work in the mines under any conditions and for as long as the bosses demanded.

Certain jobs in the coal mines were tailored to fit the size and dexterity of boys, many

Breaker boys removed with their bare hands the slate from the anthracite coal at a mine in Pittston, Lucerne County, Pennsylvania, 1911. Boys worked bent forward in the cold and dark. In 1896 a cave-in at Pittston took the lives of 58 miners.

of whom had not reached puberty. A large number had not attended school and could not even read a primer. The boys knew little of the world outside the mine village. The smallest of the boys, aged eight to ten years, worked above ground as breakers. Sitting hunched on low stools over the moving chutes, with their bare hands they pulled out the rock and slate and let the crushed coal go by, all the time breathing in the dust. Forbidden to wear gloves, their fingers became hard and cracked, their faces and arms black as the coal. For ten to twelve hours of work they were paid ninety cents a day. Many of the breaker boys lost fingers or limbs, suffered from asthma or black lung disease. In the bituminous mines there was no slate picking and all the boys worked underground. The nippers, boys eleven to thirteen, sat alone underground, ready to open the large wooden doors to ventilate the shaft or allow the mule cars full of coal to pass. The spraggers, who worked in teams of two, were the quickest of the boys, selected to control the speed of the coal cars. If the car traveled too fast, the boy would slow it down by pushing a sprag (thick pieces of wood, two feet long) into the wheels, locking them in place. And then there were the mule drivers, boys taking charge of the animals and guiding them through the narrow passageways. When a boy could properly operate a six-mule team, he received men's wages. In earlier years, the mines harnessed the young children, crawling on hands and feet, pulling carts of coal. Every morning, groups of boys carrying their full tin lunch pails could be seen trundling toward the mine, and in the evening heading home, noisily dragging their empty pails behind them.

A 1905 estimate gave the number of breaker boys as 12,800, with 3,000 door boys and 11,000 drivers, giving a total of 27,000 boys under fourteen years working in the coal fields of Pennsylvania, Maryland and West Virginia. In 1900, the mines of Alabama employed 894 boys aged ten to fifteen.

In her autobiography, published in 1925, Mother Jones, the illustrious union organizer, tells how she

> got to know the life of the breaker boys. The coal was hoisted to a cupola where it was ground. It then came rattling down the chutes, beside which ladder-like, sat little breaker boys, whose job it was to pick out the slate from the coal as the black rivers flowed by. Ladders and ladders of little boys sat in the gloom of the breakers, the dust from the coal swirling continuously up in their faces. To see the slate they must bend over their task. Their shoulders were bent. Their chests hollow.... The breaker boys are not Little Lord Fauntleroys. Small chaps smoked and chewed and swore. They did men's work and they had men's ways, men's vices, men's pleasures. They fought and spit tobacco.... They joined the breaker boy's union, and beat up scabs. They refused to let their little brothers and sisters go to school if the children of scabs went.[2]

Accidents in the American mines were frequent, with 22,000 fatalities between 1890 and 1907, with many others maimed. Deaths in coal mine accidents numbered 3,125 in 1906, 2,450 in 1908 and 2,805 in 1909. During each of these years, the number injured was

Nipper boys, aged eleven to thirteen years, sat alone in the dark underground ready to open the large wooden doors to ventilate the shaft or allow the mule cars filled with coal to pass. In 1905, the coal mines of Pennsylvania, Maryland and West Virginia employed 27,000 boys below age fourteen working as breaker boys, door boys or mule drivers. Photograph c. 1909.

three times as great. Many of the killed and injured were boys. In Pittston, Pennsylvania, the mines in 1870 employed 9,870 of whom one-quarter (2,439) were boys. In that year alone there were 53 fatalities and 90 non-fatal serious accidents. Among those killed in 1871 was eleven-year-old Corey Downs, who while

> working the Gaylord Slope, Headstrom & Co., was instantly killed by being caught in the machinery of a hoisting apparatus. His father was engineer at this place and had charge of the machinery, having much oiling to do he needed assistance. His son showing much care and pride in the business bethought him to assist his father, which he did for some time very successfully. On the day of the accident the boy had just got through oiling the breaker and hoisting machinery. In a few moments he was discovered by the engineer entangled in the hoisting engine. The poor boy was taken therefrom by his almost heart-broken father.[3]

Robert Rogers, a boy of ten years, "fell into the pony rollers. His right leg was dreadfully crushed. Sometime elapsed before he could be extricated, and after lingering a short time he expired." Frank Holliday, aged seventeen years, worked at the No. 3 Baltimore Slope driving a team of mules inside the mine when he fell under the loaded cars. He was "frightfully mangled and died instantly, sharing the fate of many of our poor driver-boys in the coal mines." Michael Groat, a fifteen-year-old driver-boy, "fell under the cars part of a train, and almost severed one of his limbs from his body. He was taken home and died in about four or five hours." Thirteen-year-old Sam Madill was luckier than others. He survived after a coal car ran over one of his leg. The one-legged boy went back to school and found a job as a clerk. Citing these cases the mining inspector concluded: "This is another proof that it is not only unwise and unsafe to put boys of such tender years to oil or having anything to do with machinery, but that it is a cruel wrong. It should be a crime." Hiring boys in the mines was cheaper than hiring men but: "In view of the large number of accidents involving children it is another question whether boys should be hired at all."[4]

The death of a boy in this mine or that, although very frequent during the nineteenth and early twentieth centuries, did not arouse the attention of the wider public. It took the disasters at Scofield, Utah, in 1900 (200 killed), Monongah, West Virginia, in 1907 (361 killed), Jacobs's Creek, Pennsylvania, in 1907 (239 killed) and Cherry, Illinois, in 1909 (259 killed) to awaken the nation to the risks of mining. In all these and other mining tragedies many young lives were lost.

The success of the Anthracite Strike of 1900 brought to the fore the remarkable John Mitchell, a founding member of the United Mine Workers of America (UMWA) and its president from 1898 (at age 28) until 1908. After the strike, Mitchell went on a victory tour of the coal towns. The highlight was a parade at Scranton, where thousands of breaker boys marched in his honor. Mitchell explained what the breaker boys meant to him. "They have the bodies and faces of boys but they came to meetings where I spoke and stood as still as men and listened to every word. I was shocked and amazed, as I saw those eager eyes peering at me from eager little faces. The fight had new meaning for me. I felt that I was fighting for the boys, fighting a battle for innocent childhood."[5]

Born in 1870 in the dirty and dull mining town of Braidwood, Illinois, John Mitchell lost his mother when he was only three years of age. His father, a miner, married again and his new wife took in washing to make ends meet. When John was six, his father was killed in a mine accident. Years later he wrote, "The poverty and hardship that followed were marked." His father, a veteran of the Civil War, brought home his heavy soldier's coat.

Drawing done in 1903 of mine boys in Pennsylvania attending a union meeting. The boys, as militant as their elders, went on strike and beat up scabs. They would not let their siblings attend school with the children of strikebreakers.

Lacking winter clothes or warm blankets, John would take down his late father's army coat to cover his little stepbrother and himself at night. When he was ten, his stepmother remarried and John took off to find work on a farm. Although Illinois law at that time did not permit boys to enter the mines before they reached thirteen, twelve-year-old John bluffed his way to work for the Vermillon Coal Company. The coal vein was barely three feet high and John spent his days bent and crouched, unable to stand erect and stretch out. In 1883, when he was thirteen, he helped in the disaster at the nearby Diamond Mine that took the lives of seventy miners. That year, he left Illinois for Colorado and New Mexico, only to find mining conditions "even worse than they had been in Illinois." At sixteen, he returned to Illinois, determined to make something of his life. He joined the Knights of Labor and rapidly made a name for himself as a labor organizer. Formed in 1890, the UMWA called for an eight-hour working day, increased pay, and better and safer working conditions. The UMWA constitution also called for the end of child labor and the strict enforcement of child labor laws. During John Mitchell's tenure as president, the UMWA increased from 34,000 to 300,000 members. Mitchell skillfully quelled the divisions between the miners coming from different countries, by declaring: "The coal you dig is not Slavish coal, or Polish coal, or Irish coal. It's coal."

The mine towns were grim places. The soot from the coke ovens killed grass, flowers and trees. The privies sited in a row between the houses stank and the muddy streets made travel difficult. At night the glow from the coke ovens could be seen from a distance. To keep wages low, the coal companies hired extra men, offering only three or four days of work a week to create competition between the different ethnic groups. To pay rent and buy food at the company store the parents desperately needed the income of their young sons, who were taken out of school and sent to work in the mine. "Men take boys to the mine actually so small that they can hardly carry their dinner buckets without dragging them."

In an article published in 1903 in *McClure's Magazine*, Francis Henry Nichols told the story of the nine hard coal counties of Pennsylvania that formed "a separate and distinct

The breaker boys of Pittston, Pennsylvania, 1911. In her autobiography Mother Jones wrote fondly, "The breaker boys are not little Lord Fauntleroys. Small chaps smoked and chewed and swore. They did men's work and they had men's ways, men's vices, men's pleasures. They fought and spat and swore."

state, called by its inhabitants 'Anthracite.'" Whether American or foreign born, the parents were largely uneducated with little vision for themselves or their children other than coal country. Education in the company school was poor; the boys expected to follow their fathers into the mines, starting around age ten or eleven as breaker boys earning 40 cents an hour, increasing after four years, to 90 cents. As mere boys they joined the union and regarded scabs with the greatest contempt. In 1901, 25,000 of the 150,000 males working in the anthracite mines of Pennsylvania — one-sixth of the workforce — were boys.[6]

Close to the mines were the silk mills and knitting factories. "The mills locate in Anthracite," wrote Nichols, "because they all employ girls, and girl labor is cheaper here than anywhere else." Like their brothers, the girls worked for 40 to 50 cents an hour. Most of the 11,216 females working in these mills were girls younger than age seventeen.

Francis H. Nichols was an adventurous soul. He was in Cuba at the time of the Spanish War. Early in the twentieth century he traveled to Shensi province in northwest China, "where hatred of the foreigner is bitterest and most intense." Despite the great risks he traveled through China on behalf of a New York newspaper to distribute money to famine-gripped Shensi. In 1904 he made his way to Tibet, where he became ill with pneumonia and died, age thirty-six. Somehow, he found the time in 1903 to report on the laboring children of the anthracite fields of Pennsylvania.

The 10 percent wage hike won from the 1900 strike did not satisfy the miners. The average annual wage for a family was $560, leaving many behind in their rent and owing money to the company store. On May 12, 1902, over 100,000 men and boys downed tools in the Great Anthracite Coal Strike and stayed out five months. The shortage of coal nationwide induced President Theodore Roosevelt to intervene. John Mitchell, president of the UMWA, agreed to call off the strike in return for a presidential commission to look into the wages and condition of work of the coal miners. Clarence Darrow, the famed lawyer, agreed to represent the miners. Among the witnesses he called to testify was twelve-year-old Andrew Chippie, "a chubby, little duckling of a boy" employed as a breaker at Jeddo No. 4 colliery. Andrew told the commission that he started working at the mine two years earlier earning forty cents a day sorting coal. However, he never received a single penny of his earnings as the company docked all his pay against the $398 the family owed in rent. Andrew's father, an immigrant from Hungary, was killed by a rock fall in the same mine four years earlier, leaving his family impoverished.

Clarence Darrow was so moved by the terrible conditions of work for little Andrew Chippie and the other boys in the mines that he wrote a story he called *Johnny McCaffery: The Breaker Boy*.

In Darrow's story, the Hungarian Chippie family became the Irish McCaffery family that settled in Scranton, Pennsylvania, where the father got a job in the coal mines. "One day a great piece of rock broke off from the roof of the chamber where he worked and fell squarely upon him crushing him to death." After paying for the funeral the family was "hopelessly in debt." Johnny was only eleven years old but: "There was nothing left to do but send Johnny to the breaker." His mother lied about his age and off Johnny went to the mine. He quickly learned the job and his nimble fingers sorted the coal from the rock as fast as it came down the chute, but the "constant stooping made his back very lame and sore." In the winter his fingers and hands turned cold, his face black, and he began to wheeze. After a few years at the breaker, Johnny was promoted to work underground as a doorkeeper. He went from one tedious job to another. After forty years of labor he retired from the mine, arthritic, asthmatic, dull and complacent, content to smoke his pipe and wait to die.[7]

Clarence Darrow became even more famous in 1925 in his defense of John T. Scopes in what became known as the Scopes Monkey Trial. In *The State of Tennessee v. John Thomas Scopes*, the high school science teacher was accused of breaking Tennessee law by teaching evolution in a state-supported school.

The 18th Annual Conference of the UMWA held in Indianapolis in 1907, with the motto "United We Stand — Divided We Fall," called child labor "the curse of this country." John Mitchell reported, "This country has more children at work than England, Germany and Italy combined." Instead of working, a child should be allowed to "develop a strong, vigorous physique, a well-balanced, cultured mind (and) obtain a good education." In 1914, the mining states enacted laws reducing the workday for children younger than sixteen years of age, and banning night and hazardous employment. In 1918, Pennsylvania legislated that no child between 14 and 16 years "shall be permitted to work more than 51 hours a week or more than nine hours a day." The Pennsylvania Department of Mines hailed the law requiring children to be "in school acquiring an education instead of wearing their young lives

Child miners accompany their hero, John Mitchell, president of the United Mine Workers of America (UMWA), on his visit to the Pennsylvania coalfields in 1902. Mitchell said of the mine boys: "They have the bodies and faces of boys but they come to meetings where I spoke and stood as still as men and listened to every word ... I felt I was fighting for the boys, fighting a battle for innocent childhood."

Miners at Tamarack in Michigan copper country, 1905. The boys carried the drills for the men. Each year miners were killed or injured by falling rock, dynamite explosions or timber collapsing. In 1913, the Western Federation of Miners struck the nearby Calumet mine. At the Christmas day party someone yelled "Fire." In the panic and stampede to the exits seventy-three people, including fifty-nine children, died.

out in the hard task of breaker work." But, there were many who opposed the law, saying that it pauperized the widows of miners killed on the job who depended on the earnings of their young sons.

The boy miners had a friend in William B. Wilson, born in Scotland in 1862, who moved with his family to Arnot, a small coal-mining town in Tioga County, Pennsylvania. At age nine, William followed his father to the mine, starting as a breaker boy. While still in his teens William organized the boys to fight for better pay and working conditions. He joined the UMWA and rose to the rank of secretary-treasurer. In 1906, he was elected to the U.S. House of Representatives and in 1913 was appointed by President Woodrow Wilson as secretary in the newly established U.S. Department of Labor. He served until 1921, advocating a "spirit of justice, of fair play" for the workers of America.

In 1845, copper was discovered in Michigan's Upper Peninsula. A group of Boston investors sent Alexander Agassiz to run the rich Calumet and Hecla mines. Alexander was the son of Louis Agassiz, the famed Harvard geologist. Copper was used for coinage, roofing, as sheathing for the bottom of ocean-going wooden vessels and in plumbing. The directors of the mine, all Harvard men, became immensely rich. Quincy Adams Shaw named the Quincy mine after himself. F.W. Hunnewell expanded into railroad ownership and was the benefactor of Wellesley College. Francis Lee Higginson, the banker, was married to a Miss Bowland, who in 1896 "created astonishment in Boston's most exclusive circles" by eloping with a man fourteen years her junior, leaving behind four children. Not to be outdone, in 1898, her former husband married Corinne Shattuck, "one of the prettiest girls in Boston Society, and is fully thirty years her husband's junior."[8]

The great profitability of the Calumet and Hecla Mining Company came in large part from paying low wages to its immigrant labor force. In the 1880s, the copper mines hired boys as young as twelve years to work underground as drill boys, earning 80 cents to $1.33 a day, with the job of carrying fresh drills to the miners and taking the dull drills away. In 1887, the Michigan legislature voted to end this practice and hired mine inspectors to uphold the law. Yet, child labor continued. In July 1913, the Western Federation of Miners called a strike against all the copper mines in Michigan, demanding an eight-hour working day and a minimum daily wage of $3. The strike continued for months. On Christmas Eve the union arranged a party in the Italian Hall to bolster the spirits of the miners and their families. Someone shouted "Fire," and five hundred people panicked as they ran for the exits. Seventy-three, including fifty-nine children, were crushed to death.

The 63rd United States Congress held hearings into the conditions in the Michigan copper mines. One witness spoke of the low wages: "If you cannot pay living wages then you have no right to keep up that industry. Otherwise you are bound to foster child labor and all kinds of underpaid labor. An industry that cannot pay a living wage is parasitic. It destroys the manhood, womanhood and childhood of the nation."

Another exchange went as follows:

Q: Mr. Rees. It was customary, as the stamp mills were run then, to have in the mills, young boys of your age as wash boys.
A: Mr. Rickard. Yes, they worked from all ages down.
Q: Mr. Rees. Do you mean to imply, do you, that the boys of 11 years of age are now, or have for a good many years, been employed in the mines, do you?

While admitting no wrongdoing the mine management indicated that there was great pressure to disregard the state law "that minors shall not be employed in dangerous occupations under the age of 18.... We shall show that there has been a very strenuous effort on the part of the miners themselves to get that reduced to 16."

Mr. Kerr elaborated: "Some of the miners with large families feel that their children ought to be able to work to help out the support of the family, and are desirous of getting their children to work at 16." This caused big problems in the one-industry towns. Boys left school at 16 and were prevented by law from working in the copper mines until they were 18 years old.[9]

The strikes and public awareness of the dismal conditions in the mines slowly led to improvements. The combination of union action, higher wages for the men, ever-stricter labor laws and technological innovation reduced the need for children in the mines. By the 1920s, employing boy miners in America finally ended. The Great Depression reduced the price of copper and drove the mines into bankruptcy, leaving behind ghost towns.

8

On the Farm

Nearly three-fourths of our child laborers are engaged in agricultural pursuits.—Edward N. Clopper & Lewis W. Hine, 1914

Daniel Webster "was a farmer's son and lived in a plain, old-fashioned house, shaded by fine elms, and separated from the broad, quiet street by a fence."

Mr. Hoyt, the storekeeper, tells the eight-year-old Daniel, "You won't need writing much when you're following the plough."

"I hope I shan't have to do that, Mr. Hoyt," replies Daniel.

— Horatio Alger, *Farm Boy to Senator:*
Being the History of the Boyhood and
Manhood of Daniel Webster, 1882

Q: When do children start working?
A: From 8 up they work right along.
Q: Work on the farms?
A: Yes, Sir, and by the time he is 10 years of age, he is as good as a plow hand as is a man.
Q: You say a boy of 10 is as good as a plow hand?
A: Yes, Sir.

— United States Industrial Commission,
Report of the Industrial Commission on
Agriculture and Agricultural Labor, 1901

In colonial America, farms varied in size from the small family farms of New England to the vast plantations of Virginia. Daniel Vickers writes, "The returns of agriculture in coastal Massachusetts were too meager to allow farmers the luxury of imported help." Instead the farmers "exploited with double intensity the only labor resource available to them — their sons.... Young boys in Essex County, much like their sisters, shortly after their fifth birthday began to help their parents." By the age of ten, the "farm boy began to acquire a workman's identity of his own." He was capable of caring for the livestock, plowing the fields and assisting with other heavy chores. By thirteen or fourteen, the New England farm boy had the strength and the experience to produce more than he consumed.[1]

George Washington's Mount Vernon plantation in Virginia with its hundreds of acres, baronial mansion and many black slaves to do all manner of work, offers the contrast with the penurious New England farm. Washington's stepdaughter, Patsy, was indulged with finery imported from England; his stepson, Jackie, much preferred horses, fox hunting and women to learning French and Latin, and grew up spoiled and indolent. In his 1917 account on farm life in colonial America, Arthur Wallace Calhoun wrote: "There was much work on the farm even for children.... Girls of six spin flax. The boys had to rise early and do chores."[2] Before independence, 90 percent of the settlers lived on farms. Apart from the large, slave-owning plantations; it fell to the father, mother and children, North and South, to do the work on the farms. With the Louisiana Purchase and the expansion to the West, thousands upon thousands of families settled on farms to raise animals and grow grains, fruit of all kinds, sugar beets, as well as tobacco and cotton. John Deere built his plow factory in Moline, Illinois, followed by Thomas Wiard of Batavia, New York, the South Bend Child Plow Company of Indiana and many other plow companies. Cyrus McCormick opened his harvester factory in Chicago in 1848, followed by Walter Abbot Wood of Hoosick Falls, New York, and dozens of other harvester companies. Displayed at the 1893 World's Columbian Exposition in Chicago, these plows and harvesters were driven by one man and pulled by horses. It was not until the twentieth century that gasoline engines powered farm machinery.

During the Gilded Age, over two-thirds of child labor was done on the farms. In 1880, the nation had nearly three million farms, with an average size of 134 acres. By 1900, the number of farms in the United States had increased to 3,269,728. Most were farmer owned and operated, with a third occupied by tenant farmers. The twelfth U.S. Census, completed in 1900, showed that 1,005,575 children, mostly boys less than sixteen years of age, were working on farms; six out of ten of the boys were the sons of farmers. With droughts, floods, sickness and infestations, farming was a precarious career, with average profits in 1910 of only $650. A farm was labor intensive. A farmer could not afford much hired help but depended on his wife and children to help with the farm work. One farmer said, "Every boy born into a farm family was worth a thousand dollars." Little wonder that large families were common.

By the close of the nineteenth century, the pull of the city was taking farm boys off the family farm. In 1881, Edmund Morris published his *Farming for Boys,* telling his young readers, "Their future respectability and happiness will be best promoted by remaining where they are." Farm life provides companionship and the opportunity to build something from scratch. Living on the farm, the boy will learn how to handle tools, plow a field, plant a peach orchard, manage the horses and pigs, plant and gather in the crop and enjoy the quiet pleasures of fishing. Farm work will teach him to handle disappointments and cope with success. With proper guidance, the youngsters will become successful farmers and perhaps rise to positions of "statesmen or public benefactors."[3] *The Boys' and Girls' Farm Leader,* a monthly magazine out of Des Moines, Iowa, encouraged children to stay on the family farm.

Reformers in many states were succeeding in reducing child labor in the factories, mines and canneries, but powerful farming interests, well into the twentieth century, continued to present farm work as wholesome, even for young boys and girls. Senator Albert Beveridge of Indiana, who regarded factory work for children as evil, spoke in favor of farm work. His Bill 17838 proposed a ban on interstate commerce of goods produced in mines and factories that used child labor. Beveridge declared that his bill "did not strike at the employment of children engaged in agriculture. Working children on the farms is good for them.... When children are employed within their strength and in the open air there can be no better training."[4] Henry C. Wallace of Iowa, president of the National Conservation Congress, claimed in 1910 that the prosperity of the typical family farm of 160 acres depended on the work of the children. "Iowa is prosperous in agriculture," he argued, "because of the labor of the farmers' children," and not having to hire outside labor. A childless farmer would soon go bankrupt, or "he would have to work mighty hard to keep from it."[5] Whether farm owner, tenant, sharecropper or itinerant worker, the labor of children helped the family survive.

Ulrich Bonnell Phillips described the role of slavery in the large plantations of the South. The child of a black slave, he wrote, "had a value purely because at some day his labor would presumably yield more than the cost of his keep." The maturing slave children owned by Robert Carter in 1840 "enabled him not only to resume tillage of the pastured tract but also to reclaim the tide-swamp of eighty-acres for corn culture." Another planter took good care of those children "who were also his, destined in time to take their parents' places." A pregnant slave was of doubtful value to the master. Her work would have to be reduced while she was pregnant and later, while nursing. If the child proved to be "an idiot, or blind or crippled," it would impose a burden on the owner. Even if the child were healthy and strong, he would only "reach a maximum [value] before the end of his teens, when he had barely begun to cover his costs."[6]

Agricultural manuals dating to the 1820s advised planters on how to use the slave children: "Negro children, after they pass five or six years of age ... should be taken from the nurse in the negro houses, and put under the tuition of the driver, who has the conducting of the weeding gang.... When any of the children becomes twelve years old, and are healthy, they are fit subjects to be drafted into the second gang, going on progressively from one gang to another." According to Wilma Dunaway, half the slave children by age seven, boys and girls, were doing heavy fieldwork, and their training was complete even before reaching adolescence.[7]

During the nineteenth century and beyond, farm children of eight years and up picked berries and apples, dug up the potatoes and the sugar beets, picked the cranberries from the bogs, milked the cows, fed the pigs, harvested the cotton and tobacco, drove the horse rake and the plow, harvested the corn, drew the water from the well, and did the myriad of other farm tasks. Some worked with their parents on the family farm, others were the little children of sharecroppers and tenant farmers and many were hired hands, brought with their parents to work in the fields during the picking season. In 1843, the French mathematician Joseph Fourier postulated that such was nature's plan: "Nature must have calculated upon the extended employment of children in the vegetable kingdom, for she has created in great abundance little fruits, vegetables and shrubbery, which should occupy the child and not the grown man. The greater portion of our gardens is composed of little plants, which are adapted to the labor of children."[8] The great demand for farm labor continued into the early twentieth century when the horse-drawn plow and harvester and other farm tools were replaced by power machinery.

According to United States census data in 1870, there were some thirteen million jobs in America, split evenly between farm and non-farm work. Over the next fifty years, the number of people working in agriculture increased only gradually, while the number in non-farm (mainly factory) workers rose steeply. By 1930, ten million workers were on the farms but nearly four times as many worked in factories or service industries. In proportion to the growth of population of the nation, the farm population in the twentieth century fell dramatically.

On February 20, 1907, an act of Congress set up a commission to study immigration

Breast-feeding her youngest and using her one free hand, and the dexterous fingers of her older children, a mother hulls strawberries. Wide bonnets shield the family from the heat of the summer of 1910.

into the United States. The great migration of Italians to the United States began in 1880, bringing five million people over the next four decades. Most were landless farmers from the overpopulated south of Italy. In America, many of these newcomers found work on the farms and followed the same patterns of family work they had practiced in Italy. The Immigration Commission (1907–1910), under Senator William P. Dillingham of Vermont, reported on the immigrant Italian families working in agriculture. "The women and all the children ... who were old enough, work with the men in the field.... Women and older children do the same work as the men, while the younger children do weeding." Not owning their own land, Italian "women and children also find employment on the farm or in the factory of a neighboring canning company as bean pickers and stringers.... The women and children assist to a large extent in the farm work, and the entire household down to the children of 10 years of age are frequently seen in the fields.... Until the age of 21, the entire earnings of children are almost invariably paid over to the father of the family.... The Italian children are bright and learn readily, as readily as the American, but most of them leave school at the age of 14, whether they have completed the eighth grade or not."

During the picking season, July to October, Calabria families were recruited from the cities to New Jersey and Maryland farms for vegetable and berry picking. They were housed

Thirteen- and fourteen-year-old boys picking tobacco leaves at the Hackett farm, Buckland, Connecticut, 1917. Northern and central Connecticut had many tobacco farms, hiring children to work in the fields and sheds.

in shacks on the farms. The Immigration Commission reported: "On going to the fields, the women take little children with them and while the parents are at work the children either play at the end of the field or sleep in old boxes or baby carriages under the shade of a tree. General living conditions are far below those of the average American farm laborer. For the three weeks of berry picking $15 a head for a family is a fair accounting. Children of 10 or 12 frequently earn 70 cents a day. The family unit is the most profitable working organization.... All who can pick do so; the little children, too small to pick, run back and forth bringing empty boxes to the pickers and carrying the filled ones to the berry shed." For this hard labor, working ten to twelve hours a day, men earned $1.50 to $2, women $1 to $1.50 and children 50 cents to $1 a day. The Dillingham Commission concluded that mass immigration from eastern and southern Europe posed a threat to American society and recommended that immigration from these regions be reduced.[9]

Citing figures from the United States Census, Edward Clopper and Lewis Hine reported that the bulk of child labor was on the farms. In 1880, there were 1,118,256 children from ten to fifteen years in the labor force, with nearly two-thirds working in agriculture. In 1900, 60 percent of the 1,750,178, and in 1910, seventy-two percent of the 1,990,225 children ten to fifteen years were engaged in agriculture. The Southern states had the greatest number of children employed, particularly Alabama, Arkansas, Georgia, Mississippi, and North and South Carolina. In 1910, Kentucky alone had 64,692 child workers aged ten to fifteen years, of which 82 percent were agricultural workers. These children were engaged in plowing, hoeing, harvesting, stripping tobacco, milking cows, feeding chickens, among other farm tasks. Many of these youngsters were hired hands, working before school, after school or in place of school.

The sugar beet industry of Colorado, Michigan and Nebraska was especially targeted for its use of child labor. Large-scale sugar beet cultivation began during the Napoleonic Wars, with the British navy blockade of French ports preventing cane sugar coming from the Caribbean. The energetic Jules Paul Dellesert found a method to extract sugar from the beet grown on French soil. His innovation was hailed as one of the wonders of the world, earning the gratitude of Emperor Napoleon himself. Sugar made from sugar beets grown in temperate climes broke the monopoly of the sugar cane fields of the Caribbean. Growing sugar beets in the United States began late in the nineteenth century. The plant grew better in the north than the south with Colorado, Michigan, Utah and northern California becoming the leading sugar beet regions. In 1909, Robert Grimshaw and Lewis S. Ware suggested using "the services of children from the schools, those being on average twelve years of age. Most of the work in the fields is done during the vacation period, when those employed may live in tents and very cheaply. This is a good, healthy life, and the labor is well paid." These experts claimed that "very excellent results have been obtained by allowing children to attend to the thinning" of the leaves.[10] The reality was less bucolic. Growing sugar beets was labor intensive, requiring hoeing and weeding before the harvesting season that begins in early October through to mid–November. The growers hired recruiters to bring in families

The sugar beet industry of Colorado, Michigan and Nebraska recruited whole families for hoeing, weeding and thinning the crop. Little children worked during the harvesting season (October to mid–November), yanking out the heavy sugar beets, and missing weeks of school. Photograph c. 1910.

from towns near and far who remained late into the fall. The heavy work of cutting the leaves and yanking out the sugar beets was done by children as young as six years.

By the start of the twentieth century farming in America had become big business with very large farms producing a single crop and requiring large numbers of workers for short periods. In Kentucky and Virginia children picked tobacco, in Maryland and Delaware they picked berries, missing many days of schooling. Farm owners and managers saw no harm in putting little children to work. Many farmers kept their own children out of school during the spring planting season and in the fall to harvest the crop. At the hearing of the Industrial Commission of the U.S. Congress in 1900, one farmer justified using children of eight or nine to pick tea: 'The labor is extremely easy. It consists simply of pinching off the leaves we choose to pluck, between the thumb and the forefinger and putting them into a Swiss trout basket suspended at the waist. It is a very easy kind of labor, and the children are very fond of it.'

In the Pacific states, California, Oregon and Washington, men were employed to pick oranges but, "in the picking of most other light crops—fruits, berries, hops etc.—able-bodied men are not in demand, the work being regarded as essentially adapted to women and children. As a rule, the labor force in the picking fields is composed of family groups, sometimes coming long distances." In the logging camps, "boys may be, and are, used as signal boys for donkey engines, and boys are also in some demand in box factories." By 1916, state laws in California, Oregon and Washington prevented boys under fourteen or girls under sixteen from competitive work, but "poverty is recognized as an excuse to issue a permit" to a younger child. Children had to be paid at least the minimum wage of $6 for a 48-hour week.[11]

Foodstuff Canneries

Preserving food in cans dates to the early nineteenth century. The abundant products of American farms were peeled, boiled, frozen or pasteurized and placed into sealed cans— to remain edible even after months or years. By the year 1897, the United States already had 2,000 canneries, one-third in meats or seafood (ham, oysters, shrimp, sardines, cod, salmon) and two-thirds in fruits and vegetables (tomatoes, peaches, pears, peas, beans, apples.) Fruits and vegetables were prepared by hand for canning. Maryland, with 500 canneries, was at that time the leading canning state. The skinning of tomatoes, pealing peaches or paring pears were repetitive tasks that did not require much training or skill. The fruit and vegetable canneries were busiest during "the few months of summer and ... engaged all the floating cheap labor in the vicinity during their busy months, paying from $2.50 to $1 a day in wages. A great deal of the work being done by women and children, who are paid by the piece."[12]

One Maryland company in 1912, with a quarter of its 586 person labor-force children aged fourteen or younger, claimed: "We never employ children; we let the mothers bring their children in with them because they've no place to leave them, and wouldn't come if we didn't." The reality was quite different as the inspectors found little children arriving at five in the morning to start a full day of work, for a sixty-hour workweek. "One hundred and fifteen were seen entering, their apparent ages ranging from 5 to 15. Approximately two-thirds were plainly under 12." Paid for piecework and with the canning season only a few months long, the children and the parents were eager to get as much work as possible. In 1912, school attendance in Maryland was compulsory only until age twelve, but even younger children were seen working well into September and even October. "There is no question that their school work must suffer."

In the Maryland canneries, the Helper System "accounts for the presence of large numbers of children who, though not employed by the proprietors, are working quite zealously as the older members of their families who are employed." The little children come in at 7 o'clock in the morning with their mothers and older siblings, "but they don't begin work until 9 o'clock."

Q: What do they do in the interval?
A: Oh, anything.
Q: Do you mean they sit idle for two hours every morning?
A: Oh, no, they sweep or scrub or anything like that we have them do, but they don't begin their regular job till 9.[13]

Whole families moved from the cities to the canneries, where they were housed and fed. The children stood alongside the adults sorting spinach, hulling berries and cherries, peeling peaches, pears and apples, skinning tomatoes, husking corn, as well as bringing in

Boy working in a food cannery in Baltimore, Maryland, 1913. By 1880 there were over 6,000 children under sixteen preparing fruits, vegetables or seafood for canning. The fruit and vegetable canneries were mainly in California and Maryland, seafood canneries in Maine, the Gulf States, California and Washington State. With advances in canning technology, fewer and fewer children were employed.

fresh supplies and carrying out barrels of processed foods. Small children battled to lift baskets of skinned tomatoes weighing 40 pounds or crates of husked corn weighing fifty pounds. If they were too small to lift these loads, the children would drag them across the floor as best they could. It took until 1918 for Maryland and Virginia to increase the age of working in the canneries from 12 to 14 years.

Delaware followed Maryland with its opulent orchards producing an abundance of strawberries, blackberries, gooseberries and raspberries as well as peaches and pears and vegetables of all kinds. Again the problem for the growers was to find enough hands to gather in the rich harvest during the months of August, September and October. Men were too expensive and difficult to manage. The growers depended on women and children "to go into the fields to pick."[14]

The march of the nation westward opened California to the cultivation of fruits and vegetables. By 1900 California was the leading state for growing and canning of fruits and vegetables. In 1902, the fecund Santa Clara County supplied 40 million pounds of canned fruits, 80 million pounds of dried prunes, 30 million pounds of green fruit and 18 million pounds of dried apricots. The county "had the biggest fruit packing house in the world and the biggest fruit canning plant in the world." As elsewhere in the fruit and vegetable growing regions of America, the picking season (August to October) was short and good labor was hard to find. Chinese and Japanese laborers were imported but a prejudiced public reaction slowed the flow of workers coming from Asia. The growers preferred the cheapness of female and child labor. With no place to leave them, these women brought their little children with them to the workplace. The small children were paid piecework and worked at their own rate. It was a combination of baby-sitting and training on the job. Growers complained that women would not come to work unless they could bring their children with them. In California at the time "the public schools do not commence the fall term until late in September ... the object being to permit the children to work in the orchards." Many of these children did not start school until late October.[15] In California in 1913, the fruit and vegetable canneries employed 8,270 women and 1,187 children.

Martin Brown and his colleagues studied child labor in the U.S. fruit and canning industries. In the 1880s, children under sixteen comprised 18 percent of all workers in the American fruit and vegetable canneries (6000 out of 30,000). By 1900 the percentage of child workers in canning declined to 7 percent and by 1920, to only 3 percent. The reasons for the decline of children in canning were the rising family incomes, increasingly strict state rules against early child labor and mandatory school attendance. Brown and his associates attribute most of the decline to advances in technology, the introduction of machines that needed a higher level of skill and better training.[16]

In 1935, Rose C. Feld wrote of child labor: "By far the greatest number, almost half a million, were found in the ranks of agricultural workers." The largest number were children on their parents' farms. There was also the problem of migratory families who "piled into the wagon seeking the high road at the first breath of spring" and individual wage earners. These youngsters worked through the summer vacations but often missed school in June and September.[17]

During the Second World War, labor shortages led to an increase in child labor on the farms. At war's end children were encouraged to stay in school. In 1971, the United States Department of Labor reported that as many as a quarter of the nation's 5.1 million seasonal farm workers were children under sixteen. Half of these, some 400,000, were children between ten and thirteen. Proponents claimed that farm work benefited children by providing fresh air, exercise, teaching the value of money, and teaching the children good work habits. Cassandra Stockburger pointed out the risks: injury, contact with pesticides, working long hours in the heat, and especially "intellectual retardation."[18]

After the war, the children of migrant workers — largely undocumented from Central and South America — made up the bulk of the exploited children. Not only were they functioning below grade level but most dropped out of school after the sixth grade. The Fair Labor Standards Act of 1938 was amended by the 92nd Congress (1971–72) to protect the children of migrant workers. In 2010, the Obama administration hired hundreds of investigators to crack down on farmers who employed children. At dawn vans filled with migrant workers and their children descended on the blueberry farms of North Carolina. To counter years of lax attention to child labor laws, the Labor Department increased the fines on farmers.[19] Yet to be resolved is whether children under sixteen years of age should be permitted to spread pesticides, operate heavy equipment or cut timber, jobs identified as hazardous by the National Institute of Occupational Safety and Health.[20]

The debate concerning government oversight versus parental control regarding farm work for children below sixteen years continues to our times.

9

Distributing the News

A gentleman from out of town stops to buy a newspaper from Dan, a poor New York newsboy with "a keen, pleasant, face." The man asks Dan why he is selling the newspapers.

"We lived in a nice house up town, and I went to a private school. But all at once father failed, and soon afterwards died, and then everything changed."

"It is a sad story," the gentleman responds. "Is your mother living?"

"Yes, sir. The worst of it is that I don't make enough to support us both, and she has to work, too."

"What does she do?"

"She makes vests for a man on Chatham Street," earning twenty cents a piece.

The man: "A mere pittance.... It is starvation wages."

— Horatio Alger, *Dan, The Newsboy*, 1893

Many of the goods produced in New York City in the early 1880s were "contributed by children of tender years." At that time an estimated 100,000 children between eight and sixteen were working, some making clothes, envelopes, paper collars, artificial flowers, toys and other items. Thousands of children worked in tobacco factories, "underground in a damp atmosphere preparing, brining and sweetening the weed in preparation for steaming." In many of these industries, the children were at risk of injury or illness. This was particularly so in the fireworks factories where children were "in constant danger of an explosion by which life or eyesight may be lost."

Connecticut and Massachusetts had earlier passed legislation to restrict the hours and age children were allowed to work. But in the New York State of 1882, there was no law to prevent "the employment of children at any age [or] fix any limit to the number of hours a child may be employed."[1]

By the close of the nineteenth-century, the streets of American towns and cities were filled with children. The younger children played there; their older brothers and sisters collected junk to sell to the junkman, hawked newspapers, sold baskets and flowers on street corners, raced on bicycles delivering messages and telegrams, tended pushcarts or shined shoes and boots.

Messenger Boys

William Frederick Cody was born in 1846 in Iowa Territory. His family was "reduced to utter destitution" after his father died and at age eleven, Bill took a job as a "boy extra" riding west with the wagon trains and delivering messages along the line. One trip, with the wagons loaded, required the crew to walk one thousand miles home. "I was not yet twelve years," recounted Bill Cody, "but I had to walk with the rest the full thousand miles, and we made nearly thirty miles a day." It took a month of "hard travel" to return home. At fourteen he sought a job on the Pony Express, "the most picturesque messenger-service this country has ever seen." Bill tells: "I was pretty young in years but I had already earned a reputation for coming safe out of perilous adventures, and I was hired." Here started the colorful life of Buffalo Bill, one of America's illustrious characters of the Wild West. The Pony Express sent its riders along a two thousand mile trail, across the Great Plains, through the desert, and over two mountain ranges to reach California. The company set up relay stations fifteen miles apart, where the riders exchanged for fresh ponies. To keep the weight down the company hired riders weighing less than 125 pounds, including many boys. "A rider's route covered three stations [but] when it became apparent to the men in charge that the boys could do better than forty-five miles a day, the stretches were lengthened." William "Buffalo Bill" Cody rode for the Pony Express for two years, earning up to $125 a month — a princely wage for those times. The mystique of the Pony Express soon gave way to the telegram as a much speedier way of sending news.[2]

In 1791 Claude Chappe in France invented the telegraph, the technological marvel that changed the way information was transmitted. In 1846 Samuel F. B. Morse set up a telegraphic link between Baltimore and New York. The telegraphic system in the United States spread rapidly and in 1861, the line reached from the east coast to the west putting the Pony Express out of business. Western Union established a network of telegraph offices in every town and city in America. In 1875, Western Union commissioned the architect George B. Post to built its nine-story head office in New York. At speeds infinitely faster than the Pony Express a message could be sent by telegraph from one city to another. It still had to get from the Western Union office to the recipient. This is where the telegraph messenger boy came in.

In his 1879 inspirational novel *The Telegraph Boy*, Horatio Alger Jr. tells the story of the street urchin Frank Kavanagh, who meets up with a kindly man who says to him: "You know where the office of the Western Union is, come round there tomorrow morning at eight o'clock, and I will give you something to do." Frank responds: "Oh, I'm very thankful to you, sir, and this will make my mother the happiest lady." Through the influence of his patron, Frank found himself in the uniform of a district telegraph messenger.[3]

Another of Horatio Alger's boy heroes undergoes many trials before he triumphs. In *Mark Mason's Victory: The Trials and Triumphs of a Telegraph Boy* (1899), fifteen-year-old Mark, out delivering messages, encounters cousin Edgar along the streets of New York. "Don't waste any time with him, Edgar," the boy's father admonishes, "He is a street boy, and his manners are fitted to his station." Mark lives "in a humble home " and supports his mother and sister through his meager earnings as a telegram boy. The rent is due and things look bleak indeed when Mark saves the life of Mr. Luther Rockwell, banker.

Mr. Rockwell feels "that I ought to do something to show my gratitude ... I should like to take you into my employ but I have no vacancy, and I do not like to discharge any of my old and trusted employees." Learning that Mark is poor "he turned to his desk, and opening his check book, deliberately filled up a check. He tore it off and handed it to Mark." Mark reads the check with amazement. It was a check for one thousand dollars,

Telegram messenger boy, Birmingham, Alabama, 1914. Thousands of boys on bicycles delivered messages from the offices of the Western Union, American Telegraph and Postal Telegraph companies.

"payable to the order of Mark Mason." Mark uses some of the money to move his family into "a handsome flat up town, and henceforth were able to live as well as their pretentious relatives." Mark takes a mercantile course at a community college in the expectation he "will eventually enter the establishment of Mr. Gilbert, with whom he is as great a favorite as ever." Mark goes out West on a knight's errand, facing many trials along the way. On his return he is rewarded with a place in Mr. Gilbert's counting house. He has another stroke of luck when Mrs. Mack, "the aged miser," dies, leaving him five thousand dollars. His trials over, Mark Mason is now well on the way to respectability and success.[4]

The blue suit and badge upon the cap of the messenger boy were familiar to every city resident. "The uniform is provided by the company, and must be paid for by weekly installments, which are deducted from the wages of the wearers.... Boys, on arriving at the office, seat themselves, and are called upon in order. A boy just returned from an errand, hangs up his hat, and takes his place at the foot of the line. He will not be called upon till all who are ahead of him have been dispatched in one direction of another." Western Union set up telephone call boxes around the city from which people called the office. Boys were dispatched to ride top-speed to pick up messages and bring them to the Western Union office for transmission, while other boys hopped on their bicycles to deliver messages from the office. The boys also collected and delivered parcels.

Wall Street stockbrokers and business were heavy users of the services of messenger boys. The United States censuses list one thousand messenger boys in 1880, five thousand by 1900 and rising nation-wide to nine thousand by 1910. For several decades after 1900 the number of messenger boys increased, despite the growing popularity of the telephone. Some businesses would hire the messenger boy for the whole day; at thirty cents an hour it was cheaper than hiring a regular office boy. They delivered parcels, and conducted market surveys. Unlike newsboys, the messenger boys generally came from intact but poor, white families who needed the extra money.

In 1881 the messenger boys in Pittsburgh, who were paid between $12 and $18 a month, demanded $18 a month for all the boys. In 1883, eighty messenger boys in Boston went on strike for more money. The company promptly hired fifty other boys to take their place. In July 1893, the messenger boys of the District Telephone Company in Wilkes-Barre, Pennsylvania, went out on strike after their hours were increased from twelve to twelve and a half per day with no increase in pay. In 1899 a wave of strikes "now spread to the telegraph messenger boys of New York City [who] think that the whole business of the city will be brought up with a jerk and paralyzed, and the telegraph companies being completely at their mercy of the messengers, will promptly capitulate and beg them to return at their own terms." The boys complained that on Sundays they had to work fourteen hours and on weekdays ten hours a day. For this they were paid two cents to deliver a message, giving them $3.50 to $4 a week, with fifty cents off to pay for their uniforms. In protest, the boys left the offices of Western Union, the American District Telegraph Company and the Postal Telegraph Company, and gathered together "with the apparent intention to create trouble, but the presence of a few policemen dampened their courage."[5] A few days later, over two hundred Philadelphia messenger boys joined the strike. In Boston hundreds of boys struck the Boston District Messenger Company, demanding an increase from 1.5 to 2.5 cents for each message delivered. The boys "ran up and down Devonshire Street, shouting and yelling."

"Wilson's Auto Hurts a Boy," proclaimed the morning newspaper in 1913. "Coming back from a run in the country beyond the eastern branch of the Potomac, one of the White House motor cars, in which President Wilson was riding, struck Robert Crawford, a telegraph messenger boy, who was knocked down and bruised. The youngster was riding a bicycle and ... swerved from his course in order to escape being hit by a stone thrown by another boy. Crawford was thrown from the bicycle."

The president's chauffeur stopped the car "in time to prevent the wheels passing over Crawford." Dr. Gary T. Grayson, the White House physician, jumped out to examine the frightened boy. Crawford was lifted into the president's car and taken to Providence Hospital. No bones were broken. Young Crawford's main concern was his bicycle. "My wheel, my wheel," he whimpered. "I'll have to carry the messages now." The next day President Woodrow Wilson visited the boy in the hospital and promised him "a nice new wheel." Dr. Grayson "bought a new bicycle and sent it to the boy, with a kindly message from the President."[6]

Dr. Gary Grayson of the United States Navy Medical Corps was one of the president's closest friends. Serving as the president's personal physician, Grayson was appointed rear admiral in the navy. On October 2, 1919, Edith Wilson placed an urgent call to Dr. Grayson saying that the president fell and was unconscious. Dr. Grayson found the president had had a stroke, leaving him with impaired eyesight and paralysis of the left side of the body. Grayson did not declare Wilson incapable or tell the nation just how ill the president was. Instead, Edith Wilson, Grayson and a few confidants formed a circle of silence regarding the severity of the president's condition. Wilson was bed-ridden and did not attend meetings for six months; his cabinet was shocked to see his decline. In 1921 Wilson left the White House and remained an invalid until he died on February 3, 1924.

The telegraph companies took messages from any callbox and delivered messages to any address. In this way the telegraph boys became involved with the seamy side of life. According to Edward Clopper (1911), during the day hours the messenger boy went about his regular business "but after nine o'clock at night the character of his work undergoes a radical change; from that time until two or three o'clock in the morning his work is almost exclusively the running of errands in connection with the three great evils of gambling, drink and prostitution. Calls come to the messenger offices over the telephone from hotels, drug stores and saloons, asking these messenger boys to be sent at once to where the patrons are to visit them. Prostitutes call in messenger boys to perform for them a surprising variety of services. The boys get them chop-suey, chili-con-carne, liquor, tobacco, opium, and articles used in their trade, deposit their money in the bank.... The boys are drawn into close association with the denizens of the underworld." Some of the boys stayed on the job a few years and went on to better things, but most, according to one observer, got stuck there: "The messenger service is a blind alley; it leads nowhere."[7]

Horatio Alger's fictional heroes occasionally had real life equivalents. Charles M. Higgins started his work life at age fourteen in Cleveland as the messenger boy to John D. Rockefeller at the start of the Standard Oil Company. Higgins was promoted to vice president of Standard Oil of New York. George C. van Tuyl, Jr., once a lowly messenger boy at the National Exchange Bank of Albany, rose to be president of the Metropolitan Trust Company of New York. The messenger boy William A, Nash became president of the Corn Exchange Bank. Few personified the "messenger boy to company president story" more than Belvidere Brooks, born in 1859 in Wheelock, Texas. Western Union had arrived in town in 1871 and hired the twelve-year-old as its local telegraph messenger boy. He taught himself Morse code and the following year was promoted to key operator at a salary of $8 a month. Belvidere Brooks "worked his way up" in forty years from messenger boy to general manager of "the entire Western Union Telegraph Company," in charge of 28,000 offices and 50,000 employees. Moving to company headquarters in New York City, Belvidere Brooks gave his sons the advantages of a college education. His son Belvidere Jr. attended Williams College where he was captain of the football team. In August 1918, Captain Belvidere Brooks of the United States Expeditionary Force was killed at Fismes, France, in the American offensive during the second Battle of the Marne.[8]

Messenger boy strikes occurred periodically into the twentieth century. In 1935, "one of the fastest strike settlements on record" took place. In the morning of January 14, the messenger boys of the Western Union and Postal Telegraph Companies threatened a walkout over wages. By the afternoon the strike was settled with an increase of $1 to $1.50 extra per hour, plus the end of the seven-cents a day charge for uniforms. This was a 50 percent pay increase for the boys.

Train Boys

These children rode the line selling newspapers and candy. The most famous train boy was Thomas Alva Edison, born 1847, in the village of Milas, Erie County, Ohio. At age twelve, Edison got a job on the Grand Trunk Railway traveling from Port Huron to Detroit and back, all in one day. He sold newspapers and candy to the passengers and did his scientific experiments in the luggage car. One day the train jerked, the chemicals spilled and caused a fire. Edison was kicked off the train but continued to sell his newspapers on the station platforms. In *Cab and Caboose: The Story of a Railway Boy* (published in 1891) by Kirk Munroe, the young hero, Rodman Ray Blake, was "among the boys, decidedly the most popular fellow in the place. He was a slightly-built chap; but with muscles like steel wires and possessed of wonderful agility and powers of endurance." Known as "Railroad Blake," he was unjustly driven from his own home to become a vagabond, traveling on the railroads. "I am a runaway," he explains, "That is, I was turned away first, and ran away afterwards." He experienced many misfortunes and disappointments coolly and courageously and was justly rewarded to become a brakeman.

Newsboys

Newsboys were drawn from the legions of orphaned and abandoned children who survived in the cities by forming their own world, living, sleeping and eating together, protecting each other and going on strike together. In the business of selling newspapers, they were independent operators, each with his own turf, spending a little money for supplies, and providing a service in the hope each evening of making a small profit from the day's labor; enough for a meal, a bed, entertainment and perhaps some money left over as savings.

Little boys selling newspapers were long a feature of life in the fast-growing American cities. Seven years before the Civil War an observer wrote that these feral New York newsboys were "a distinct class among themselves ... they eat and sleep, and make their living, and amuse themselves, in their own way, preferably independent of the world, so long as the world will buy their newspapers." They were "little fellows from 10 to 13 years of age [but] they had all the manners of little men." The boys slept six to eight together in alleyways, in "a dark stairway under the sidewalk" or found warmth "curled up around the grating by the sidewalk where the steam comes through." They went to the theater, smoked, drank and gambled. A few saved their money. They helped each other and were even generous. The boys were very sharp businessmen. Each had his own beat "and if one invades the range of the other he is well pummeled."[9]

By the close of the nineteenth century every American city had its daily newspapers. New York had a dozen, Boston, Philadelphia and Chicago almost as many. The armies of impoverished and homeless boys in American cities formed the distribution system to sell the newspapers to the general public. The newsboys, or "newsies," were not employees but got up early in the morning to buy their supplies at distribution points and then rushed off to their regular corners to sell the newspapers. Each boy was an independent operator paying fifty cents a hundred. Since he was not refunded for returns he would stay out on the streets until the last paper was sold. For all this effort a boy usually made a profit of fifty cents a day, $1 if he was lucky. In New York alone, there were 10,000 boys out each day carrying and selling newspapers. It was a harsh and competitive world that daily faced these small, impoverished boys. Selling newspapers was a way to survive.

In 1854, the Children's Aid Society of New York opened the Newsboys' Lodging House

Even before the Civil War, newsies were a common sight on the streets of cities large and small. The children would congregate early in the morning outside the distribution centers to collect their papers and then rush off to their chosen corners to shout out the headlines to sell their supply. New York City alone had 10,000 newsboys, many of them orphaned or abandoned. Founded in 1854, the Newsboys' Lodging House in New York offered a filling meal and a clean bed. John L. Sullivan, seen on the poster in this c. 1908 photograph, was the world's heavyweight boxing champion from 1882 to 1892. For years after, out of shape and overweight, he continued to hold exhibitions. Known as the Boston Strong Boy, he died poor in 1918, aged 59 years.

at 9 Duane Street, and, over the next twenty years, built separate shelters for boys and girls, each housing up to 250 children. The Newsboys' Lodging House on Park Lane, near Broadway, "is always full at night.... The boys pay five cents for supper and five cents for bed.... It requires a great deal of tact to keep the boys under proper supervision, without, at the same time, letting them feel that the restrictions are too severe.... Some of the newsboys have considerable savings and are well-conducted lads.... Some of the boys are eager to learn to write." Other boys, accustomed to self-reliance from an early age, were unwilling to accept the morality of their "betters."[10] The city of Buffalo had its Newboys' and Bootblacks' home for boys between 10 and 18 years, who either worked or attended school.

One of the first newsboy strikes in the United States took place in Pottsville, Pennsylvania, in October 1884, after the *Evening Chronicle* raised the price to the newsboys from fifty to sixty cents a hundred. Seventy-five boys went on strike. When four others crossed the line to collect their papers they were set upon by the crowd and "severely beaten."[11] In New York City in 1889, "Several hundred newsboys went on strike because they had been told that *the Evening Sun* and the *Evening World* had been advanced from 50 to 60 cents a hundred.... A number of fights followed and some of the boys were very roughly handled."

Newsies were up early to sell the morning edition and out late for the evening edition. Mostly boys but girls also sold newspapers as this 1910 street picture from Wilmington, Delaware, shows. There were claims that allowing girls to sell newspapers led to vice, including prostitution.

The police arrested Arthur Lutt, an eleven-year-old Polish boy, for hitting a police officer and Joseph Baldi, an eleven-year-old Italian boy, for destroying newspapers. The boys were taken to the Tombs Police Court, where Justice Hogan committed them to the city prison.[12] In Chicago in 1877, the newsboys came to the aid of the striking printers of *the Chicago Post* by picketing and refusing to sell the paper on the streets.

The largest and most dramatic of the newsboy strikes started on Wednesday, July 19, 1899, after Joseph Pulitzer, publisher of the *World*, and William Hearst, publisher of the *Journal*, increased the price of their newspapers sold to the newsboys from fifty to sixty cents a hundred. Pulitzer's action against the newsboys was all the more shocking since he experienced similar hardships when he came to the United States as a boy. On July 19, hundreds of newsboys, led by Kid Blink, a small boy so-named because he had only one seeing eye, gathered at City Hall Park, and agreed not to sell these two newspapers. On July 22, Kid Blink, Dave Simons and several of the strike leaders met with Hearst in his office at the Journal building, asking him to bring down the price of his paper. William Hearst told them he would give them an answer early the next week. Without telling the boys in advance, Hearst and Pulitzer hired several hundred burly men at $2 a day to deliver their papers in an effort to break the strike of the newsboys. On July 24, Kid Blink gathered 5,000 newsboys at the Irving Hall on Broome Street. Two thousand filled the hall and three thousand gathered outside. They heard the Kid declare: "I'm here to say that if we are going to win the

An above-knee amputation did not stop this boy from selling newspapers. In 1899 five thousand newsboys in New York went on strike against the papers of Joseph Pulitzer and William Hearst.

strike we must stick together like glue and never give in, Am I right?" The newsboys "howled like demons" and voiced their approval, cheering and singing union songs. To protect their business, gangs of the little boys attacked the newly hired men.

To their dismay the newsboys discovered that Kid Blink, whose real name was Louis Ballatt, and the other strike leaders had sold out and made their own deals with Pulitzer and Hearst. Calling Kid Blink a traitor, the boys managed to keep the strike going, causing the *World* and the *Journal* to lose circulation. After holding out for two weeks these great newspaper tycoons made a deal with the boys: the newspapers would remain at sixty cents a hundred but the newspapers would buy back from the boys any unsold copies. The newsboys' strike of 1899 was the inspiration for the Disney musical movie *Newsies* of 1992.

Hordes of newsboys could be seen early in the mornings and again in the evenings hanging on to the delivery wagons eager to get their deliveries. On July 30, 1885, one delivery wagon crashed into a passing streetcar, throwing several of the boys to the ground. John Abbott, 12, and Patrick Shea, 13, were run over by a beer truck and sustained injuries to their limbs and head. The boys were taken to the hospital "but neither was dangerously injured." Despite the pain and bruising, the stoical boys went back to work. Not only did the newsboys of New York occupy every corner shouting out "Extra! Extra!" to get attention but they swarmed on the streetcars and subway trains with their bundles of newspapers. Claiming they were acting to defend the riders and the boys themselves the owners of the streetcar companies collectively banned the newsboys from their cars.[13]

The messenger and newsboys became, in fantasy if not in truth, a symbol of the American rags to riches saga. Frederick William Vanderbilt, grandson of Cornelius Vanderbilt, was a major stockholder in Western Union. For twenty years (from 1893 to 1913) his wife, Louise Vanderbilt, held a special Thanksgiving party at Memorial Hall near her grand Newport, Rhode Island, mansion, Rough Point, sitting on a ten-acre oceanfront property at the end of Bellevue Avenue. Four to five hundred boys came each year for dinner, and "practically every poor boy in Newport was present." Frederick and his wife also owned large homes in New York City, Hyde Park and elsewhere. They had no children of their own and took pleasure in "adopting" the telegraph and news boys — if only for a day.

In April 1902, Randolph Guggenheimer, one of New York's wealthiest men, hosted a party for twelve hundred newsboys. On February 23, the next year, Guggenheimer held a Washington's Birthday dinner for four hundred New York newsboys at the Newsboys' Lodging House on Duane Street. He gave each boy an American flag and assured them they too could rise to fame and fortune. "It was the sons of ordinary people and lads who worked their way upward through hardship and poverty," hectored Mr. Guggenheimer, "that made great discoveries and inventions of science. The locomotive, the steamship, the modern printing press, the telephone, the telegraph and a thousand other wonderful things came from the brains of men whose parents were not blessed with overmuch money.... Anything is possible to you if you will steer clear of follies and vices." Guggenheimer, the son of a wealthy tobacco grower, offered the boys his own story of starting low before achieving success. After finishing New York University law school, he worked briefly in a law office earning only 75 cents a week.[14] The newsboys of New York were a favorite charity of the elites. In 1915, a group of prominent men collected $250,000 to enlarge the Newsboys' Clubhouse at Eleventh Street and Seventh Avenue, to which 2,000 boys belonged.

The rapid spread of the telephone to businesses and homes early in the twentieth century was the lurking threat to the telegraph companies and the messenger boys who worked for them. On February 1, 1918, three hundred messenger boys went out on strike against Western Union. Violence broke out when "the strikers tried to tear off the uniforms of the boys who continued to work." A company official warned: "We are more than able to make up for the loss of messages by using the telephones for delivering messages; and if these boys don't look out they will find that the telephone will take their places."

The newsboy tradition continued in the suburbs where boys on their bicycles delivered the newspapers to homes early each morning. The tradition of praising newsboys continued at least until October 5, 1957, when President Dwight Eisenhower said that "delivering papers has been part of the early chapters of America's greatest success stories."

10

City Work

James Wainwright, the wealthy banker, sends Fred Fenton to retrieve $15,000 worth of stolen bonds. He explains to a friend:

> *"I have sent a messenger to recover them."*
> *"Who is it?"*
> *"My office boy."*
> *"I suppose that is a joke?"*
> *"By no means."*
> *"What is the age of your office boy?"*
> *"I should judge from his appearance that he is sixteen."*
> *"Do you mean to say you have entrusted a boy of sixteen with so important a commission?"*
> *"I do."*
>
> —Horatio Alger, *The Erie Train Boy*, 1891

> *We moved from Rivington Street to Brooklyn and then to the Bronx. I had a lot of jobs when I was a kid—paper boy, grocery boy, all kinds of things.... All the kids I knew were poor kids. Some turned out bad, some just ordinary, and some turned out nice.*
>
> —Jacob Julius Garfinkle (1913–1952),
> better known as the actor John Garfield

The plethora of jobs specifically for boys and girls can be readily ascertained by examining the Classification Index of Occupations from the various United States censuses. These bottom-of-the-ladder jobs included office boys and girls, bundle boys who carried bundles, cash boys and girls who handled money, parcel boys and girls, wrapper boys and girls, the butcher boy, the delivery boy and the grocery boy, errand boy and factory boy, store boy and store girl, the shop boy and the stock boy, the tool boy, wagon boy and the messenger boy; there was a draper's boy, a bobbin boy and a bobbin girl, flower girl, cabin boy, and the house maid. The quilt boy worked in the cotton mill, the mold boy in the glass works, the screen boy in the paper mill, the farm boy, the quarry boy, the band boy worked in the rope factory, the dilly boy in the coal mine, the heater boy in the iron works, rivet boy in the boiler works, the spool boy in the hosiery mill, water boy on the railroads, kitchen boy and kitchen girl, chore boy in the lumber camp, signal boy, scrap boy in the steel mill, door boy and, of course, the ball boy and the altar boy. These were lowly and poorly paid positions. Even when fully grown they were still called boy or girl.

Domestic Servants

Catharine Esther Beecher (1800–1878) was the oldest of the remarkable brood of the preacher Lyman Beecher. In 1823 she opened the Hartford Female Seminary, one of the first school for girls in the United States. A decade later, she moved with her father to Cincinnati where she operated a similar school. Based on her long experience teaching the daughters of the wealthy, she wrote in 1842 *A Treatise on Domestic Economy: For the Use of Young Ladies at Home and at School*. These "young girls, especially of the more wealthy classes, are not trained for their profession," as wives, mothers and housekeepers. They lack the "muscular and nervous strength" necessary for the "happiness of marital life." In order to prepare for her adult roles, "a little girl may begin, at five or six years of age, to assist her mother and, if properly trained, by the time she is ten, she can render essential aid.... All the sweeping, dusting, care of furniture and beds, the clear starching, should be done by the daughter of the family, and not by hired servants." A mother, even of the wealthy classes, should "train her daughters to aid her in domestic service." Catharine's ideas had an influence on her younger sister, Harriet who was a pupil at the Hartford Female Seminary. In 1836 Harriet married Calvin Ellis Stowe and in 1852, as Harriet Beecher Stowe, she wrote the great novel about the evils of slavery, *Uncle Tom's Cabin*. The notion of physical exercise and housework, however, did not sit well with the daughters and wives of wealthy men of the 1840s. Instead of following Catharine Beecher's advice they chose instead to hire domestic servants at cheap rates from among the daughters of German and Irish immigrants coming to the United States.

Between 1840 and 1860, some four and a half million immigrants came to the United States, mainly due to the potato blight in Ireland and political upheaval in Germany. These destitute people faced a difficult life in the New World. In Buffalo, New York, the historian Laurence A. Glasco measured the level of family disruption among the different ethnic communities. While native American girls remained with their parents until age sixteen or later, the young children of the Irish and German immigrants had to go to work. "Irish girls began leaving home at age 11, and by age 14 about 60% no longer lived with their parents.... Irish girls left home invariably to become live-in servants.... Virtually every Irish girl during adolescence spent several years as a live-in domestic." The girls of German immigrants followed the same pattern as the Irish girls. "Nearly all the German girls at some point during their adolescence served as live-in domestics." These young girls often worked as domestic servants seven days a week without any pay, beyond board and lodging.[1]

Francis Amasa Walker was born to a prominent Boston family in 1840. He attended Amherst College, fought in the Civil War and, at age twenty-nine was appointed chief of the United States Bureau of Statistics. As superintendent of the national censuses for 1870 and 1880, and later, president of the Massachusetts Institute of Technology, he had a great deal to say about trends in American life. In 1875 Walker wrote that the nation was becoming more prosperous. "Not only had rapid progress been made in the Upper Ten Thousand toward European standards of equipage and service (but) the middle class of our population had made a decided movement in the same direction." The 1870 census showed the United States had 951,354 people working as domestic servants. Half of these were former slaves in the South whose daily lives had barely changed despite the Civil War. The remaining half of the domestic servants lived in the "sixteen free states" where, on average, one household in seven had the services of a domestic servant. Largely female, the domestic servant workforce comprised largely the American-born young daughters of Irish and German immigrants.[2]

In Ireland at the time of the Potato Famine and beyond, families were large. Very few could afford the dowries needed for their daughters to marry, resulting in the emigration of young girls seeking work as domestic servants, despite the low status of such work in America. With many native-born Americans entering the middle class, there were plenty of jobs. In Springfield, Illinois, Abraham and Mary Lincoln employed a succession of Irish domestic servants. The teen-aged Catherine Gordon was live-in help to the Lincoln family in 1850, followed by Sarah Harper, Mary Johnson, Ruth Stanton and Harriet Hawks. In 1888, fourteen-year-old Sarah Bryne found work with a Vermont family and remained there for the rest of her life. In 1912, fourteen-year-old Sarah Brady left County Galway for Boston to find work as a housemaid.

Emily Blackwell (1828–1910) was denied admission to several medical schools but persevered to graduate in 1854 from Western Reserve University in Cleveland as the third woman in the United States to be awarded a degree in medicine. With her sister Elizabeth, she moved to New York to open the New York Infirmary for Indigent Women and Children. In 1868 she helped establish the Women's Medical College. Dr. Blackwell became an authority on the working lives of women and girls. In 1883 she wrote on "how pressing and increasing an evil is the lack of skillful and reliable servants" in the well-to-do American home. "The Irish girl finds work from the day of her landing, and begins almost immediately to send remittances of money to her friends at home," wrote Dr. Blackwell. "The American girl, thrown upon her own resources, struggles miserably to keep soul and body together upon the scanty wages of the shop or the factory. Yet so decided is the disinclination to domestic service, the largest and most profitable field for women to work, that American women have virtually abandoned it. The Irish girls gradually absorb the same distaste and are less available as they become Americanized. We already hear the suggestion in favor of the Chinese that they are needed to supplant the Irish servants, as the Irish have taken the place of the Americans."[3]

The 1880 census showed that 10 percent of all female domestic servants in the United States (numbering 93,000) were fifteen years or younger. In the 1900 census, 120,000 girls ten to fifteen years of age (9.4 percent of all domestic servants) were in domestic service, after which date the number began to decline. In the 1920 census only 30,536 (3 percent) of domestic servants were fifteen or younger. The electric-powered vacuum machine, dishwasher, clothes washing machine and other household gadgets made twentieth-century housework manageable without live-in servants. Girls increasingly turned from domestic work to office, factory and shop work instead.

Office Boys

In the nineteenth century the dusty ledger books and letters written with quill and ink were replaced by the telephone, typewriter, adding machine, dictation machine, filing system, and cash register. The large corporate offices that mushroomed across the United States needed a new type of employee at the bottom of the ladder — the office boy. Mr. J.

New York office boy, 1917. The great corporations of the twentieth century kept a large number of office workers busy. Office boys were employed to answer telephones, file papers, sweep the floors, carry messages from desk to desk and, above all, collect and distribute the mail. In some large offices the boys glided from desk to desk quickly and quietly on rubberized roller-skates.

W. Deitz of the Western Electric Company, based in Chicago, explained in 1917 how these boys were trained: "The office boy comes into a progressive organization ... Western Electric employs about twenty thousand people, we have over one hundred boys who are on office boy work," answering telephones, filing papers, sweeping the floors, carrying messages and, above all collecting and delivering the mail. "The tremendous size of the Loose-Wiles Biscuit Company's office ... makes it necessary, in order to handle their mail and the delivery of letters, from one department to another, to put the office boys on skates.... It is interesting, indeed, to see the boys glide noiselessly from desk to desk. It is the last word in efficiency." Western Union on Walker Street, New York, occupied two entire floors of the building and had "more than one hundred boys who will do their work on rollers." Ordinary steel-wheeled skates were too noisy and special rubber rollers were substituted, permitting the boys to "glide on roller skates from desk to desk, without even stopping, and scarcely slackening their speed." By 1919, office efficiency experts had made the office boy redundant by introducing the "mechanical messenger boy," an overhead carrier system. This innovation provided "a saving in time and labor and eliminated much of the confusion which invariably arises from having a number of persons involved in handling and distributing documents."[4]

Published in 1919, the book *The Girl and the Job* offered guidance to girls who started work at an early age: "A few years ago there were practically only two fields open to the fourteen-year-old girl on leaving school to go to work,—the department store and the factory. Today there are three; for so many girls of fourteen are becoming office girls.... The office girl is fast succeeding the office boy. She runs errands, addresses envelopes, stamps letters, attends to the mail, receives callers, delivers cards of introduction and in every way tries to see what she can do to aid others.... Many firms today are utilizing the services of girls from 14 to 16 instead of the much joked about gum-chewing office boy. Girls are more willing and cheerful." Salary in 1919 was $6 a week. Girls, who show ambition, can aim to become typists, stenographers, Dictaphone operators or even private secretaries.[5]

In 1889 Parker Brothers, the board games company based in Salem, Massachusetts, took advantage of the great popularity of Horatio Alger and his plucky band of poor boys that worked their way up in the world by issuing Office Boy. In this popular game, the players tried to avoid the places marked "careless," "dishonest" or "inattentive," and aim for "earnest," "capable," and "ambitious." The winner of the game got to be the Head of the Firm.

Pin Boys

Bowling became popular in nineteenth-century America with the introduction of indoor alleys in New York in 1840. Small boys were hired to sit on a raised platform behind the ten-pins, and after a game, to jump down and re-set the pins and pass back the balls

Arcadia Bowling Alley, Trenton, New Jersey, c. 1910. Small boys found jobs in bowling alleys as pin boys, placing the pins in position and returning the bowling balls to the players. Children worked late into the night, often past midnight. After 1945, pin boys were rapidly replaced by electrically operated machinery that set the pins and returned the balls.

for the next player, earning a nickel a game. Bowling alleys were set up near billiard-rooms, attracting gamblers and a rough element. In 1906, "In the city of Peoria, a man keeps a café, billiard-room and bowling alley, all in the same building and on the ground floor. In this place were five boys from twelve to fifteen years of age, employed as pin boys in the bowling alley; also in bringing liquor and cigars to the patrons.... All the boys worked from 10 o'clock A.M. to 11 and 12 o'clock P.M., every day, Sunday included, working from twelve to fourteen hours a day, seven days a week."[6]

Teachers complained that the boys were missing school or falling asleep in the classroom. Legislation banned the employment of little boys, requiring bowling alley owners to hire older boys at greater cost. The problem was solved in the 1940s when the Brunswick Company and the American Machine and Foundry Company introduced electrically operated machinery to set the pins and return the bowling balls. The machine was as fast as the best of the pin boys and operated around the clock, and "unlike pin boys never has to go home."

Bellboys

They worked in the lobbies of fancy hotels, where people, who had not previously met, would arrange to meet. The uniformed boy with his characteristic hat, cocked to the side, "hopped" at the ring of the bell at the front desk, given a name and walked about the lobby "Calling John Smith" or whomever was being sought. The most famous of the bellboys was not a boy at all, but the diminutive Johnny Roventini who worked at the New Yorker

The cobbled streets at Scollay Square in Boston, c. 1910, were busy with horses, customers and boys selling goods from the pushcarts.

Wearing her apron and bonnet, a girl sells vegetables from a sidewalk stall, near city hall, Wilmington, Delaware, 1909.

Hotel, 481 Eighth Avenue, New York City. Weighing only 59 pounds and 47 inches tall, little Johnny was hired at age twenty-three years in 1933 as the spokesman on radio, television and in the press for Philip Morris cigarettes. His "Calling Philip Morris" in a perfect B-flat tone, made him an American legend. His wages, during the Depression rose, from $800 a year as a bellboy to $50,000 as a booster of cigarettes.

Grace Hoadley Dodge (1856–1914) came from the wealthy New York Dodge family of Phelps & Dodge fame, with interests in cotton, mining, and the railroads and lumber. Her sympathies lay with "the condition of the work-girl in our great towns. Her working and wage-earning life begins at fourteen often, indeed, at thirteen.... If the parents are poor, the girl knows how valuable will be her weekly earnings at home; should her parents be in easy circumstances, wage-earning people, themselves in constant work, the girl may be apprenticed or learn a trade.... The day will come when the long hours of fatigu-

Carrying a homemade wooden box with his brushes and shoe polish, the young boy walked the streets and parks calling out, "Shine your shoes, sir?" For a nickel or a dime he would get to work.

ing labor will make the child regret those happy schooldays she has so joyously quitted." Bored and fatigued "after ten or eleven hours of monotonous work," these girls are likely to, "follow other temptations, the easy sliding into greater sin, the degradation of all womanly virtue."

Grace Dodge established the Working Girls Society in 1884 where members could pass the evening, attend classes, read books and make friends. The hope was to keep the girls off the streets at night and to foster the "development of higher and nobler aims." The girls were drawn from tenement factories as well as shops, department stores and offices. Their average wage was $5 a week. Within ten years, New York alone had nineteen Working Girls clubs with more in other cities. Miss Dodge became the president of a nationwide Association of Working Girls Societies. These groups had some success among American-born girls but had little appeal to immigrants. Grace H. Dodge died in 1914, leaving an estate of $7 million. Her Working Girls Societies did not long survive her death.[7]

Girls and women have always worked, declared Edith Abbott, but until the nineteenth century, did not receive wages. Factory work and domestic service, and later, work in shops, department stores and offices, opened many opportunities to girls to earn wages. These new jobs required skills in reading, writing, typing, and calculating as well as in poise. With education, upward mobility was possible. "The granddaughters of the first mill girls," wrote Edith Abbott in 1918 with a Ph.D. from the University of Chicago and another of the remarkable Hull Street Settlement House women, "are now to be found in the women's colleges, while the women who have taken their places in the mills are immigrants or the children of immigrants."[8] E. W. Weaver wrote a popular book on *Profitable Vocations for Girls* in 1913. She advised "that girls should remain in school as long as possible." Many jobs were opening for educated young women, but employees "do not want girls under sixteen years of age and many will not take them under twenty-one." Girls in factory or domestic work were earning around $450 a year while skilled stenographers, social workers, journalists and nurses were able to earn twice as much or more.[9]

Flower Girls

Perhaps the most adorable of the Charlie Chaplin films was his 1931 *City Lights*, featuring Virginia Cherrill as the blind flower girl. Using his last cent, the Little Tramp buys a flower from her. On the mean streets of New York girls sold flowers, while boys sold newspapers. The flowers were grown in nurseries and greenhouses in New Jersey, especially at Union Hill, near Orange. As the following 1871 account will show, selling flowers was a harsh life for little girls. The flowers were cut early in the morning and taken to New York to be sold at street corners or at the stalls near Astor House, Vesey Street. In the afternoons the flower merchants sold "the remainder of their stock to the children ... sent out by

A boy hawker busy at work in Boston, 1915. Sidewalk fruit and vegetable stalls and pushcarts were a familiar sight in American cities. In 1883, Massachusetts issued a law banning children from selling goods at night.

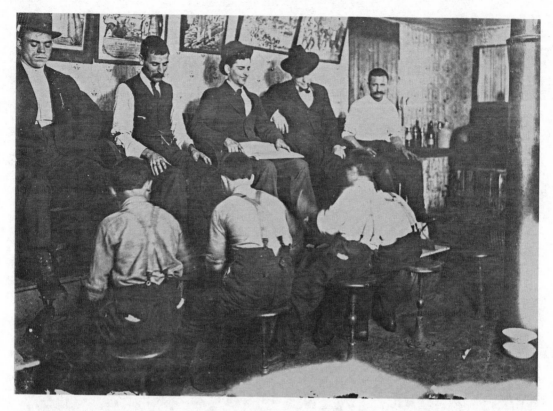

At the start of the twentieth century shoeshine parlors opened in many American cities. Kept in a state of ignorance, from five to as many as twenty immigrant boys worked from morning to night for $2 to $3 a week with room and board. The reformers viewed this system of child labor as akin to servitude.

drunken parents ... from whom they receive four, five and six cents a bouquet." The girls freshened up the flowers with a splash of water and took "their stations along Broadway, between 5 and 6 o'clock when gentlemen are returning home from their offices." Here the girls sell most of their stock and take what remains to the theaters where the "poor little girls accost all the gentlemen accompanied by ladies." On wet nights the girls went to the ale houses and saloons, "but [did] this with reluctance because the men in these places are coarse and brutal, and seldom give them more than five cents.... Little things of seven and eight years old may on such nights be seen taking furtive naps under porticos and under kitchen stoops, curled up in an uneasy ball." In the winter, the flower sales are suspended and instead the girls go about "over frozen snow and cold pavement ... with their poor little naked feet, their faces blue and pinched, their fingers cramped with cold," trying to sell matches or toothpicks.[10]

The flower girls were hardly noticed but occasionally were the object of pity of the wealthy and the privileged. Mrs. Grover Cleveland, wife of the president of the United States, volunteered to sell flowers for up to $25 each for a charity to aid the "poor immigrant girls." Hundreds of people came to buy expensive flowers from the hands of Mrs. Cleveland.[11]

Bootblacks, Hawkers and Chimneysweeps

> *Tom Grey earned his keep in all weathers along the streets of New York since he was ten years old. Now fifteen "with an open, prepossessing face, and an air of one ready to fight his own battles without calling for assistance. His position in life is humble, for he is a street bootblack."*
> —*Tom, the Bootblack*, Horatio Alger, 1889

A boy with a homemade wooden box, carrying his brushes, shoe polishes made by Whittemore Brothers or Bixby, a lot of strength, determination and self-confidence was ready for work. Boys like Tom set up early each morning at street corners and parks calling, "Shine your shoes, sir," to every pair of men's shoes passing by, charging five cents a shine but hoping for a good tip as well. William O'Neill was a young boy, "always poorly clad," but wearing a medal on his tattered coat. William was a shoeshine boy working on the Sylvan Steamship Line to support himself and his widowed mother. When he saw a small boat capsize throwing three boys into the icy water, William quickly stripped off his shoes, dived into the cold waters and swam towards the drowning boys, keeping them afloat until the boat came alongside to lift the frightened, shivering boys out of the water. William was proud to tell all that he was the last to be pulled out of the icy Hudson River. A medal was

In 1885, Martinez Ybor moved his cigar factory from Cuba to Ybor City, near Tampa, Florida. Other companies followed, making Tampa the center of the American cigar industry. The image shows boys rolling cigars at the Filogamo & Alvarez factory. Many of the boys smoked cigars while they worked.

A large group of girl workers outside the American Tobacco Company plant in Wilmington, Delaware, 1909. The company was founded in 1890 and was one of the original twelve listed on the Dow Jones Industrial Average. American Tobacco, known as the Tobacco Trust, was fined for violations of the child-labor laws.

given to him by the American Benevolent Life-saving Association together with an award of $25 for rescuing a total of fourteen people from drowning in the Hudson River during 1878 alone.[12]

By the beginning of the twentieth century the self-employed shoeshine boy was being replaced by shoeshine parlors under the illegal padrone system where the boss employed six to twenty-five immigrant boys paying them $2 to $3 a week with room and board in return for their labor. Large American cities had dozens of shoe-shine parlors. The boys were recruited abroad and came alone virtually as indentured labor, housed in unsanitary conditions and expected to work fifteen-hour days to repay their travel tickets. The boys were kept in ignorance without family or friends, learning only enough English to conduct their business, shining shoes. The North American Civic League for Immigrants regarded the shoeshine parlor system as akin to servitude and peonage.

The streets of New York and other cities were abuzz, day and night, with the sounds of girls selling flowers, boys hawking chewing gum, peanuts, chickens, baskets, vegetables and fruit. One reporter at the start of the twentieth century described the chaos of the

Joseph Severlo, an 11-year-old peanut vendor in Wilmington, Delaware. Lewis Hine took this picture on May 21, 1910. Joseph told Hine that he started selling peanuts two years earlier, working for his father six hours a day.

Lower East Side of New York at Rivington, Delancey, Essex and Hester streets, so filled with pushcarts that "it was almost impassable for pedestrians." Some five thousand pushcarts filled these streets. These were owned by men working in the garment industry "who used their wives and children" to sell their wares. These pushcarts served the sweatshops and other tenement industries of the neighborhood. The fishmongers "threw the fish scales into the gutter causing a horrible stench that comes from the putrid fish." The meat and poultry carts attracted "a huge swarm of great blue flies which buzzed about and laid their eggs on the meat." Children such as "a dirty boy, about fifteen years of age" manned many of the carts. Nearby milled about "children covered with sores and hundreds of them are nearly blind with sore eyes. There was hardly a person among the whole crowd of street vendors who had not sores underneath the finger nails and between the fingers."[13] The new immigrants who inhabited this section of New York, concluded the writer, lived in such squalor as to make it unfit for uptown New Yorkers. The pushcarts were family enterprises, offering goods for sale from early in the morning till late at night. The owner shared the work with his family. "When the children came home from school," wrote another reporter, "one of his children comes out and takes his place. If business is good he may hire another pushcart for his wife or one of his children to run after school hours or during the holidays."[14] Massachusetts tried to regulate peddling and hawking in 1883, requiring peddlers to be licensed and forbidding minor children from peddling goods on the streets after dark. In 1912, the Chicago City Council banned child peddlers from selling chewing gum, fruits and vegetables between eight o'clock at night and five o'clock the next morning.

Chimney Sweeps

Five year-old boys in England once climbed down chimneys to clean out the soot. In 1859, Ralph Chipman wrote, "It is known that boys have been sold frequently and taken from their native place to a strange part of the country.... When I was five years old I was taken and put up chimneys."[15] These boy chimney sweeps were susceptible to lung diseases as well as a form of cancer of the scrotum, thought due to the irritation of coal dust. Percival Potts in 1775 was the first to describe Chimney Sweep's Cancer, a squamous cell carcinoma affecting the scrotum. This was the first report of an environmental cause of cancer. Largely based on Potts' accounts the British Parliament in 1788 passed the Chimney Sweep's Act, barring children less than eight years from the chimney sweep trade. In February 1875, twelve-year-old George Brewster got stuck in the flue of a chimney of the Fulbourn Hospital, the county pauper lunatic asylum for Cambridgeshire, England. This shocking death galvanized the British Parliament to pass the Chimney Sweeping Act of 1875 banning the employment of children under sixteen from the trade.

In the United States sending little boys to climb up the chimney was less done; instead long brushes and chemicals from above or below were used. Yet in 1910, the dermatologist Dr. Jay Frank Schamberg reported on nineteen cases of scrotum cancer among chimney sweeps treated in Philadelphia hospitals.

11

At Sea

Early in the seventeenth century fishermen from the West Country of England knew of the abundance of fish off the coasts of Newfoundland and New England. With cod and herring already an important part of the diet of Europeans, a great fishing industry soon developed. The coastal towns of Gloucester, Salem, Marblehead and Newburyport prospered with fishermen, sailors, boats and fish-processing plants.

For generations the sons of New England fisherman followed their fathers to sea. In 1887, George Brown Goode wrote: "Along the coast of Maine, where the old methods of fishing are still practiced by the boat fishermen, small boys are taken out to help their fathers and brothers as soon as they are old enough to be of practical assistance. It is not uncommon to see boys of eight or nine handling fishing nets as large as themselves." Over the course of two or three years, the small boys were taught how to handle a boat, know the winds and the ocean, recognize the fish and haul in the catch. On the mackerel boats the boys started from age ten, but on the halibut and cod boats, where strength was needed, boys did not go out to sea until age fifteen or sixteen when they could do "a man's work." Boys attended school in the winter and went fishing in the warmer weather. Maine boys usually left school on reaching fourteen years of age, while the girls stayed longer and were, on the whole, better educated.[1]

In 1847, the great fishing town of Gloucester, Massachusetts, had 287 sea-going vessels giving employment to 1,687 men and 186 boys. Twelve years later, the town had 301 vessels employing 3,434 men and 134 boys. When the catch came in the boys and girls of the town were kept busy cutting off the heads and removing the entrails to prepare the fish for drying and salting. In 1885, the United States had 101,084 professional fishermen with Maryland (17,000), Massachusetts (17,000) and Virginia (10,000) having the largest concentration of boats and fishermen. Whaling, mackerel, cod, halibut, sardine, oysters and shrimp were major industries.

"The fisherman's son," wrote Samuel Eliot Morison in 1922, "was predestined to the sea. As soon as he could walk, he swarmed over every Banker or Chebacco boat that came into port, began 'hand-lining' for cunners off wharves and ledges, and begging older boys to teach him to row. At six he was already some aid in curing the catch.... Boys of nine to twelve did the cooking for Marblehead and Gloucester fishermen.... After a voyage or two he became an apprentice, learned the secrets of luring codfish to hook, and the art of heading, splitting and salting with quick precision. A strong boy of fifteen or sixteen might be as accomplished a fisherman as any.... The boy's ambition was to save enough money to acquire a fishing vessel and to live ashore on her earnings." By the age of sixteen many a son of a fisherman was working steadily during the ten-month fishing season, could turn a boat in the dark and feel the direction of the wind on his face. He still paid most of his wages to his parents but by twenty-one had proven himself a fisherman, with a dream one day of skippering his own boat.[2]

Thomas Nickerson, a fourteen-year-old cabin boy, took part in the heroic but tragic story of the American whaling ship *Essex*, a tale that inspired Herman Melville's 1851 *Moby-Dick*. As an orphan boy, young Nickerson sailed August 12, 1819, from Nantucket with twenty other sailors on a thirty-month journey around Cape Horn to the whaling grounds of the Pacific Ocean. Following the custom on American whaling ships, none of the sailors was paid a fixed wage. Rather each received a percentage of the catch. The captain received the largest share, while the cabin boy got the least, only one three-hundredth of the value of the catch, even though he was expected to take a full part in the capture of the whales. Fifteen months out on its voyage, *Essex* was struck and sunk by a sperm whale. The surviving seamen managed to board the three small whaling boats, collect 600 pounds of dry bread and all the water they could find, and head east 3,000 miles for the coast of South America. The eight survivors, among them Thomas Nickerson, ate the bodies of those who died. After three months in the small open boat young Thomas Nickerson lay down to die. On February 18, 1821, the brig *Indian*, out of London, spotted and saved them. Thomas and the others were given food and drink and slowly recovered. They returned to Nantucket a few weeks short of three years from their date of departure. The ordeal did not stop Thomas from returning to sea. Later he became a captain and then retired to Nantucket. Near the end of his life he wrote an account of his ordeal.[3]

Apprentice Sailors

In 1823, the British Parliament passed the Merchant Seaman Act requiring British merchant ships over eighty tons to carry apprentices. On May 1, 1826, the United States Congress established a similar ruling for American shipping: "Vessels engaged in the whale fishery are required to have on board one apprentice for every thirty tons.... All these apprentices are exempted from impressments until they are eighteen years of age." The apprentices could be as young as eleven years and were bound to remain in service for seven to ten years. In return the captain was instructed to "support, clothe and instruct" the apprentices on his ship. In the West Indian trade the captain was obliged to take one apprentice under the age of seventeen for each one tons of his vessel.[4]

Around 1828, Thomas Goin of New York, at great personal expense and effort, "took about 150 boys and young men, from ten to twenty-one years of age, out of the House of Refuge in this city, and sent them to Nantucket and other Eastern ports, where they were shipped out on whaling voyages." Within ten years, forty of these boys had risen in the ranks to first mate or captain. By the 1830s only ten thousand of the 100,000 seamen sailing on American ships were American born. The *Delaware*, a proud American man-of-war, had only 182 Americans among its crew of over 1000 sailors. Using these figures, Thomas Goin traveled to Washington to campaign for a naval apprenticeship system with the idea of setting apprentice schools in Boston, New York, Philadelphia and Norfolk to train American boys for service on American ships. His idea caught the attention of James K. Paulding, secretary of the navy, and on March 2, 1837, Congress passed a law "to enlist boys to the navy, with the consent of their parents or guardians, not being under thirteen or over eighteen, to serve until they shall arrive at the age of twenty-one years." The boys received $5 a month for the first year of service, $6 a month in the second year and $7 a month in the third and final year of their apprenticeship. The boys were to be "thoroughly instructed as to best qualify them to perform the duties of seamen and petty officers." The boys signed their indentures with the promise that each would receive a new uniform, accommodation, food and training. Each boy had to show that he could read and write and do arithmetic, and comply with orders. The goal was to enlist 20,000 apprentices within two years to the ensure that the United States Navy would be "manned solely by American seamen." John W. Finch was appointed principal of the naval apprentices school.[5]

Sailor boys. USS *Brooklyn* was a 9,215-ton armored cruiser, built in Philadelphia. It served in the Spanish-American War and was later used as a training ship. Photograph by Edward H. Hart, 1898.

The sailing ship USS *Hudson*, berthed at the Brooklyn Navy Yard, was the first home of the apprentice school. By 1839, nearly three hundred boys were enrolled in training. That year, President Martin van Buren visited the ship to meet the apprentices "all dressed in their sailor uniforms, viz. white shirts and trousers, trimmed with black nankeen, blue jackets with a white anchor on the right sleeve, and black tarpaulin hats, with broad flowing ribbons." The president made "very particular inquiries as to the manner of instruction and manifested great interest in the system of thus preparing young Americans for the naval services of their country." To offer the boys real experience at sea, the navy converted the steamer *North Carolina*, "a ship of the line," into a training ship under Captain John Gallagher.

In 1852, the sailing master William Brady published his *Kedge Anchor, or Young Sailor's Assistant*, "for those who have just entered the sailor's life, and particularly those destined for the navy." Brady's beautifully illustrated book described the "evolution of modern seamanship," with detailed information on rigging, knotting, splicing, sails, provisions and other skills "applicable to ships of war." Twenty years later, on June 7, 1872, the Laws Governing the United States Merchant Service were issued. With the consent of his father or guardian a boy who "has attained the age of twelve years, and is of sufficient health and strength," could enter into a naval apprenticeship. "Said apprenticeship shall be terminated when the apprentice becomes eighteen years of age." The master of the ship who accepted boys to sea service received $5 for each indenture. Foreign vessels in American waters were required on demand to "produce the indenture by which the apprentice is bound." Failure to do so could lead to a fine of up to $100.[6]

The apprenticeship system was introduced eight years before the establishment of the United States Naval Academy at Fort Severn, Annapolis. Several hundred boys joined but promotion was slow and the apprenticeship system was abandoned in 1843. During the Civil War it was again tried but not until 1875 did the apprenticeship system finally take hold, with a training school near Newport, Rhode Island. The Naval Academy Preparatory School has now set the age of admission as no younger than seventeen and no older than twenty-two years of age.

Cabin Boy

Many an English tar began his naval career as a cabin boy, carrying messages for the captain as well as helping with the cooking and the cleaning. Cloudseley Shovell (1650–1707) started as a cabin boy but rose through the ranks to become commander-in-chief of the British navy. Rufus Daniel Isaacs evolved from a fifteen-year-old cabin boy in 1875 to a man of great fame and fortune. The son of a Jewish fruit seller in London, he went on to a distinguished career at law; he served at various times as lord chief justice of England, secretary of state for foreign affairs, leader of the House of Lords, solicitor-general of England and as viceroy of India. He was elevated to marquess of Reading shortly before he died in 1935. He espoused a close friendship between Britain and the United States. The *Daily Telegraph* rated him as "the most eminent and most versatile British public servant of his race and faith since Disraeli. There could be no higher eulogy."

Tales from the nineteenth century about cabin boys abound. In 1861 the ship *Mary Ann* left New Bedford on its way to hunt whales in the Pacific Ocean. While at anchor off the Florida Keys the ship was seized by a privateer loyal to the Confederate cause. The ship was taken to New Orleans where the crew was clapped into prison. Henry W. Kelly, a 14-year-old cabin boy, with two of his shipmates managed to escape by jumping out of a window thirty feet above ground level. Without any money the three youngsters traveled north to Albany, New York, where the "skeleton-like" Henry Kelly told his story. After fattening up, the boy caught the train back to New Bedford and vowed "he will remain at home during the remainder of the war."[7] John Anglin of Portland, Maine, volunteered his services to the U.S. Navy when only fourteen years old. He was assigned as cabin boy on the USS *Pontoosuc* built in his town. In January 1865, the ship took part in the Second Battle of Fort Fisher, off Wilmington, North Carolina. In the battle young John was exposed to heavy enemy fire but conducted "his duties faithfully." For his gallantry, skill and "cool courage while under the fire of the enemy," he was awarded the Medal of Honor, one of the youngest to receive this high award.

In 1865, the steamer *Brother Jonathan* hit submerged rocks on its way from San Francisco to Oregon. Only sixteen of the 150 crew and passengers survived. The ship carried nine cabin boys, including Edward Franklin, Charles Laws and Stephen Morran.[8] In 1876, seven masked men boarded the schooner *Joseph Morse*, bound from New London to New York, demanded money and valuables and threatened the life of William Saterlee, the cabin boy, as well as other members of the crew.[9] In 1881, James O'Neil, a lad of twelve, told the police in New York that he had served as cabin boy on the packet ship *Black Hawk,* recently arrived from San Francisco. The captain "turned him adrift in the streets with only a fifty-cent piece." The story was a fib and James was turned over to the Society for the Prevention of Cruelty to Children. In 1895, fifteen-year-old Lucy Dewhirst ran away from Lawrence, Massachusetts, to Boston where she boarded the steamer *Bostonian* disguised as a cabin boy. Explaining her odd behavior, Lucy said she missed her mother, who lived in England.[10]

But the days of the cabin boy were drawing to a close. An old sea captain in 1907 observed that the "cabin boy has completely disappeared, or at least, how extremely rare he is, now." The cabin boy served the crew and the passengers and was regarded as the "scapegoat for anything that went wrong." Grown men and women have taken his place.[11]

Fish Canneries

Along the Pacific and Atlantic coasts as well as the Bay of Mexico, fish canneries were notorious as heavy users of child labor.

> *The boys and girls who cut fish—well, they're children.... There is not much winter work in this town. Men are out of the habit of winter working. They earn so much in the summer that they won't work for low wages in the winter. It's astonishing! They put up with misery and cold, and whistle in their shanties and think about the next season when it'll be warm and there'll be plenty of money.*
>
> —Charles Poole Cleaves, *A Case of Sardines:*
> *A Story of the Maine Coast,* 1904

Eastport and Lubec, in Washington County, Maine, are the easternmost towns in the continental United States. A few miles offshore lies the Canadian island of Campobello, where Franklin Roosevelt and his family spent happy summers. The Bay of Fundy

Using sharp knives, young children were employed to cut off the heads and innards of the fish, in preparation for washing, pickling, cooking and canning. By 1910, an estimated one thousand children under fourteen years of age worked in the Maine fish canneries. Largely of French-Canadian stock, they worked from April to the cold of December, and barely attended school. Serious cuts from the sharp knives were common.

was teeming with fish. In 1875 Julius Wolff of New York came to Eastport to start a sardine-packing factory. He was soon earning twelve dollars a case, arousing the envy of the local fisher-men. Within the next quarter century seventy-five sardine-canning factories opened along the northeast coast of Maine; Eastport alone had thirteen. Sardine canneries stretched along the coastline of the Washington County, creating much of the wealth and many of the jobs of Downeast Maine. The Maine industry grew to rival the famous sardine industry of France. By 1900 the plethora of factories made sardine packing unprofitable. The Continental Sardine Company — a sardine trust — was formed to control three-quarters of the trade.

    The Downeast fishing season for herring started in mid–April and continued until mid–December. The fish were trapped in weirs, collected in boats and ferried to the wharf, where workers, many of them children, using sharp, long knives cut off the heads and removed the innards. The fish were washed and pickled, cooked for fifteen to thirty minutes and taken to the packing room where workers arranged the sardines in rows in the cans, added oil or mustard, sealed and heated the cans to 250 degrees F to kill off bacteria. Charles Poole Cleaves describes the tedium and blight of Eastport, Maine:

> The long line of sardine factories crowned the spider-limbed wharves, their cutting sheds open to view. The fish-boats had come in early, and their shining, slimy cargoes of young herring were fast losing their heads under the long knives of the boys and girls; bare-armed, bare-footed and more or less bare-limbed — brown as the shore that stretched eastward; some in their common garb, rolled and abbreviated, some with aprons of oilcloth or sacking; some draped in

grain-sacks inverted with arms and head thrust through slits in the bottom.... Girls must work in the factory.... There are girls who never saw the inside of a really nice house, or beautiful pictures, or were ever told beautiful things.[12]

In a 1909 report, Everett W. Lord estimated that over one thousand children, largely of French-Canadian stock and under fourteen years of age, were employed in the Maine sardine canneries. "The one industry in New England in which children are practically without legal protection," Lord reported, "is the canning industry of Maine ... no less than a thousand children under fourteen years of age are so employed ... a good many children as young as eight or nine work in the flaking rooms." The children came with their parents from the hardscrabble nearby towns and were housed in shacks near the canneries. Working from April to December the children barely attended school and were unlettered. The children "were always cutting themselves" on the long and sharp sardine knives. A nine-year-old girl lost her hand in a machine. No damages were awarded since "the girl was supposed to know that the machine was dangerous." For their work the children in the Maine canneries were paid from 8 to 12 cents a day.[13]

The oyster and shrimp industries developed after 1840, attracting families to settle near the canneries. As areas were overfished, the families had to travel to canneries that were still active. In 1910 A.J. McKelway "was amazed by the number of small children who are employed in the oyster shucking factories." These children, largely from Bohemian and Polish immigrant families from Maryland, where they canned fruits and vegetables in the summer months, were recruited with their parents in the winter months to the oyster and shrimp canneries of the Gulf States. At one such factory McKelway saw "acres of oyster shells fifteen feet deep, and a great proportion of these oysters had been taken out of the shells by children."[14]

After working until late summer in the fruit and vegetable canneries of Maryland and Delaware, whole families moved down to the Gulf States to work in the oyster and shrimp canneries. In the oyster sheds, little children played amongst the heaps of shells. As soon as they were able — age four and upwards — the children helped their parents shucking oysters, putting the meat into bowls and tossing the shells to the floor. Paid 5 cents a pound, a small child could earn 20 to 30 cents a day. Older children could earn $1 a day. Cuts from the shucking knives were frequent.

The photographer and investigator Lewis Hine was "horrified to see how many minutes and hours of actual work these little tots do put in." Hine tells the story of children laboring in the shrimp and oyster canneries, situated along the Gulf Coast from New Orleans to Florida and along the Atlantic coast from Georgia to Maryland. The season begins in October when the trawlers bring in the catch. Immigrant families, father, mother and all children, collect at the canneries ready to work, for the more hands the more the pay. The families are housed in dilapidated shacks without running water or sanitation. The canneries smell of dead fish. Along the Gulf Coast, the heat, flies and mosquitoes plague the workers while along the Atlantic coast it is near freezing with the coming of winter. Before daybreak, the families assemble at the shucking tables ready to handle the catch. The oysters are steamed, making shucking easier for little fingers but the shrimp is frozen, hardening the fingers, which crack and bleed.

The three- and four-year-olds play alongside their working mothers "learning the trade." Four-year-old Mary worked "irregularly through the day shucking about two pots of oysters. Little Olga, five years old, pick[ed] shrimp for her mother.... Boys and girls, six, seven and eight years of age, take their places with the adults and work all day." Mother says of her five-year-old: "He kin make fifteen cents any day he wants to work, but he won't do it steady." Annie, at seven years, is already accomplished at shucking oysters. "She kin beat me shucking," says the proud mother, "and she's mighty good at housekeeping, too."

A shrimp cannery in Biloxi, Mississippi, 1911. As with oysters, hundreds upon hundreds of children worked in the shrimp canneries. The acid in the head of the shrimp burned the tender skin of little children. The children worked alongside their fathers, mothers and older siblings, earning money for the good of the family.

Sardine canneries in Washington County, Maine. The fish were collected in boats and taken to the canneries. In 1900, the Commercial Sardine Company — a sardine trust — was formed. Overfishing led to the collapse of the Maine sardine industry.

Hine added: "You see little ones, from four upward, working until physical strain and monotony become unbearable; and then, for relief, go over into the corner and rock the baby or tote it around until they feel like working again."

"Hundreds of these children," reports Hine, "from four to twelve are regularly employed." The three- and four-year-olds play around "learning the trade." At five or six they are working steadily and at seven are putting in a full day like their parents. A large family can earn $15 to $20 a week, children under seven can earn 25 cents a day, children eight to ten 50 cents a day and up to $1 if they work very hard. The children are docile and generally do as their parents tell them. They are too tired for school, leaving parents and children alike illiterate but content to return north after the fishing season is over with a little money to spare.[15]

From 1918 to 1919 the United States Children's Bureau conducted a study of child labor in the oyster and shrimp canneries of the Gulf Coast. At the start of the twentieth century the fish canning industry had moved from Maryland to the Gulf Coast and families were hired from Baltimore to work in the South for the fishing season that lasted from October to May. Five hundred and forty-four children under the age of 16 were found working in 22 canneries. Of these 322 were 6 to 14 and the rest were aged 14 or 15. For the employers, it was easy enough to circumvent any state laws by locating the canneries in remote places and relying on poor surveillance. At that time Louisiana had only one labor commissioner with two assistants to cover the whole state outside of New Orleans. Florida and Mississippi each had only one inspector. Workers were paid 5 cents for every pound of oyster or shrimp meat. The average wage was $10 a week for men, and $5 for women. "The children's earnings were, of course, lower." Parents were eager to put their children to work just as soon as they could earn 50 cents a day.

The families were housed in barracks close to the canneries. Work started early in the morning when the oyster and lobster catch came in. The fresh oysters were steamed for a few minutes to partially open the shell and make shucking easier. The working children and their mothers arranged themselves on either side of long tables covered with steamed oysters. Using sharp knives, the workers cut into the oyster to remove the meat, threw the shells on the floor and placed the meat in their bin. When the bin was full, the worker carried it to the weighing station for payment. Infants and children too little to work were left on the floor next to the mothers, to play among the heaps of shells or run around the factory.

On the boats, shrimp was packed in ice, making the meat contract and easier to peel. The children and their mothers took the shrimp off the table, broke off the head and squeezed the flesh out of the shell into the bin. As with oysters, once the bin was full it was carried to the weighing station for payment. The children worked to their capacity, those 14 and 15 years old expected to work the full 60-hour week. To abide by state laws, the employers offered the children a perfunctory education early in the morning or after work when they were too tired to absorb much of anything. Illiteracy among these children was high. They suffered cuts from the knives and the ragged oyster shells. Acid from the head of the shrimp ate into their fingers and hands, leading to rawness of the skin and infections. A 13-year-old-boy, reported the Children's Bureau, "shoveling oyster shells on the wharf had his leg caught in the derrick and was crippled for life. Three children, one 2 years old, another 5 and a third child of 10 who had fallen in the path of the oyster cars, had their hands crushed."[16]

Roger Deniston Hume was born in Augusta, Maine, in 1845. At eighteen he crossed the nation to find work in a salmon cannery in California. From there he moved north to Oregon to set up a salmon cannery along the Columbia River. Hiring Chinese labor, he prospered and became known as the salmon king of Oregon. Salmon and sardine canning became big business in California, Oregon and Washington. Long before John Steinbeck made it famous, Monterey's Cannery Row was the center of the West Coast sardine canning industry. When Chinese labor was restricted, boys and girls were employed and stood all day at long tables, wielding long, sharp knives to cut off the heads and viscera to prepare the herring and salmon for canning. Oregon established a Child Labor Commission in 1903. In the twentieth century the Pacific states were generally successful in keeping children out of the canneries.

12

Bottles, Silk, Meat and Shoes

In all directions the family is being dissolved by the labor of wives and children, or inverted by the husband's being thrown out of employment and made dependent upon them for bread.
— Friedrich Engels, *The Condition of the Working Class in England in 1844,* translation into English by Florence Kelley

Glass Workers

In 1820 the Englishman Thomas W. Dyott opened a glass factory near Philadelphia, close by the Delaware River. His Dyottville Glass Works employed 225 boys "some of whom are not more than eight years of age." In his community Dyott provided a night school to train the boys in the art of glass blowing and teach them to read and write. He was a stern taskmaster but the boys were too tired to learn after laboring twelve hours a day in the sweltering glasshouse. Dyott grew wealthy selling patent medicines in glass bottles made cheaply by little boys. Early in the nineteenth century the New England Glass Works, Cambridge, Massachusetts, also used boy labor. One commentator, writing in 1833, observed that manufacturing establishments such as Dyottville Glass Works "extinguished the flame of knowledge."

Glass and bottle factories were established in other parts of the United States in the nineteenth century. The industry was based on the centuries-old skill in which the master blower dips his blowpipe into molten glass and blows into the pipe to form a container. The bottle might need reheating to get it to the desired shape and size. When the bottle is formed it is broken off the blowpipe. The standard work team consisted of two or three skilled glassblowers, with three or four young boys as their helpers. One boy carried the still red-hot blowpipe from one glassblower to a second. The mold-holding boy helped the blower shape the bottle. The carrying-off boy conveyed the still hot bottle to the finisher and from the finisher to the cooling kiln. The cleaning-up boy cleaned the end of the blowpipe between uses. All these jobs were done in intense heat, running the risk of severe burns or blinding by fragments of molten glass entering the eye. If a boy broke a bottle the cost was taken out of his pay. The boys, constantly on the move, were regarded as unskilled labor and were poorly paid despite the dangerous work. "In the center of the room," wrote Edwin Markham in 1906 about the glass factories, "stand the red-hot, reeking furnaces [around which are] the glassblowers and their boy minions.... Sometimes as many as fifty boys are shuffling about the furnaces." The boys used asbestos shovels to carry the hot glass bottles. "Studies show," continued Markham, "that many of the children of the glass factories are absolutely illiterate." The intense heat and thirst of the glassworks "make boy and man turn to stimulants." Boys are sent out to the local store to buy alcohol. "We find," wrote Markham, "young boys even going the drunkard's way!"[1]

The Illinois Glass Company of Alton was an especially egregious exploiter of young children. The company employed 1800 workers, of whom 800 (44 percent) were under the age of sixteen years and "of these last about 200, were under 14 years of age." There were even 24 children aged 7 to 12 years. In her last report as chief factory inspector of Illinois, Florence Kelley announced that "the Illinois Glass Company was the largest employer of child labor in the state."[2]

Each adult glassblower worked with two or three boys; one boy closed the mold, the second picked the bottles out of the mold, and the third carried the bottles to the furnace.

Woodcut showing boys working at the red-hot furnace of a bottle factory, 1906. The mold-holding boys heated the glass to a molten state and carried it to the adult glassblower. Once the bottle was shaped, the carrying-off boy took it to the finisher and from the finisher to the cooling kiln. The cleaning-up boy cleaned the ends of the blowpipe between uses. Image from *Cosmopolitan Magazine*, September 1906.

Boys working the night shift at a glass factory. Each adult glassblower had a team of two boys. Child labor was a common practice in glassworks. In the 1890s, the Illinois Glass Company of Alton employed 1,800 workers of whom 800 were boys under sixteen years. The children were at risk of burns from fragments of the molten glass.

The larger boys earned 40–45 cents a day, but boys under fourteen years earned less than 40 cents a day. Florence Kelley reserved some her most pungent language for use against the glass industry. In 1903, she wrote: "The earnings of the blowers depend upon the speed of the boys to fetch and carry." The job was dangerous. "Young boys, with heads and hands bandaged, where they have received burns from the melting glass, or red-hot swinging rods, dodging in all directions to escape the danger." Some boys worked the day shift, others at night. The work had its toll on these immigrant boys. "None of the children go to school. [They] are an unusually wretched-looking set. They are ill fed, ill clothed, profane, obscene, and in many cases, unable to work without stimulants. Boys 7 to 10 chew tobacco, and boys 10 to 14 are in some cases, habituated drinkers of beer and whisky."[3]

After the Civil War, the glass industry expanded greatly with the spread of bottled patent medicines, canning jars, and table lamps. Glass factories were established in Pennsylvania, West Virginia, New Jersey, Maryland, Ohio, Indiana and Illinois. Companies worked day and night, requiring the little boys to work the night shift every other week, returning home in the early hours of the morning, winter or summer. In New Jersey glassworkers told the governor's commission, "Children of six or seven years of both sexes worked seventeen to eighteen hours a day, with but a few minutes of rest. They were told of women and children dropping at their toil, worn out and driven back to finish their long hours of work for which they were paid two or three cents an hour." In 1893, Gillinder & Sons, a

Baseball team of boy workers from an Indiana glass company, c. 1910. Many of the boys smoked cig-arettes or pipe tobacco. The great demand for patent medicine bottles and canning jars kept the industry active until the early twentieth century. Technological advances in glassblowing and stringent state laws steadily eliminated child labor from the glassworks.

Philadelphia glassmaker, paid skilled laborers $1.50 a day but "boys from 50 to 90 cents a day." The Obcar Glass Works of St. Louis estimated that the living costs of a workman and his family were $55 a month, yet he earned barely that much. Boys were paid only 40 to 50 cents a day.[4]

On leaving Chicago in 1899, Florence Kelley and her children moved into the Henry Street Settlement House in the Lower East Side of New York. From her new position as general secretary of the National Consumers' League, headquartered in New York City, Florence continued her battle against *The Needless Destruction of Boys*, working in the glass-bottle factories. Writing in 1905 she described the tragic lives of boys working the night shift in New Jersey glassworks. "The boys work at a rate of speed determined by the blowers whose pay depends on the speed of the group; the boys are, therefore, under the highest possible pressure to keep their speed up steadily.... Night work, heat and speed pressure are terribly wearing on growing boys, fourteen years of age." Who are these unfortunate boys? Kelley writes, "Only the orphan sons of blowers.... No well-situated workingman sends his son into the glass-bottle trade; only the sons of recently immigrated laborers with large families and small wages.... Boys from certain orphan asylums and reformatories have long been imported into New Jersey to supply the dearth created by the cruel hardships attending night work," for which the boys were paid 43 to 63 cents a night.[5]

On September 1, 1903, a child labor law was scheduled to go into effect in New Jersey making it a misdemeanor to employ children younger than fourteen years of age. If convicted a manufacturer would be liable to a fine of $200 or one-year imprisonment. The glass companies of the state opposed the legislation arguing "they cannot make the business pay without child labor," and the law would ruin them.[6]

Change was slow. It took a decade of inspections and prosecutions before the Illinois glass companies significantly reduced the number of working children. Even by 1907 many children, despite their small size, were still working in the glass factories having been certified as older than fourteen years. Rather than the problem's being solved, child labor in glass factories spread to Indiana, West Virginia and Pennsylvania, where many children worked the night shift, and where the laws were poorly enforced. By 1880, a recorded 5,648 boys under sixteen years worked in the American glass industry. The number reached its peak in 1889 with 7,116 children (representing 13 percent of the total work force). With regular reports in the press condemning child labor, the number of children working in the glassworks fell to 6,435 in 1904. Advances in technology also played a big part in the decline of child labor. With the introduction of bottle-making machinery only 1,413 boy laborers remained in the nation's glassworks in 1919.

Silk Mills

Some industries in the United States, including iron and steel, employed the heads of households, especially immigrant men, but little child labor. Near the steel mills a curious phenomenon emerged, the building of "cigar and tobacco factories, silk mills, and men's and women's manufacturing establishments" to take advantage of the plentiful supply of "cheap women and child labor." With its anthracite coal, the fertile valley of Wilkes-Barre attracted thousands upon thousands of immigrants in the nineteenth century. The Vulcan Iron Works in the city manufactured locomotives and iron goods. The sons of the miners and ironworkers found jobs as breaker boys and the mothers and girls worked in the Wilkes-Barre Lace Company and in the garment factories of the town. Allentown and Bethlehem (home of Bethlehem Steel) became major centers of the American silk industry, due to generally lower wages in Pennsylvania and lax laws regarding child labor. In the Lehigh Valley there were hundreds of silk and clothing mills, including the mammoth Adelaide Silk Company. In 1900, over 10 percent of the silk workers in Pennsylvania were children under sixteen years. A 1909 report states that in the nine counties of anthracite in Pennsylvania, the silk and cotton factories employed 11,216 females of whom 2,403 (over one in five) were girls aged twelve to sixteen year. Many more fibbed their age in desperation to get the jobs. The youngest girls were paid the lowest wages. A 1911 investigation found that men in the silk trade received on average $485, women $345 but girls under sixteen years only $144 a year.[7] The decline of iron and steel in eastern Pennsylvania saw grown men walking the streets looking for work, while their young sons and daughters abandoned their studies to go into the silk, cotton and woolen mills.

Poultry and Meat

Chicken houses were labor intensive. In 1913 the Kansas State Department of Labor and Industry reported on the hiring of children ostensibly "merely assisting older workers. This was a popular plan followed by those who wish to evade the child-labor laws." Once these underage children were identified by state inspectors, they were summarily fired. The stockyards and meat cutting plants were among Chicago's greatest industries. By 1900, machinery was introduced making the work simpler and allowing the packers to hire less-skilled and cheaper workers, especially children. By 1900, over five hundred boys under age sixteen were employed in Packingtown, working as messenger boys or assisting older workers. Ernest L. Talbert of the University of Chicago studied in 1911 the children growing up in the stockyard district. On average they were performing a year below appropriate grade level. One-third of the boys and girls left school to go to work on reaching age fourteen. Before reaching the seventh grade well over half of the boys and girls of the district had left school and applied for work certificates. The main reasons given for stopping school were the illness of one or both parents and the urgent need to earn money, even though wages were as low as 4 cents an hour. Child labor was "the cheapest labor of all."[8]

In her 1896 report Florence Kelley wrote the there were 320 children under fifteen years of age working for Armour, Morris Nelson, Swift and other Chicago-based meat cutters. The boys "cut the hides from the quivering flesh of newly stunned cattle," sort entrails or pack meat. "In several places, a boy has been found at work at a dangerous machine,

An Underwood & Underwood stereoscopic image of boys working in a meat cutting plant, probably in Chicago, c. 1900. Sharp knives and power machinery led to many injuries. In his book *The Jungle*, Upton Sinclair described the appalling working conditions in Packingtown.

because his father was disabled by it, and keeping the place pending recovery depended on the boy's doing the work during the father's absence."[9]

It was the journalist Upton Sinclair who most vividly described the horrors of Chicago's Packingtown that once employed 27,000 men, women and children, who slaughtered cattle, hogs and sheep and butchered the meat. In 1904, Sinclair worked incognito in the meat-packing business to collect material for *The Jungle*, telling in novel form the plight of the Rudkis family, immigrants from Lithuania. Coming to America full of hope for a better life, Jurgis Rudkis plans to support his family through his labor and send his children to school. Instead he sinks into drunkenness and unemployment. The reason "that Jurgis did not starve," wrote Sinclair, "was due solely to the pittance the children brought him." His mother-in-law, Elzbieta, reasoned that "with all the children working they could get along." Thirteen-year-old Kotrina remained at home to do the cleaning, cooking and washing. "Little Kotrina was like most children of the poor, prematurely made old."

Upton Sinclair questions the laws governing child labor. "It was against the law for children to work before they were sixteen," he writes, but "the law made no difference except that it forced people to lie about the age of their children. One would like to know what the lawmakers expected them to do; there were families that had no possible means of sup-port except the children, and the law provided them no other way of getting a living. Very often a man could get no work in Packingtown for months, while a child could go and get a place easily ... the packers could get as much work out of a child as they had been able to get out of a man, and for a third the pay." Both Upton Sinclair and Florence Kelley were founding members in 1905 of the Inter-Collegiate Socialist Society. Kelley, on Marxist grounds, opposed children working before age sixteen, without exception; the less doctrinaire Sinclair would have allowed it if there was "no other way of getting a living."[10]

Shoes

> *Once upon a time there was a shoemaker's apprentice. He was really a pastor's son, and was to have studied for the Church, and to have been a pastor, too; but when he was fourteen years old, he lost both his parents, and there was no one left to look after him and keep him at his books. So, he was apprenticed to the village shoemaker. [Three years later] he had now mastered all there was to know in the trade; he could cut out, and sew, and make a seam, and peg, but he never had any liking for the occupation, which he had been bound to.*
> — Svend Grundtvig, *Fairy Tales from Afar*, 1902

Village and itinerate shoemakers were part of the lore of Colonial America. Armed with a few tools and the knowledge to tan, cut, and sew leather these early shoemakers could fashion a pair of shoes from start to finish. Early in the nineteenth century a number of shoemakers who settled in the town of Lynn, Massachusetts, decided to divide the work among them. One tanned the leather, a second did the cutting, a third the sewing and a fourth did the polishing. Specialization was efficient but expensive. "In time," wrote the historian W. J. Rorabaugh, "master shoemakers hired women and children at low wages to displace journeymen."[11]

The influx of Chinese workers into the San Francisco labor marker so alarmed the government in 1877 the 44th Congress conducted an investigation. Several congressmen voiced their concern that Chinese laborers worked for lower wages and were replacing white workers in the San Francisco shoe factories. One observer reported that the manufacturers "are getting boys and girls, and working them in as apprentices, so that they can gradually dispense with Chinese labor, and conduct the manufacture successfully with white [child] labor alone."[12] A 1913 United States government report lamented: "There are shoemaker apprentices who have never made an entire shoe, but have always been employed in mending.... The task of the shoemaker is now being more and more reduced to mending; since most shoes are bought in the stores and are made almost exclusively in the large factories."[13]

The American shoe industry had its start in Lynn (women's shoes) and Brockton (men's shoes) in Massachusetts. Labor strife in the 1860s prompted the move to rural towns in Maine and New Hampshire. But it was not long before these workers demanded better conditions, inducing the owners to look to the Midwest for a cheaper and more compliant workforce. In 1922, Isaac A. Hourwich wrote: "The principal inducement for locating new shoe factories in the rural sections of Missouri appears to be the availability of cheap labor of native American women and children who can underbid the male immigrants employed in the shoe factories of Massachusetts."[14] Early in the twentieth century shoemaking was one of the crafts taught to boys in the Indian schools of the United States. "In the shoe shop it is designed to teach the boys to mend and make shoes that they may be able to do this for themselves after they leave school. Training continued over three years," by which time the boys would be sufficiently advanced to assist the shoemaker in instructing new pupils.[15]

Men who came up the hard way built the American shoe industry. William Lewis Douglas (1845–1924) started his apprenticeship at age seven, learning the trade under the guidance of his uncle. He built the W.L. Douglas Company in Brockton, Massachusetts, making men's shoes. He was elected mayor of the city and served one term as governor of Massachusetts. George F. Johnson was born in 1857 in the small shoe-town of Gilford, Massachusetts. His education ended at age thirteen when he started work at Seaver Brothers boot factory in nearby Ashland. He made rapid progress and eight years later, moved to Binghamton, New York, as a supervisor at the Lester Brothers shoe company. A few years later the brothers sold out to the wealthy Henry B. Endicott of Boston. By the start of the twentieth century Endicott-Johnson was one of the largest shoe companies in the world, making 18,000 pair of shoes a day.

Its principal rivals were the up-and-coming shoe factories of Missouri. By 1904, Missouri had thirty-four shoe companies and by 1909 the number had increased to fifty-nine, employing 18,891 "men, women, boys and girls." The largest of the Missouri shoe companies was Hamilton-Brown. Most of the factories, however, were much smaller and tucked away in small towns. In its annual reports the Missouri Bureau of Labor Statistics trumpeted shoes as a "thriving and progressive industry." Success, however, came by paying its workers less than in New England and New York. In 1910, the annual average wage of a St. Louis shoe worker, working fifty-hours a week, was $459.81, which fell $100.19 short of $560 as "the lowest tolerable budget without charity for a man, wife and three children from eight to fourteen years of age." Boys and girls, who received $4 to $5 a week, had to work to help the family.[16] Lewis Hine in 1910 visited the Hamilton-Brown Company in Columbia, Fargo & Phelps and Friedman-Shelby in Kirksville and the Robert Johnson Rand Company in Washington, Missouri. At each of these locations he photographed groups of small boys and girls who worked for these shoe companies.

13

Children at War

Children fought in the Revolutionary War. In his *Washington: A Life*, Ron Chernow quotes two European officers attached to George Washington's army. Baron Von Closen, an aide to Washington, commented: "It is incredible that soldiers composed of men of every age, even of children of fifteen ... can march so well and withstand fire so steadfastly." Count de Clermont-Crevecoeur was shocked by the condition of Washington's army: "The men were without uniforms and covered with rags; most of them barefoot. They were of all sizes down to children who could not have been more than fourteen."

One of the youngest boys to fight for American liberty was Israel Trask, born in 1765 in the fishing port of Gloucester, Massachusetts. Aged ten years, little Israel accompanied his father, Jonathan, who was a lieutenant in an Essex County regiment. Israel's job was to take care of the baggage and to prepare food for the officers. Later, he served as a cabin boy on a privateer. Ebenezer Fox, born in Roxbury, Massachusetts, in 1763, was twelve years old when he walked to Boston harbor to sign up on a privateer "for the cause of liberty." His ship was captured by an East-Indiaman of eleven hundred tons, carrying twenty-two guns. James Forten, age fifteen, was a free African American from Philadelphia. He signed up as a powder-boy on the *Royal Louis,* only to be captured and taken aboard HMS *Jersey,* a British prison ship. James was exchanged for a British prisoner and returned to Philadelphia in 1780 to start an apprenticeship as a sail-maker.

Yet another spirited young patriot was Christopher Hawkins, born in Providence, Rhode Island, on June 8, 1764. He came from a large but poor family and at age twelve years was apprenticed to the farmer Aaron Mason. In May 1777, young Christopher left the farm and made his way to the port of New Bedford where he signed up as cabin boy on the privateer *Schooner*, armed with twelve guns. The officers and crew were eager for booty and "had promised themselves many British prizes." But it was the *Schooner* that was captured and escorted to New York where the crew was imprisoned on HMS *Jersey*. In his autobiography, written many years later, Christopher Hawkins tells of his adventures and his escape from the prison ship by swimming to shore.[1]

During the Civil War, the Battle of Chickamauga, September 19–20, 1863, one of the bloodiest battles of that bloody conflict, the Twenty-Second Michigan Infantry fought a Confederate force. In the confusion twelve-year-old Johnny Clem, carrying his sawed-off musket, ran headlong into a Confederate colonel. The bemused colonel told Johnny: "You are a little fellow to be in this business, but war is war, and I think the best thing for a mite of a chap like you is to drop that gun." Instead, Johnny put his gun to shoulder, fired at the colonel and ran for all his worth back to the Twenty-Second Michigan.

Johnny Clem, an orphan boy, was only ten years old when President Lincoln issued his first call for volunteers. The boy in May 1861 tried to join the Third Ohio Regiment but was told he was far too small and far too young. He pestered the Twenty-Second Michigan and was taken along as the regimental mascot and drummer boy. Along the way he exchanged his drum for a musket, explaining, "I don't want to stand and be shot at without shooting back." In addition to Chickamauga, Johnny saw battle at Perryville, Murfreesboro, Kennesaw Mountain, and Peach Tree Creek at Atlanta, where he was thrice wounded. For his bravery, General William Rosecrans promoted Johnny to sergeant, the youngest non-commissioned officer to serve in the Union Army.

John Clem at Point Lookout, Tennessee. Lithograph by James Fuller Queen. At age eleven Johnny joined the 22nd Michigan regiment. For his bravery he was promoted to sergeant and was the youngest non-commissioned officer in the Union army.

Before the Civil War began in April 1861, the U.S. Army was a force of only sixteen thousand men, all over seventeen years of age. On July 22, 1861, the United States Congress authorized a volunteer army of 500,000 men, aged from eighteen to thirty-five years. On April 16, 1862, the conscription act passed by the Confederate Congress made all white men between eighteen and thirty-five years eligible to be drafted for military service. With the high rate of casualties, recruiters on both sides paid less attention to the age of the eager young recruits. Over three million soldiers took part in the Civil War. Six hundred and twenty thousand men — on the Union and on the Confederate sides — were killed and another half million seri-

Drum Corps of the 93rd New York Infantry Regiment, shown on parade at Bealeton, Virginia, August 1863. The regiment of 998 soldiers left Albany on February 14, 1862, and took part in several battles, as well as the siege of Yorktown. The drummers led the troops into battle, communicated messages and sometimes engaged in fighting. In the war, many boys were killed, wounded or captured. An estimated forty-eight boys under 18 (including eleven under 16) were awarded the Congressional Medal of Honor for showing extraordinary valor in combat.

ously wounded between 1861 and 1865. Many underage boys — estimates run as high as a half million — lied, saying they were already eighteen years old. Among these an estimated 200,000 enlisted boys were age sixteen or younger, determined to fight in the Civil War.[2] The Union forces employed 40,000 boys, the Confederate side 20,000 boys as buglers and drummers. The buglers played "Taps" signaling bedtime; the drummer boys kept the beat during marching drills, led the men into battle, and signaled turns to left or right, to advance and retreat. Hundreds of drummer boys were killed and thousands more wounded. Other boys delivered messages, collected and buried the dead or attended to the wounded. William C. Richardson of the 104th Ohio Regiment carried water to the soldiers, helped care for the wounded and buried the dead. He sent home $65. Many of the boy-soldiers carried muskets and saw battle. William Black was nine years old when he joined the 21st Indiana as a drummer boy. Three years later his left hand and arm were shattered by a shell, making him one of the war's youngest casualties.

Fifteen-year-old William Bircher grew up on a Minnesota farm and was determined to become a soldier and help the Union Army defeat the Confederacy. He was rejected several times before being taken, in late summer of 1861, as a drummer boy to Company

K of a Minnesota regiment. "The happiest day of my life," wrote young William in his diary, "was when I donned my blue uniform and received my new drum [and was] going South to do or die for my country if need be."

Johnnie Wickersham fought on the Confederate side. Born in 1846 to a successful dry goods merchant, he lost his mother in 1859. When his brothers Richard and James signed up for the Missouri State Guards, the 14-year-old Johnnie slipped out of the house at night and followed them into the Confederate Army. Richard was appointed commander of his company, with young Johnnie carrying messages for him. Johnnie took part in the battle of Pea Ridge in 1862 and was captured at Vicksburg. After he was pardoned, he joined General John Bell Hood to fight Sherman outside Atlanta. After the war, he settled to a family life in Missouri. Toward the close of his life he moved to California as a traveling salesman. John Wickersham wrote his memoirs shortly before his death, still espousing the elitist and racist attitudes of his youth.

Elisha Stockwell was born on June 28, 1846, in the central Massachusetts town of Athol. The coming of the railroad carried away many families, including the Stockwell family, which moved to Wisconsin. Elisha wrote: "In the summer of 1861, I was fifteen years old, and worked in the fields earning fifty cents a day, "but my father collected my wages as he was a very poor man." In September he heard there was going to be a war and went to the little log schoolhouse to volunteer. His father objected and scratched out Elisha's name, "which humiliated me somewhat." His sister "called me a little snotty boy, which raised my anger. I told her, Never mind, I'll go and show you that I am not the little boy you think I am."

One day in February 1862, Elisha told his family that he was going to the Dutch dance. His sister told him: "Hurry back, the dinner will soon be ready." Instead he went off to the recruiting office and "told the captain the circumstances, and the captain got me in by my lying a little, as I told the recruiting officer I didn't know just how old I was but thought I was eighteen." On February 15, 1863, the fifteen-year-old Elisha Stockwell enlisted in Company 1, Fourteenth Wisconsin Volunteer Infantry. He left for the front on March 8 and took part in the Battle of Shiloh on April 7. He was twice wounded, and promoted to corporal. He remembered the shells flying and soldiers crying for help. "My thoughts went back to my home," he writes, "and

Edwin Francis Jemison joined the 2nd Louisiana Regiment of the Confederate Army and served in the Peninsula Campaign under General John B. Magruder. He was shot and killed at Malvern Hill, Virginia, on July 1, 1862, aged sixteen years. Owing to the mounting deaths of children, the War Department in 1864 ordered a halt to enlistment of boys younger than sixteen.

I thought what a foolish boy I was to run away and get into such a mess as I was in." Nonetheless, he re-enlisted and received a bonus of $300 with a thirty-day furlough. Elisha did not return home for two years. He was mustered out October 9, 1865. He married and settled on a farm in Wisconsin.[3]

Boys as young as thirteen officially registered with the army but many more lied about their age. The young ones started as drummer boys, but many soon gave up the drum to fight on the line. Nine-year-old George H. Wilson went off with the 17th Maine Regiment, writing home that he "likes the soldier's life and is the pet of the regiment."[4] Orion P. Howe, a fourteen-year-old drummer boy of the Fifty-fifth Illinois Regiment, was awarded the coveted Medal of Honor for gallantry at Vicksburg for remaining on the field despite his severe wounds. A large number of the boys, on both sides, paid with their lives. Seventeen-year-old W.W. Dutton of the Tenth Vermont Regiment was killed in July 1864 at Monocacy.

Under-aged boys found it easy to enlist, especially if they were tall and muscular. Thomas Galway became a soldier at age fifteen; Ned Hutter joined the Confederate Army at fifteen; Edwin Francis Jemison, at sixteen, was a private in the Louisiana infantry and was killed in the Battle of Malvern Hill in July 1862. Many children, like twelve-year-old drummer boy William Black, who lost his left hand and arm, were severely injured during the war. The boy soldiers had the same privations as the adults and experienced the same harsh conditions as prisoners of war. The boys smoked and gambled, sent money home and showed increasing maturity and resilience as the fighting continued. Most remained common soldiers with but a few achieving fame.

Girls During the Civil War

Before the Civil War there were no medical corps or army nurses. Soon after President Lincoln issued an appeal for soldiers, Dorothea Dix was appointed superintendent of female nurses to work with doctors in the field hospitals. She imposed strict standards, officially taking only women over twenty-one and under thirty. Still, a number started earlier. Mary Alice Smith was "but eighteen years old" when she tended to the sick and the dying at the battles of Antietam and Gettysburg. Neither the Union nor the Confederate side officially enlisted women to fight. "I met two soldier girls who donned the blue," wrote Martha A. Baker. "One, Frances Hook, alias Harry Miller, served two years and nine months; the other was called Anna. She was put in our charge [to work in the kitchens] until the military authorities could send her north."[5] Richard Hall estimates that there were several hundred females, mostly young girls, who cut their hair short and copied the mannerisms and dress of beardless boys in order to pass the perfunctory test for age and physical fitness to bluff their way to the front.[6]

Brigadier General William Emile Doster kept a diary during the Civil War. In 1864 he wrote about a pair of soldiers who had been through the Battle of Bull Run:

> One day the officer of the guard arrested two puny looking soldiers supposed to be drummer boys. They refused to give the names of their regiments. To cure them of their obstinacy, they were ordered to be showered, when the discovery was made that they were girls. Then they told that they were from Hagerstown, Md., had enlisted in the service to be with certain of their friends in the field. General [James Samuel] Wadsworth gave them a kind admonition for the folly of their course and sent them home on the cars.[7]

In her remarkable 1863 book Virginia Penny writes about the women and girls who filled the jobs of the men battling in the Civil War. Her book was the first of its kind published in the United States to help women and girls find work. Penny dedicated her book to the "worthy and industrious women in the United States striving to earn a livelihood." She wrote:

> A million men are on the battlefield, and thousands of women, formerly dependent on them, have lost or may lose their only support. Some of the mothers, wives, sisters and daughters of soldiers, may take the vacancies created in the business by their absence — others must seek new channels of labor.

Virginia Penny traveled the nation by stagecoach, wagon and train to learn how women and girls could make their living. She identified five hundred different jobs, learning that women regularly were paid less money than men for equal work, and young girls earned even less. She accepted the notion of child labor, and in particular the labor of girls, as a fact of life, but was critical of the low pay. Along her travels she found many girls and women at work.

A job suitable for girls was selling flowers, "most profitably at opera houses, theatres and other places of amusement. They buy of those who devote themselves to the raising of flowers, and arrange them in bouquets. A number dispose of flowers on Broadway." Penny wrote: "I have been told there are probably 10,000 women and children employed in making artificial flowers in New York," earning $1.60 to $6 a week. One candy company employed "ninety girls in busy times" at $3 to $6 for a sixty-hour week. A daguerreotype apparatus maker in New Haven employed one hundred and fifty girls, earning 50 to 75 cents a day. "It does not take a smart girl more than eight days to learn to color" the photographic plates. Young girls were employed making parasols, paper boxes, hoop skirts, pens and buttons. Girls were often employed as domestic servants. "The number of white female servants in New York City was estimated at 100,000, that of Boston 50,000, Philadelphia 30,000 and Baltimore 20,000." Girls were employed in the early department stores such as Levy's, Sharpless and Evans of Philadelphia earning $3 to $6 a week. In pottery factories, "the girls receive one-third as much as men working at the wheels." A hat factory in Philadelphia employed three hundred girls trimming bonnets at $1 a day.

Girls were employed sewing clothes, making cigars, brushes and mattresses and "binding, mounting, stitching and coloring maps." The American Bank Note Company of New York employed sixty girls in printing, making impressions, drying and sorting banknotes. Girls were hired to strip the leaves from the stems of the tobacco plant. At a canvas bag factory, "men cut out the bags. The folding and trimming is done by little girls, who receive $1.50 a week." At the Sedgley & Warrington Pin Factory, girls began to work as early as five years of age.[8]

One field of employment for girls and young women that Virginia Penny could not imagine was government work. The carnage of the Civil War left both the Union and the Confederacy short of men to run their treasury departments. In Washington, Brigadier General Doster observed in 1865: "A notable feature in the streets of the capital is the female government employees, especially the treasury girls. They are generally young and of good families — for it takes some influence to get into a department."[9]

On the Confederacy side, the need for treasury girls was even greater. Starting in 1862 and until 1865, the Confederacy's treasury departments in Richmond, Virginia, and Columbia, South Carolina, hired several hundred teen-age girls and young women to sign and number bills. The jobs were in high demand, with one hundred candidates for each position. The jobs went largely to girls from formerly upper-class families with connections. From the treasury, jobs for girls and young women opened in other government departments. Before the war, girls from well-to-do homes never worked, but hard times made it necessary.[10]

With the death of over six hundred thousand men the Civil War left in its wake numerous fatherless children. Starting July 1862 the government gave pensions to the widows according to the rank of the deceased. The wives of dead privates received $8 a month, and the wives of senior officer upwards of $30 a month. Children went to work in factories or earned a living on the streets selling newspapers, flowers or baskets. Orphanages across the land took in children, training the girls for domestic service and the boys for a craft. The children of deceased or injured farmers took over the tilling and reaping, the care of the animals and the responsibility of running the farm. Many of the battlefield orphans were placed out to other families as domestic servants or farm workers. The soldier Daniel Goodnow wrote to his three sons to "remember always that your mother has the right to your help.... You can never do too much for her." He told his boys to collect the wood, make the fires, milk the cows, help with the washing, and generally "take all work off her hands that you can do."[11]

With their father in the Confederate Army, Cecile and Leon Fremaux of Louisiana learned to take care of themselves as well as care for their young siblings. Daily life for the wealthy Hawthorne family of Fayette, North Carolina, changed suddenly after their slaves disappeared. Eight-year-old Sally learned to wash and dress herself as well as sweep the floors and set the table. Her brother fetched the wood, lit the fires and did other chores. Lieutenant Theodorick Montfort wrote to his 13-year-old son "to attend everything, see to it yourself, don't delay. Never go to sleep of a night until you see that everything is attended to."[12]

Virginia Penny sold thousands of copies of her book and was credited with helping many girls and women find work, occasionally at a decent salary. Her advice did not long keep Penny herself out of poverty. A public appeal for money in 1893 informed the wider public that "Miss Penny is now sixty-five years old and destitute.... Women owe it to her to make her last days comfortable."[13]

During the Second World War children were encouraged to stay in school. With millions of American men enlisting to serve their country, an army of women was recruited to fill the jobs at home. Their work was personified by Rosie the Riveter, a tough women dressed in overalls, sleeves rolled up, riveting tool in hand, who was "part of the assembly line," building the ships, tanks and airplanes for victory. Skilled teams of men and women workers built the Flying Fortresses and B-17F bombers that saw action over the Pacific and Europe. America admired the patriotism of women who went to work during the war but worried that their latchkey children were neglected and at risk of becoming delinquent. In 1942, greater New York set up a program "to curb delinquency: Mothers in war jobs create problems."[14] A quarter century earlier, child labor was blamed as the cause of delinquency. Now, parental neglect was the alleged cause.

14

Health and Education
of Working Children

The American people should know under what conditions [children] are living, and working and becoming invalids, thousands of them dying in childhood or early youth.

— Florence Kelley, December 8, 1905

[Ragged Dick tells a customer:] "I ain't always goin' to black boots for a livin." [He is told:] "All labor is respectable, my lad, and you have no cause to be ashamed of any honest business; yet when you can get something to do that promises better for your future prospects, I advise you to do so." He had four dollars left in his pocket-book…. In fact he had formed the ambitious design of starting an account at a savings' bank, in order to have something to fall back upon in case of sickness or any other emergency…. Hitherto he had been content to live on from day to day without a penny ahead.

—Horatio Alger Jr., *Ragged Dick*, 1895

Reformers were eager to show that children sent to work at an early age suffered permanent damage to body and soul. There were others who believed that labor taught children responsibility and the drive to better themselves. In 1859, James Hogg published in London his *Men Who Have Risen*, the inspiring stories of humbly born lads who rose to greatness. Among his heroes were George Stephenson, born in 1781 in a coal-miner's cottage, who was the inventor of the steam locomotive; John Scott, also a coal miner's son, who became Lord Eldon, Lord Chancellor of England; and Humphry Davy, born in 1778, the son of a wood-carver who rose to become a famous chemist and inventor. Charles Altamont Doyle, a mediocre artist and alcoholic, illustrated Hogg's book. Doyle happened to be the father of Arthur Conan Doyle, whose fictional detective, Sherlock Holmes, still thrills today with his superior intellect but all too human weaknesses.

Newell Avery, of Puritan stock, was born in 1817 in Jefferson, Maine. In the late 1820s the Avery family traveled by wagon to Michigan to start a new life. "Newell was but eleven years of age when his father died, leaving to his widow little beside the farm for the support of herself and ten young children." Living was hard and primitive. Newell "began so early to labor in aid of the family, that he scarcely can be said to have had an education." Newell grew into a six-foot, well-built and athletic man. Newell Avery bought timberland and rose to be one of the foremost lumbermen in the United States.

American frontier history abounds with real-life tales like that of Newell Avery. The writer Horatio Alger Jr. specialized in fictional inspirational tales for boys. Born in Chelsea, Massachusetts, in 1832, Horatio was the literary hero of the American waif. He grew up in genteel poverty and attended Harvard Divinity School before ministering to a Unitarian church in Brewster on Cape Cod. There he was charged with committing sexual acts with two teenage boys of the parish. Alger moved to New York where he befriended and wrote about poor boys. During the second half of the nineteenth century Alger wrote dozens of books with titles like *Sink or Swim, Strive and Succeed, Risen from the Ranks, Sam's Chance,* and *The Road to Success.* His books are peopled with homeless bootblacks, boy peddlers, luggage boys, newsboys, and street musicians who use their wit, drive, hard work and honesty, and with the help of kindly adults find their way into middle-class morality, with the bonus of money and respectability. His rags to respectability tales reflect as much Horatio Alger's own demons as they do the hopes of children. More fantasy than reality, the Alger novels gave buoyancy to the American spirit, even in hard times.

Horatio Alger's most notable book was *Ragged Dick,* set in New York City before the Civil War. Dick is a fourteen-year-old homeless but street-smart bootblack who sleeps in a box filled with straw "without taking the trouble undressing." His clothes are in tatters and he goes around carrying his "little blacking box" ready for use, looking sharply in the faces of the men who pass by and asking each one, "Shine yer boots, sir?" at ten cents a go. Despite his desperate circumstances, young Dick has his dignity and tries to stay honest. "You don't catch me stealin'.... Lots of boys does it, but I wouldn't." Dick does not save his money but enjoys going to the Old Bowery Theater and occasionally inviting his friends to have an oyster stew. His life is filled with trials and tribulations. Others try to rob him and accuse him of trying to rise above his lowly station in life.

Dick saves a little boy from drowning and is rewarded by the boy's father with a new suit and the offer of a job in a mercantile house where he takes on the persona of Richard Hunter, Esq. "He is Ragged Dick no longer," but is on his way to become a respectable and successful member of the middle class. Alger's inspirational novels generally had happy endings. *Ragged Dick* was highly popular for years after its publication and is still a brisk seller a century and a half later.

During the nineteenth and early twentieth centuries, industrial accidents were frequent. Gilbert Lewis Campbell analyzed the figures of the Pittsburgh Survey for the year ending July 1, 1907, and found 526 industrial deaths and 2000 cases of serious injury that required "extended hospital treatment." In Cook County, Illinois, during 1908, a total of 524 workers lost their lives and a further 2,494 had serious injuries, In 1907, Campbell calculated, one in 206 workers was killed on the job.[1] Work accidents were especially high on the railroads and in the coal mines. Until the twentieth century, workers were compensated little after suffering injury on the job. A sickness or injury quickly plunged families into poverty due to loss of income and inability to pay rent or buy food. By the start of the twentieth century records were kept by several states listing injuries suffered at work. Most of the injuries suffered by child workers were minor but some caused dismemberment and even death. Public outrage, legal action and the rising costs of compensation were among the reasons why child labor declined.

Whether or not early employment stunted the intellectual and moral development of children and whether children were more prone to accidents was debated occasionally during the nineteenth century. John Orne Green was born in 1798 and entered Harvard College at age fourteen. Upon graduation he apprenticed to the noted Boston physician Dr. Edward Reynolds. In 1822 he moved to Lowell, which at that time "had no more than 200 inhabitants," and treated many of the mill workers. In 1846, he addressed the Massachusetts Medical Society on the subject of industry and health. In less than a quarter of a century, Lowell had grown from a small farm community into a textile manufacturing city with over 20,000 workers. "We still believe factory labor is," concluded Dr. Green, "on some counts, injurious." On average, the workers were on their feet twelve hours a day with little time to smell the flowers or see the sun. Many developed varicose veins, became depressed and nervous or contracted tuberculosis. Life was short. Laborers and factory workers lived on average only 27 years and 5 months, compared to 45 years and five months for the farming folk. The long hours of work breathing air filled with cotton dust, concluded Dr. Green, caused pneumonia (cotton phthisis) and a rapid decline in health.

In 1907, Senator Albert Beveridge, a leading foe of child labor, evoked an even more ominous threat to the nation's health. Putting children to work, he warned, leaves them permanently stunted in body and mind, passing on their impairments to their offspring, leading to the degeneration of the race and the decline of civilization. This line of thought reached into the highest levels of government. On January 19, 1920, the President's Industrial Conference assembled under the chairmanship of W.B. Watson, secretary of labor, and vice-chairman Herbert Hoover. Members of the committee included some of the nation's leading industrialists and economists. Section 5 of Part IV of the report states:

> The Federal Government has already recognized the unsoundness of the economic use of the nation's resources of permitting the entry of young children into industry. Such a practice results in the progressive degeneration of the race.... The entrance of young children of tender years into the mill or factory tends to stunt their development, and injure the race.... We must not only protect our children from the physical degeneration which results from an early entrance into the mill or factory but we must enable them by education to take their place in society.[2]

President Woodrow Wilson's Industrial Conference separated child farm labor from factory labor. The report says: "The employment of children in agriculture may, if wisely supervised, develop physique and lay a good foundation for their more formal education in the country school."

Robert M. La Follette served as governor of Wisconsin (1901–1906) and then as its United States senator from 1906 until his death in 1925. Addressing the American Federation of Labor on June 14, 1921, La Follette noted that once "it was desirable or even commendable to employ young children in exhausting labor in factories, mines and shops." It was medically proven, claimed the senator, "that such labor was not only a crime against childhood, but that it degraded adult labor as well, and was a menace to the nation." La Follette quoted from Senate Report No. 368, issued by the 64th Congress in 1916 that "unregulated child labor does not promote healthy citizenship; that it tends to the deterioration of the race physically; and the dwarfing of children mentally through the denial of a full opportunity for education." Getting into his stride, La Follette also claimed that child labor led to criminality and drunkenness.

Mill Disasters

After the dramatic expansion of textile mills along the Merrimack River at Lowell, the brothers Abbott and Amos Lawrence built a second textile city downriver in a town named Lawrence in their honor. The Pemberton Mill, financed by John Amory Lowell, nephew of Francis Cabot Lowell, started production in 1853. On January 10, 1860, some six hundred workers, men, women and children, were busy at work when the building collapsed. "At five o'clock in the afternoon the floors of the large structure, five stories in height, suddenly gave way, the walls were overthrown, and stone, bricks, timber, machinery, and this vast crowd of human beings lay in one confused mass of ruins." With many trapped under the rubble fire broke out, killing more. One in five of the workers was younger than fifteen years of age. An estimated eighty-nine workers lost their lives, among them Irene Crosby, Peter Callahan, Catherine Hannon, Michael O'Brien and Catherine Kelleher. "Give this to my father, I shan't see him, but you will," said little Mary Anne Bannan, an Irish child of ten years to a girl near her, as she gave her the pay roll certificate she had received that afternoon.... Mary Anne was never seen again." A further one hundred and thirty-four were seriously injured.[3]

On September 19, 1874, a fire engulfed the fifth and sixth floors of the Granite Textile Mill of Fall River, Massachusetts. The mill "employed a considerable number of young children.... The employees on the sixth floor were mainly girls between the ages of twelve and eighteen." The children worked twelve-hour days with an hour off for dinner. Nine of the nineteen people killed in the fire were children twelve years of age or younger. Among those killed was James Smith, a boy of nine years, who started working in the mill only two days before the fire. According to the inquest report: "It was his first work in a mill, his mother having several younger children ... had kept him at home to assist about the house. For this reason he had never been to school." James Newton, born in Ashton-Under-Lynde, England, was aged ten. "He had not attended school since his arrival in this country but had had a little schooling in England.... He was killed and his remains so badly burnt as to be recognizable only by a small portion of his shirt." Albert Fernley, aged ten, started working at the mill soon after his arrival from England, "consequently he had never attended school in this country." Albert sought refuge in the attic and then jumped out of the window and "received such injuries that he died in two hours." Noah Poitros, aged twelve years, also "leaped from the attic window and survived the fall but two hours." His sister Lydia, aged fifteen years, was lucky. A mattress placed on the ground softened her fall from the same window. "Her injuries were internal, except a few scratches, and probably were not of a serious nature." Many other children including Edward and John Goss, George Stinton and Joseph Lynch were injured but survived the fire. One of the strong reactions of the board of inquiry into the Granite Mill disaster was that: "Children have no right in mills at all."[4]

The Massachusetts Factory Act of 1876 was passed as a response to the Granite Mill disaster. This law stipulated that no child under ten be allowed to work in a mill, and that children under fourteen years be required to show that they had at least twenty weeks of education in the year before taking up employment. Owners who hired under age children, or parents who allowed their underage children to work, would be subject to stiff fines.

On April 15, 1896, at the Chicago Fireworks Company a group of young girls was busy rolling and pasting firecrackers. Nearby a fourteen-year-old boy was stuffing the crackers into a box that contained a mixture of potash and antimony. The crackers exploded, killing the boy and seriously injuring Emma Simski, a fourteen-year-old girl.

Based on her work as chief factory inspector of Illinois, Florence Kelley railed against the illnesses and injuries suffered by young children in the workplace. As early as 1895, she listed how children in the tobacco industry suffered nicotine poisoning and the sufferings of boys "who are voluntary devotees of the weed." Children working in frame gilding suffered from stiffness of the fingers. Children in the sweatshops suffered "spinal curvatures, and, for girls, pelvic disorders." In the bakeries "children slowly roasted before the ovens." Working in confined, dirty and airless places children developed tuberculosis, smallpox, scarlet fever, typhoid and other contagious diseases.[5]

Claiming that child labor dulls the mind and stunts the body was a recurring theme of Florence Kelley's, and it was shared by Jane Addams in Chicago, Julia Lathrop in Washington, Lillian Wald in New York, and by the National Child Labor Committee. In 1913, Florence Kelley delivered a series of lectures at Teachers' College, Columbia University, on the theme of "Modern Industry in Relation to the Family, Health, Education and Morality."[6] Kelley combined Friedrich Engels' analysis with American morality, strident prose and sweeping generalizations. Power machinery, she wrote, has taken the grunt work and the thinking out of labor. Modern industry uses cheap and compliant child labor to replace grown men. As a result men are laid off, or their wages are reduced. The school system has become the servant of the capitalists, displaying "unthinking willingness to surrender children — under pretext of their poverty — to the greedy hunger of the mills, mines, sweatshops, cotton-fields, and the city street trades." The schools, she continued, "serve as feeders for industry.... Modern industry tends to keep the wage-earner spiritually poor and dull." In the workplace, these young children run a high risk of physical injury with "young legs and backs made crooked, young eyes strained by continuous watching [and] young minds cramped, stupefied and deadened."

Children of fourteen are too young, she wrote, to leave school for monotonous, mindless "machine tending." They are usually illiterate and lack judgment. Machine tending "habituates them to irresponsibility and monotony, to the utter absence of thought, inventiveness, of judgment, of ambition." Children destined for the factory should remain in school at least to age sixteen and attend manual-training schools to gain maturity and knowledge to be fitted "to become foremen, managers, superintendents," performing white-collar rather than blue-collar work. Instead of being a servant of industry, the schools should train children "to resist monotony, and to organize their activities for themselves, so that they may combat successfully the deadliest foe of this Republic, the lowering of the citizenship by industry."

Does a child worker grow into adult life with his health and vigor intact? If a child leaves school early to go to work, does he have enough education to make him a good citizen? To answer these important questions Julia Lathrop, chief of the Children's Bureau of the U.S. Department of Labor, hired the economist Helen Sumner Woodbury to conduct a study. Woodbury was educated at Wellesley College and the University of Wisconsin. She focused on the early school-leavers of greater Boston. Children were interviewed in 1914 and followed up three years later. The conclusions were stark. The three-year period after leaving school at an early age "was in nearly all cases, almost, if not completely, wasted, and

... for many, it was worse than wasted." These children "had only a rudimentary education" that left them ignorant and inexperienced and excluded them from more complex jobs. As a result "these children drifted about restlessly from one simple task or errand position to another," earning an average of only $16 a month, with periods of unemployment. These children were "permanently handicapped, in most cases for life, by an educational training inadequacy," rendering them unable to adapt to new tasks or take on "the duties of citizenship."[7]

Handicapped by only "rudimentary education," the early school-leavers often had health problems as well. A survey of 88,851 Milwaukee school children examined from 1913 to 1918 found that many had "defects that required correction." One third had enlarged tonsils or adenoids, two-thirds had tooth and gum disease and one in four had defective vision. In 1915 a total of 30,204 New York City children aged fourteen or fifteen applied for employment certificates. One thousand were denied because they were suffering from malnutrition. Again, defective teeth, poor vision and enlarged tonsils were the common health problems. A study of one hundred boys in Baltimore who had been employed in factories for an average of two years each showed that on average they were a half-inch shorter than the 5 foot 1 inch standard and weighed 8 pounds less than the standard 100 pounds for boys of their age.[8]

Julia Lathrop used these findings to launch her education initiative. During her last years as chief of the Children's Bureau, when the United States entered World War I, Lathrop embarked on ambitious, nationwide "Stay-in-School," "Go-back-to-School" (1918), and "Every Child at School" (1919) programs. These federal initiatives were "a safeguard against child labor and illiteracy." The programs were aimed at the one million children "who had been drawn into work by the war-time demand for labor and the high cost of living." Lathrop reassured children that the war effort did not need them and by leaving school they "were wasting an irretrievable opportunity and should be encouraged to return to school at once." It was vital, she wrote, to keep children "from the ranks of premature laborers who in later years, if they don't become public charges, at least, rarely develop into children able to give valuable service to their country." The programs also called for keeping children in school until age sixteen "except in agriculture and domestic service," for better teacher training and raising the minimum teacher salary to $1,000 a year, at a time when many teachers "receive no more than $10 a month."[9]

Julia Lathrop issued a patriotic appeal to children to support the entry of the United States into the Great War by staying in school and receiving the education necessary to become productive citizens. The "Stay-in-School" appeal came at a time when most of her Hull-House colleagues had rallied around Jane Addams and Florence Kelley to actively oppose the war and America's participation in it. In 1915 these women declared themselves pacifists and formed the Women's Peace Party, later to become the Women's International League for Peace & Freedom. Jane Addams' advocacy for world peace would win her, in 1931, the Nobel Peace Prize. Florence Kelley, however, was vilified as unpatriotic and a Russian agent.

The Federal Report on Women and Child Wage-Earners in the United States, done in 1910, found that in the cotton mills of the South, children age fourteen and fifteen had 48 percent more accidents than children a year or two older. Massachusetts had long since enacted laws to prevent children working with power machinery but the practice persisted.

Lucile Eastes at Simmons College, Boston, published a study, *One Thousand Industrial Accidents Suffered by Massachusetts Children*, for the year ending June 30, 1917. There were a total of 1,730 accidents involving children of fourteen and fifteen years. Boys had a much higher rate of accidents than girls. Most of the accidents were fairly minor and with only temporary impairment. There were seventy-six cases where children suffered permanent disability with loss of fingers or arms, head injuries and burns. There were seven deaths. The most common accidents came from work with machines that cut, punched or stapled, causing amputation of the tips of fingers or crushed hands. A number of children had their clothes or hair caught in the gears or belting of the machinery.[10] Children of fourteen and fifteen suffered a higher rate of machinery injuries than did sixteen-year-olds.

Raymond Garfield Fuller concluded, "From two to three times as many children as adults in proportion to the number employed are killed or injured in industry." The accident rate at work for children fourteen or fifteen years old was 48 percent higher than for children sixteen or older. In Massachusetts, New York, Pennsylvania and other industrialized states one child in twenty suffered some level of injury "as a direct result of his employment."[11] Amy Hewes, at Mt. Holyoke College, found in 1920 that working children age fourteen and fifteen had an annual accident rate of 37.1 per hundred while the rate of accidents for those twenty or older was only 21.7 per hundred. Fuller attributed the high rate of accidents among adolescents to their lack of physical maturity, poor coordination, lack of fine motor coordination or just plain carelessness and a desire to play.[12]

More and more states enacted compensation laws that applied also to children. Under the impetus of these laws, "gigantic efforts have been made in the whole country ... to reduce industrial hazards." In its 1921 report the Metropolitan Insurance Company paid out the compensation claims for forty-three boys who died from their injuries. Of these, eight died in mines or quarries, seven from machines, thirteen while working on the railroads, three were killed by electricity and six in vehicular accidents. In West Virginia a boy under fourteen years of age was injured while working at the Proctor-Eagle Coal Company. He severely injured his hand while hooking a loaded coal car to a cable, receiving $3,000 in compensation. The State of Wisconsin enacted a law to make companies pay triple damages to injured children who were "employed in violation of the child labor laws." Injured boys entitled on average to a settlement of $100, instead received $300. This law was a strong deterrent against employing below-age children. New York and New Jersey also adopted double or triple compensation laws.[13]

One of the most vociferous, persistent and influential of the critics against the National Child Labor Committee and its attempts to ban child labor was David Clark of Raleigh, North Carolina. Trained as a mechanical engineer, Clark ran a cotton mill before founding and editing the *Southern Textile Bulletin*. He was one of the founders of the Southern Textile Association. So incensed was Clark by the criticism of the Southern mills by the NCLC that he appeared uninvited at its annual meeting in Washington in January 1915, demanding to be heard. He emphatically "denied that children were oppressed and overworked in the mills of North Carolina." He protested against Lewis Hine's pictures showing "thin, emaciated children that look too weak to stand." Clark issued a challenge: "I am willing to wager that the children in the mill district, boy for boy, can lick any of their class of boys in America." Clark charged that the NCLC reports "exaggerate conditions and tell half-truths. They take isolated cases and create the impression that they are representative."

Finally, thundered Clark, the liberals of the North should not come to North Carolina to find fault; it was "none of their business."[14]

Rosa M. Barrett, a wealthy English lady living in Dun Luoghaire, County Dublin, Ireland, became concerned over the plight of the poor women in the seaside town. Reasoning that these women could support themselves if their children were properly cared for, Rosa, in 1878, opened a crèche in the town. The idea grew and soon Rosa was in charge of the larger Cottage Home for Little Children. So started the career of Rosa M. Barrett as an expert on the "child life among the less-favored classes" and as a leading campaigner on behalf of the homeless and destitute children. Rosa collected statistics from industrialized countries, including the United States, on the care of children in need.

She believed that it was the duty of the parent "to feed and maintain his own child." When through illness, death or neglect the parent could not take care of his child, it became the duty of the state. Rosa Barrett wrote a number of books to show that neglected and destitute little children grow to become vagabonds and criminals. It was better and cheaper, she argued, for the state to intervene early rather than covering the expense of reformatories and prisons. Rosa Barrett was particularly upset to see children hawking goods on street corners. These little children fail to attend school and when they reach adulthood "are too old to learn a trade, and they increase that difficult class of next to no value in the labor market, living always on the verge of starvation, our unskilled laborers.... It is from this class that the ranks of paupers and criminals are largely recruited."[15]

Thomas A. Smith, chairman of the Bureau of Industrial Statistics of Maryland, reported that in 1900 there were 331,904 children of "school-going age," five to seventeen years, but nearly one-third of them (115,535) "were at work or kept at home [and were] deprived of the educational facilities so liberally maintained by the State." Many of these children were employed in fruit, vegetable and oyster canning or in sweatshops making clothes. In these industries men on average earned $550 and women $270 but children only $120 a year. This translates to a daily salary for men of $1.50, women 75 cents and for children, only 30–40 cents.

"The question of the employment of children below the age of 16 years," wrote Smith, "has long agitated the labor organizations of the State and ...various humanitarian societies of ladies" who sought legislation "prohibiting the employment of these little ones. There are two sides to the question, one humanitarian and the other economic." Smith bluntly wrote that his state could not afford to give up child labor "in the present age of fierce competition in the manufacturing and commercial world as it will place its citizens at a disadvantage with the industries of all other States [and will] hamper the growth of such industries, especially if there is no other means available to perform the work now being done by children." Thomas Smith acknowledged that new machinery was available to replace the work of children, but these machines were expensive and children's wages (in 1899) of "$130 or 42 cents a day probably accounts for the demand of child labor." In 1899, 11 percent of the workers in the fruit and vegetable canneries of Maryland were children. The high season for canning fruits and vegetables was from early August to the end of October. The average wages in these seasonal industries for adults was $182 but for children only $92.15 cents per annum.[16]

The race degeneration theories, popular during the first half of the twentieth century, are now fortunately no longer in fashion. Still, the debate over the risks of early work continues. Child labor in the United States has persisted longer in agriculture than in factories, or mines. On August 21, 1998, Congress received the results of the study into *Child Labor in Agriculture*. At that time an estimated 155,000 children aged 15 to 17 were working in agriculture, of whom 116,000 were hired workers. Each year 400 to 600 children "suffer work-related injuries." Between 1992 and 1996, fifty children lost their lives while working in agriculture. The report concluded "agriculture is a hazardous industry for children."[17]

15

National Child Labor Committee and the U.S. Children's Bureau

The National Child Labor Committee considers the Alabama Child Labor Committee as its mother. It was organized first, and its organizer, Edgar Gardner Murphy, was one of the moving spirits in the organization of the National Child Labor Committee.
— Alexander J. McKelway, 1911

Edgar Gardner Murphy (1869–1913) was born in Fort Smith, Arkansas. Abandoned by his father when aged five years, Edgar moved with his mother to San Antonio, Texas, where she operated a boardinghouse. After the University of the South, Sewanee, Tennessee, he moved to New York in 1889 to attend the General Theological Seminary of the Episcopal Church. He served in Episcopal communities in Texas, Ohio and New York before his appointment as rector of St. John's Church, Montgomery, Alabama. Murphy was an odd mixture of white supremacist and foe of child labor, in particular the labor of white children.

Factories and mines expanded child labor in the South. On February 28, 1887, Senator Daniel Smith, representing Mobile County, secured the first child labor law in Alabama, fining companies $50 for allowing children under eighteen years to work longer than eight hours a day. On December 5, 1894, business interests ensured that the law was rescinded. In 1897, efforts to reinstate child labor laws failed in the committees. In 1901, Murphy formed the Alabama Child Labor Committee, whose members included justices J.B. Gaston and Thomas G. Jones as well as Dr. J.H. Phillips, superintendent of schools in Birmingham, Alabama. Murphy fought hard to get a bill passed by the Alabama legislature to prevent children under twelve years from working in the cotton mills, and limit older children to daytime work only. Murphy met strong opposition from the Dwight Manufacturing Company of Chicopee, Massachusetts, which had built a subsidiary mill in Alabama City, Alabama. The Dwight Company of Chicopee had long opposed the abolition of child labor, raising wages and shortening the workweek. Its move to the South was intended to take advantage of a cheaper and more compliant workforce. In the 1901 hearings of the Alabama legislature, representatives of the Dwight Company succeeded in blocking stringent child-labor laws by threatening to leave the state.

In his 1904 book the Reverend Murphy laid out his views on the labor of children. The South lay prostrate after the Civil War, with farmers, black and white, eking a subsistence living off the land. Change came after 1880 with the textile mills: "The mills came to the cotton." From 1880 to 1900, over one hundred million dollars, coming mainly from the North, was invested in Southern textile mills. The four years from 1900 to 1904 saw the dramatic expansion of textile mills in the South, increasing from 412 to 900 mills, "more than double." Faced with stricter labor laws, strikes, and wage increases in the Northeast, the owners moved to the South to take advantage of its "tractable and cheap labor." The source of the Southern labor "lies in the unfettered masses of the white population," especially the labor of children. In 1900, out of 97,559 textile workers in the South, 24,459 (25 percent) were children under sixteen years of age. By 1904, the mills in the South employed some 50,000 children, 20,000 of whom were under twelve. The "labor of the cotton factory," wrote Edgar Murphy, "has been almost wholly white." He claimed that black children lacked the endurance or the skills to work twelve-hour days.[1]

Attempts to persuade the legislatures in the South to impose limits on the labor of little children in cotton mills ended in failure. Murphy put the blame on the Northern mill owners and their local supporters who "have thronged the lobbies of Southern legislatures in an effort to defeat such an elementary law as the prohibiting of factory labor for children under twelve.... The effort for the passage of a child labor law was defeated before the legislature of 1900, largely through the skillful and aggressive opposition of the representative of one of the New England factories in Alabama." Murphy decried "the heartless policy with which capital is using and is striving to perpetuate the defenselessness of the children of the South." These little children "were called to work before sunrise and were dismissed from work only after sunset, laboring from dark to dark.... I have seen children of eight and nine leaving the factory as late at 9.30 o'clock at night, and finding their way home with their own little lanterns, through the unlighted streets of the mill village, to their squalid homes." Not only were the children exploited by the owners, but they were also being cheated by their own parents "who make every effort to get their children into the mill." Murphy issued a public appeal to the people of New England, and in particular to the shareholders of the textile mills, asking them to stop the Northern mill owners from blocking child labor legislation in the South.

The Reverend Murphy was the first to broker the idea of a national organization to combine the various child labor committees. In 1903, Murphy traveled to Atlanta, Georgia, to attend the annual meeting of the National Conference of Charities and Corrections, where he gave a talk on May 9 on "Child Labor as a National Problem." "With all emphasis," he said, "the practice of child labor is a national problem. North and South, it belongs to all of us." There he met Jane Addams and Florence Kelley who spoke on the topic of destitute children. Finding they had mutual concerns Addams and Kelley met with Murphy to plan a National Child Labor Committee. On returning to New York, Florence took the idea to the New York Child Labor Committee, which appointed a three-person group to confer with Murphy and his Montgomery organization. In addition to Florence Kelley and Professor Felix Adler, William Henry Baldwin Jr. was selected. Baldwin was born in Boston in 1868, attended Harvard College and found employment with the railroads. At the start of the twentieth century he was president of the South Railway Company, headquartered in New York. Like his father, he was civic minded and philanthropic. Baldwin fell ill, leaving the work of organizing the National Child Labor Committee to Florence Kelley

On the evening of April 14, 1904, and the following day representatives from across the nation gathered at Carnegie Hall in New York City to form a National Child Labor Committee (NCLC). The aims of the committee were: (a) to develop a clearing house for information on child labor practices, and (b) to go beyond remedial work and initiate legislation that would create "fair industrial conditions for child life." Felix Adler of Columbia University was elected chairman of the committee, with Homer Folks vice chairman and Edgar Gardner Murphy as secretary. Joining them on the thirty-five-member committee, Lillian Wald and Florence Kelley assembled their friends in the settlement house movement (Jane Addams, Robert Hunter), wealthy and influential bankers (Isaac N. Seligman and Paul M. Warburg), and industrialists (Stanley Robert McCormick of Chicago, William H. Baldwin, and V. Everit Macy). The proprietor of the *New York Times*, Adolph S. Ochs, and former president Grover Cleveland also lent their names to the committee — a veritable Who's-Who of society. The NCLC began small with only fifty members in 1905, but by 1912 its membership was over 6,400.

Felix Adler was the founding chairman of NCLC. He was born in Alzey, in Rhein-Hessen, Germany, in 1851, the son of Rabbi Samuel Adler. In 1857, his father was invited to become the rabbi of Temple Emanu-El in New York City. At age fifteen, Felix entered Columbia College and later studied for the rabbinate at the University of Heidelberg. While in Germany he was much influenced by the writings of Immanuel Kant, believing that ethical values can develop independent of theology. "Deed, not creed" was his guide. He believed that ethical values should drive behavior and that people are put on earth to do well to others. On his return to New York he established a kindergarten to care for the children of poor workers, believing that education helps the children of the poor to take care of themselves. In time, the kindergarten evolved into the Ethical Culture School, at 63rd Street, New York. Adler also established a school for working people. In 1902, Adler was appointed professor of ethics at Columbia University. Adler shared with Florence Kelley the fundamental belief that children should go to school, not to work. "Moral education," added Adler, "is the most important part of all education." Adler was married to Helen Goldmark, older sister to Josephine Goldmark, assistant to Florence Kelley.

Isaac N. Seligman, Paul M. Warburg and Adolph S. Ochs — trustees of the NCLC — were members of the same German-Jewish elite as Felix Adler. They all attended Temple Emanu-El. Seligman and Warburg were prominent banking families. Ochs began more humbly and worked as an office boy before becoming a newspaperman and publisher of the influential *New York Times*.[2] Stanley Robert McCormick was the youngest son of Cyrus McCormick, inventor of the mechanical reaper. Stanley excelled at Princeton and seemed ready for a brilliant career at International Harvester and as a Chicago philanthropist before he descended into madness. Yet another member of the committee was Alexander Johnston Cassatt, born in Pittsburgh. President of the Pennsylvania Railroad Company, Cassatt was the man who authorized building Pennsylvania Station and the railroad tunnels under the Hudson River. He was brother to the painter Mary Cassatt.

These men paid the rent and the salaries of the permanent staff of the NCLC as well as using their clout to pass legislation. Two thirds of the members of the committee were from the North and Midwest and one-third from the South. The committee appointed Samuel McCune Lindsay, of the University of Pennsylvania, as its first general secretary with Alexander Jeffrey McKelway, a Southerner, and Owen Lovejoy, a Northerner, as assistant secretaries. Florence Kelley prided her National Consumers League as "a sort of great grandmother of the NCLC" to take up the fight to improve conditions for the "young clerks, cash boys, cash girls, bundle girls, delivery boys, messenger boys," and the masses of other children put to labor.

Sensitive to criticism of the South, Edgar Murphy and his followers refused to support the enactment of federal child labor laws because "conditions of industry vary so greatly and so decisively from state to state." Differences between the delegates of the South and the North came to a head in 1906 when Senator Alfred Beveridge of Indiana sought out the NCLC to support his federal bill to ban the interstate shipment of goods by companies employing the labor of children under fourteen years of age. When the majority of the NCLC voted to back the senator and his bill, Edgar Murphy objected.

On January 13, Murphy detailed his opposition to the Beveridge bill in a letter to the *Advertiser* of Montgomery and two months later in the *Evening Post* in New York City. For good measure he published his argument in pamphlet form. He acknowledged that the nation had a responsibility to care for its citizens, especially the defenseless, such as working children. However, it would be "a day of peril for the Nation when we must depend upon the federal congress to rush to the correction of every evil and support every virtue." Murphy argued that the individual states were best able to make their own laws, and more wisely and efficiently employ resources to combat problems. The Beveridge bill would extend federal authority. "I have opposed," wrote Murphy, "such exercise of federal power." The Reverend Edgar Murphy with his fellow Southern members resigned from the NCLC and campaigned to defeat the bill.[3] Despite Murphy's claim that the states could act more effectively, his Alabama for years lagged far behind. On August 9, 1907, the Alabama legislature voted that no child under 12 years be permitted to work in a mill, mine or other manufacturing establishment. Two years later the legislature raised the bar to 14 years, allowing children to work no more than 60 hours per week.

The Beveridge Child Labor Bill (S 6562) had only lukewarm support from the trade unions and President Theodore Roosevelt. The leaders of the child labor reform movement were also divided. Business leaders heavily opposed the bill, which was debated in the United States Senate on January 23, 28 and 29, 1907, only to go down to defeat. As compensation to Beveridge, the Congress voted funds for a federal study of child labor in America.

The National Child Labor Committee conducted studies across the nation to expose child labor in the mines, mills, fields and factories as well as children on the streets selling fruit, newspapers, flowers and baskets. The committee held annual conferences highlighting the harm done to children by work and the advantages from staying longer in school. These reports were meant to shock and were regularly reported by the press. The NCLC set out to influence politicians to see child labor as an evil to be outlawed and replaced by compulsory education, at least to age sixteen years.

In their 1907 booklet on *Child Labor Legislation*, Florence Kelley and Josephine Goldmark were critical of "the lack of protection for working children in the United States," leaving many thousands of "little boys and girls" laboring at night in the mines and mills. The authors called for laws "to exclude from interstate commerce all products of mines and factories which employ children under the age of fourteen years" and to protect children from night work, "the greatest menace to children." With 578,000 children aged ten to fourteen illiterate, Kelley and Goldmark called for compulsory school attendance until age sixteen.[4]

On November 14, 1907, Florence and Josephine traveled to Boston to ask Louis D. Brandeis, another of Josephine's prominent brothers-in-law, to defend the state of Oregon's maximum ten-hour a day work law in the case of *Muller v. Oregon*, Brandeis agreed to represent the state. Josephine Goldmark completed a lengthy brief to show that women, especially of childbearing age, were harmed by long hours of work. Louis Brandeis, a future Supreme Court justice, won his case (*Muller v. Oregon*, 208 U.S. 412, 1908). This was the first time that social science was used as law before the Supreme Court. The "Brandeis Brief" became a model for many future Supreme Court presentations.

A forceful and passionate speaker, Florence Kelley came year after year to the annual conventions of the National Child Labor Committee to beat the drum of reform and to impose her views. Her experience in Illinois convinced her that progress on the local level could be undone by political change. Federal child labor legislation — one set of laws for the entire country — was the goal, rather than piecemeal state action. "Never again can the problem of working children in the Republic be regarded as merely a local one," she stressed on December 8, 1905, at the 2nd annual conference. Child labor leads to illiterate children and criminality. Philanthropy is not the answer: "a feeble volunteer society to collect a few hundred dollars, here and there" is no substitute for federal action to respect the rights of children. At the 4th conference (Atlanta, 1908) Kelley spoke about the "Responsibility of the Consumer" to refuse "outright to buy papers from little newsboys" or to accept messages from little messenger boys or to shop at stores employing "undersized girls." These children, she said, should be in school.

In 1911, at the 7th NCLC conference, held in Birmingham, Alabama, Florence Kelley asked, "What Should we Sacrifice to Uniformity?" by allowing each state to promulgate its own laws. Rather, there should be nationwide standards of no night work for children, an eight-hour work day, no employment of children on the streets, no work for children under fourteen years, and even "banishing children from the stage." In 1915, at the 11th conference, she spoke on the "Responsibility of the Federal Government." "It is exceedingly difficult to get a law enforced" at the state level, she complained. Corruption, inertia, local magistrates and local juries all conspire to prevent progress: "We shall never get laws — state child labor laws — enforced so long as we rely on local jurors." Her solution was the "speedy passage of the Federal law to take out of interstate commerce those goods which implicate the employment of children under 14 or older children at night, or more than 8 hours, or in dangerous occupations.... Uncle Sam comes down with a very heavy hand in perjury."

Following the assertive position of Florence Kelley, in 1911 NCLC crafted the Uniform Child Labor Law for approval by the states and engineered a bill before Congress to prohibit the interstate transportation of goods manufactured by the labor of children under the age of fourteen. The NCLC believed that any employment under age sixteen was "wasted time." Florence Kelley was no longer satisfied with banning children below fourteen years and now insisted that children stay in school full-time until age sixteen. In 1918 she dismissed "the agitation for letting children between 14 and 16 working half-time — half-time in school and half-time in industry." She was determined to move the United States from unfettered capitalism where people "find their own level" to a society that cares for and protects its people. To achieve children's rights she was willing, even eager, to use a full range of state and federal laws, factory inspectors, health inspectors, truant officers, a national birthdates register, and other means to ensure that children remain in school and prevent them from working before age sixteen. If children are left destitute, they should not have to go to work, as it is the government's responsibility to provide for them.

Felix Adler remained chairman of the board of the NCLC until 1921, when he was replaced by David Franklin Houston, an academic, who served from 1913 to 1920 as the United States secretary of agriculture and briefly as U.S. secretary of the treasury. Writing in 1922 in the magazine *Current History*, Owen R. Lovejoy, general secretary of the NCLC, bemoaned the decision of the United States Supreme Court on May 15 that the child labor law passed by Congress was invalid as an "encroachment on States rights." Lovejoy reported that there was still no federal protection for working children in agriculture, tenement work, street trades, restaurants, hotels, movie houses or in domestic service. There were still "countless thousands of children who do work regularly." These children were at serious risk. "Illiteracy," he declared, "is one of the most widely felt effects of child labor." In the year 1919 alone, "some 15,000 children were killed in the United States, and the greatest proportion of these accidents occurred to children while engaged in some occupation." Child labor led to juvenile delinquency and adult crime. Lovejoy gave the impression that child labor was the root cause of social disruption. Only by its abolition, replaced by education, could America's children grow up healthy in mind and body.

In 1926, Owen Lovejoy retired as general secretary of the NCLC and was replaced by his assistant, Wiley Swift. It was a low time for the committee, with little to show for its efforts. The National Association of Manufacturers had come up with a plan to put to work children age 14 to 16 years who did not seem to benefit from their schooling. Eager for some success, Swift was willing to work with the NAM by compromising on the NCLC rule to prohibit all children working before reaching 16 years. Florence Kelley, in particular, saw this as a sell-out to the manufacturers and protested strenuously, forcing Swift to back down. Swift resigned from the NCLC in 1930.

On December 16, 1929, the National Child Labor Committee celebrated its twenty-fifth birthday at Hotel Roosevelt, New York City. The principal speaker was Franklin D. Roosevelt, then governor of New York, who spoke on "The Function of Government in Child Protection." Roosevelt insisted that the Empire State would continue to protect its children despite threats from industry that the high cost would compel them to move where labor costs were lower.

The rising star in the next generation of administrators at the NCLC was Gertrude Folks Zimand. Her father, Homer Folks, was a graduate of Harvard, who served as New York City's commissioner of public charities and was among the founders of the NCLC. After graduating from Vassar College in 1916, Gertrude joined the NCLC as a field worker. She served as editor of *American Child,* the agency's magazine. She rose quickly through the ranks and was general secretary from 1943 until 1955. Gertrude Zimand recorded the decline in child labor in America. In 1910 one child in twelve under the age of 14 years was employed, in 1930 only one in eighty. Among children aged 14 or 15, one-third were employed in 1910 but only one in ten in 1930. In the age group of 16 and 17 years more than half were employed in 1910 but one in three twenty years later. In the period between the two great wars children were staying longer in school. With labor shortages during World War II, many children quit school early. An American middle class was expanding as people moved from the rural South to the industrialized North, and took up managerial positions. Minority populations had not yet found a place in the new prosperity. Zimand shifted the focus of NCLC to find careers for the poor and minority city youngsters.[5]

U.S. Department of Labor, Children's Bureau

The idea of a federal agency to take care of the interests of children came to Lillian Wald and Florence Kelley while having breakfast. The two women were troubled by the high death rate among children in the summertime. Lillian observed: "I wish there was some agency that would tell us what can be done about these problems." They turned to the daily newspapers and read a report that the secretary of agriculture that day was traveling to the South to examine the damage done to the crops by the boll weevil. This news inspired an idea. "If the Government can have a department to take such an interest in what is happening to the Nation's cotton crop," exclaimed Lillian Wald to her friend, "why can't it have a bureau to look after the Nation's crop of children?" In 1903, President Theodore Roosevelt heard about the idea and thought it "bully," inviting Wald to "come on down and tell me about it." Using the offices of the NCL and the NCLC, Kelley and Wald worked tirelessly to gain the support of women's groups, the clergy and the press. In January 1909, Lillian Wald appeared before the House committee on expenditure of the Department of the Interior. Her vision was to create "a clearing house, a source of information and reliable education on all matters pertaining to the welfare of children and child life." After a nine-year struggle the Children's Bureau was finally established during the administration of President William Howard Taft on April 9, 1912, by act of Congress, with a first appropriation of $25,640. The act directed the bureau "to investigate and report upon all matters pertaining to the welfare of children and child life among all classes of our people." President Taft said at the time: "We have the power to spend the money on a Bureau of Research to tell us how we may develop good men and women." Taft appointed Julia Clifford Lathrop (1858–1932) as the director, making her the first woman ever to head a federal bureau.

Child labor was but one of several issues on Lathrop's list of concerns. In 1912, the United States had an infant mortality rate of 12 percent. Malnutrition, infectious diseases, disrupted families, truancy, delinquency, juvenile crime and juvenile courts were among the other issues on her agenda. During her tenure as head of the Children's Bureau, Lathrop was given the responsibility to administer the Child Labor Law of 1916. This law specified that "no child under 16 shall be allowed to fall in the great field of industrial life." However, with parental permission and proof of age, a child 14 to 16 could be issued a certificate of employment. This loophole led to widespread cheating, making it difficult to abolish child labor. Using the reports of her bureau, Lathrop showed the harm done by putting young children to work.

Julia Lathrop and her Children's Bureau launched an ambitious Children's Year, from April 1918 to April 1919, with the slogan "Save 100,000 Babies." The bureau encouraged the states to set up children's departments to ensure that newborns were properly fed and received health care. Lathrop stressed that childhood was for schooling, recreation and play. She linked the end of the World War with child labor. It was the patriotic duty of working children to give up their jobs to make room for the returning soldiers. A popular poster of the Children's Bureau read: "Children Back to School Means Soldiers Back to Jobs."

In its ninth report (1921) the bureau outlined the unhealthy conditions in the sugar

The health of the child is the power of the nation

APRIL 1918 Children's Year APRIL 1919
UNITED STATES CHILDREN'S BUREAU AND WOMAN'S COMMITTEE OF THE COUNCIL OF NATIONAL DEFENSE

U.S. Children's Bureau poster celebrating Children's Year, April 1918 to April 1919. Children were encouraged to have exercise and fun. Jobs should go to the returning servicemen, and children should stay in school.

beet farms of Michigan and Colorado. Early in the spring, immigrant families from the surrounding towns or as far away as Chicago and Detroit, lured by the promise of good wages, were recruited as contract laborers to tend and harvest the beets. "Nowhere in agriculture are children exploited more than in the beet fields of Colorado, Michigan and Nebraska." The families were housed in caravans or wooden shacks on the farms. Children as young as six years worked "beside their mothers and older siblings," who supervised them. In one region the Children's Bureau identified 861 children under the age of fourteen, with 215 of these ten or younger. The children and their families started work in March, tending to the young plants. Then came the heavy work of weed control. When the beets, each weighing five to ten pounds, were ripe, the small children pulled them out of the ground, cut off the tops with a sharp knife and threw the beets into piles. The children worked long hours until the end of the harvest, missing school for months on end. With both parents and all the children working together, a family could earn $800, less $200 for food, for six months' contract work on the sugar beet fields. These contract families returned to the fields year after year. During the cold months they would seek work in the cities. With luck, they could even save a little money.[6]

In Hill County, Texas, the center of the cotton-growing district, "Practically every child 10 years of age or over—girls and boys—had worked in the fields" for an average of twelve hours a day. The children did not go to school. "Many of these children will, in mature life, be handicapped by illiteracy." The Children's Bureau reports received nationwide attention and helped improve conditions, including schooling, for the working children.

Julia Lathrop was a diligent public servant. According to Jane Addams, Lathrop "usually was found defending the actions of the courts, insisting that we must proceed by precedent broadening into precedent." As chief of the Children's Bureau she accepted the decision of the Supreme Court that the child labor law was unconstitutional. In 1917, she was elected president of the National Council of Social Work. In 1921, aged sixty-three years, she retired as chief of the Children's Bureau. President Calvin Coolidge appointed her to a federal commission looking into the conditions at Ellis Island. She served as president of the Illinois League of Women Voters. The *Rockford Register-Republic* wrote that she "was born with the gift of human sympathy" and devoted her life "especially for the care of the insane, for the health and happiness of children, for the guidance and reform of youthful offenders." Julia Lathrop remained active to the end of her days, dying in her hometown of Rockford, Illinois, on April 15, 1932.

Over the years, the Children's Bureau took on additional duties. In 1921 the Children's Bureau administered the Maternity and Infancy Act to improve health services to infants and mothers. With the passage of the Social Security Act in 1935, the Children's Bureau was responsible for awarding grants to the states for maternal and child health, child welfare and aid to handicapped children. The bureau expanded into adoptions, recreation for children, the control of rickets, and children born out of wedlock and into poverty. During the Great Depression, the Children's Bureau organized the school lunch programs.

During the 1920s, the Children's Bureau was at the center of the struggle to pass the child-labor amendment to the Constitution. Child labor declined in the prosperous 1920s, as adult workers took the place of children. In 1924, Grace Abbott, the new chief of the Children's Bureau, told a congressional hearing that "child labor and poverty are inevitably bound together."

During the Great Depression, children were again hired for the cheapness of their labor. Allentown, Pennsylvania, became an important industrial city with a population close to 100,000 people. In 1929, the city supported 283 manufacturing plants, giving employment to 18,000 workers. Within three years half the jobs were lost and those who still worked saw their wages cut by 75 percent. The textile factories in the city kept going by paying child workers a pittance of less than $1 a week. In April 1933, the children went on strike. On April 17 a delegation of four hundred "baby shirt-worker strikers," aged fourteen to sixteen, traveled to Harrisburg to call on the governor, Gifford Pinchot, to tell him about their terrible condition of work. The government responded by issuing fewer child-work permits.

During World War II, the Children's Bureau saw a return of child labor, with children filling the jobs of men off to fight the war. Boys and girls, many as young as fourteen years, moved away from home to take jobs, some of which were hazardous. Children were again exploited, working long hours for little pay. The bureau fought efforts to relax child-labor laws. In January 1943 the Children's Bureau, along with the War Manpower Commission, issued a "Statement of Policy on the Employment of Youth under 18 Years of Age," declaring that the young could best serve the nation by staying in school, and if needed, accept work during vacations. Despite these statements children as young as fourteen continued to fill jobs. A study done in 1945 in New York State found that two out of five school children over fourteen years of age had part time employment. Many worked thirty or more hours a week as sale clerks, delivery boys, in restaurants and in manufacturing. Some held two jobs, working into the night and on weekends. Their schoolwork suffered from the heavy workload. Despite long hours these children were poorly paid, averaging $10 a week.[7]

In 1968, the Children's Bureau became part of the Social and Rehabilitation Services. Two years later, the bureau was integrated into the Office of Child Development, and later it was submerged into the Administration for Children and Families of the Department of Health and Human Services.

16

Lewis Wickes Hine,
Photographer Extraordinaire

Lewis Wickes Hine showed the laboring child to the American public. He was born in Oshkosh, Wisconsin, in 1874. After his father died, Lewis took a job as a laborer in a furniture factory, working thirteen hours a day, earning barely $4 a week. His passion was education, and he attended the State Normal School before taking up the study of sociology at the University of Chicago. In 1901, Hine moved to New York to teach at Felix Adler's Ethical Culture School. While employed at the school, Hine became interested in photography, visiting nearby Ellis Island to take pictures of the immigrants. In 1908, he was hired by the NCLC to tour the mills, mines, tenements of the nation, documenting the use and abuse of children as laborers. For ten years, using a 5- by 7-inch box camera that made glass-plate negatives, with a magnesium flash for night or indoor photography, Hine criss-crossed the country taking pictures of children working in mills, mines, canneries, tenements, and on the streets as delivery boys, newsboys, shoeshine boys or flower sellers. He developed over 5,000 photographs. Hine noted the location of the pictures and recorded the children's names, ages and occupations. He was a small, meek-looking man who gained access to mines and factories, lugging his heavy equipment, to take his pictures. Posing sometimes as a Bible salesman or an insurance agent, he put himself at risk when the management realized what he was up to. The pictures were taken from Maine to the Gulf States and from New York to California. The children, with faces and clothing covered with dirt or lint, mostly looked directly at the camera, rarely with a smile on their young faces. His poignant pictures remain a haunting testimony to the once nationwide acceptance of child labor.

Lewis Hine also wrote essays showing empathy and understanding of the children he observed. In February 1911 he wrote: "I have witnessed many varieties of child labor horrors from Maine to Texas, but the climax ... regarding the exploitation of children has been among the oyster-shuckers and shrimp-pickers" of the Gulf States canneries. Hundreds of women with their young children in tow arrive early each morning to shuck oysters and clean shrimp. At one canning factory Hine "found boys and girls whom I judge to be from three to eleven years of age." He was "amazed and horrified to see how many minutes and hours of actual work the little tots do put in.... The earnings of the little ones are not usually over five cents a day, but ... they are not only being kept out of mischief but are getting their early training." Children aged eleven or twelve, with more skills, were earning a $1 a day. "It is not an uncommon sight to find children with swollen or bleeding fingers, but still keeping bravely at it."[1]

In 1911 and 1912 Lewis Hine gained access to tenement houses in New York and other cities seeing children and their parents at work in the kitchen, parlor or bedrooms. The children worked long hours after school; others did not go to school at all. Many of these photographs were published in 1912. Hine added somber and pithy captions to his photographs. Fourteen-year-old Annie told Hine that she could not go to school because she did not have shoes. The children, "under the direction of their parents," worked in dirty rooms with poor light and little heat. Hine worried that the work and conditions would undermine their health and their morals. He found one family making dresses. "The older boy, aged 12, operates the machine ... and helps the little ones, 5 and 7, break the threads; the family earning 25 cents for a dozen dresses." In another home, ten-year-old Rosie is busy making dresses but she would rather "read library books." Her father "earns $9 a week and Rosie must help in supporting the family of six." Rosie earns 4 cents for sewing thirty-six buttons. "That is more tangible than fairy tales." In another home a mother and her seven-year-old daughter are busy embroidering skirts, earning together $2 a week. "See how smart she is," says the mother, "I show her how and right away she makes them," Katie, age thirteen, and her sister, Angelina, aged eleven, "are making cuffs of Irish lace.... You go blind for thirty or forty cents a day." Sitting together in a grubby basement apartment is a family opening nuts, using dirty jack-knives. The children have runny noses, the mother "has a cold and her much-used handkerchief reposes comfortably on the table." Four-year old Johnny, five-year-old May and eight-year-old Mabel help their parents crack open the shells to remove the nuts. The children go to the factory to pick up the 50–to 100-pound bags of nuts to crack open. The children work to please their parents and to compete with each other. Despite laws forbidding the practice the inspectors turn a blind eye. The parents have no one to mind the children at home and, for a great want of money, put their own children to work at the earliest possible age for the extra money.[2]

In Oklahoma in 1918, Lewis Hine found "a very complacent attitude toward child labor ... and a general feeling that 'we haven't any of it here.'" A new state with little industry, Hine still found that "in street trades and rural work a large number of children are employed.... Boys begin selling papers at four and five years of age, helping their older brothers.... Many of these children rise early in the morning as some of the papers are on the streets by 6 A.M." The two leading newspapers in Oklahoma City estimated that 265 boys from six to fifteen were in their service, of whom sixty-three were from six to ten years of age. Small children could be seen selling newspapers even in smaller Oklahoma towns and cities. Boys also delivered groceries and packages.[3]

Lewis Hine, as a loyal member of the NCLC staff, attempted to debunk the common belief that the profitability of industry depended on the cheap labor of children. Based on his visits to mines and factories, Hine was convinced that child labor did not come cheap. Child workers were prone to accidents and sickness, and more likely than adults to break machinery. Early work left the children ill educated and ill prepared for life. The low wages of children forced down the wages of adults. More telling, Hines felt, was the moral cost — the loss of innocence and hope.

> The street child seems so well able to take care of himself that sympathy is abundant for the little newsie who seems to need our patronage, and in our superficial way, we drop a nickel in his hand and hurry on; not realizing that his bundle of newspapers is an open sesame to all kinds of baneful influences, which train him in the ways of the world. He knows salon life, he gambles,

he wastes his money, he becomes acquainted with the underworld. The messenger boy carries notes between a prostitute in jail and a man in the red light district. He knows the whole correspondence, and ere long his familiarity with vice leads to crime. Whatever industry saves by child labor, society pays over and over.[4]

Hine analyzed the 1910 United States census regarding the employment of young children. There were 673,057 children aged ten to thirteen years working on their parents' farms compared with 121,758 working as hired hands on farms owned by others. In the fifteen- and sixteen-year age group, 484,407 worked on the family farms and 135,437 as hired help. Of the total 1,417,659 children sixteen years and younger working on farms, 18.1 percent were hired help. Alabama, Arkansas, Louisiana, Mississippi, North and South Carolina, Texas and Tennessee had the largest numbers of children working on farms.

During his photographic tour of California in 1915 Hine noted that the ills of the East and South had found their way across to the West. "I found children from 5 years of age upward selling newspapers in Sacramento, Los Angeles, San Diego and San Francisco.... The problem of street trades is just as important as factory work." As elsewhere in the United States, "a large part of the illicit traffic in drugs is done by messenger boys."[5]

After 1918, with his salary at the NCLC cut, Hine promoted himself as a freelance photographer, finding work for the American Red Cross, taking pictures of the war in Europe. In 1930, he was hired to photograph the construction of New York's Empire State Building, then the world's tallest. Unlike his child labor pictures, those of the construction of the Empire State Building show the dignity of labor. He photographed men high above the ground assembling the steel framework. One picture shows eleven men casually eating their lunch and reading the newspapers while sitting on the beam supported by steel ropes; another shows a workman gripping tightly to a rope as it swings a beam into place, a thousand or so feet off the ground. The adventurous photographer faced the same risks as the intrepid workmen. In 1932 he took the pictures of the raising of the mast of the Empire State Building, 1,454 feet above ground level.

The Great Depression was hard on Lewis Hine. He could not find employment in photography and his work was forgotten. Like so many others of those times, he lost his home and lived off welfare. Some years after his death in 1940, his son offered the Hine collection of photographs — including his child labor pictures — to the Museum of Modern Art, but the collection was not accepted. The Lewis Wickes Hine Collection, a national treasure, is now at the Library of Congress, Washington, D.C.

17

The Legal Battle

Intense labor, beginning too early in life, continued too long every day, stunting the growth of the mind, leaving no time for healthful exercise, no time for intellectual culture must impair those high qualities that have made our country great. Your overworked boys will become a feeble and ignoble race of men, the parents of a more feeble progeny, nor will it be long before the deterioration of the laborer will injuriously affect those very interests to which his physical and moral interests had been sacrificed.

— Lord Thomas Babington Macaulay,
House of Commons, May 22, 1846

Massachusetts and Connecticut led the way in the mid-nineteenth century seeking to curtail the employment of underage children. At first the barrier was set low with children under twelve barred from work. Later the age of entry into work was increased to fourteen or even sixteen years. Laws were enacted to prevent children from working more than twelve hours a day, then ten and then eight. Night work was prohibited. Policing these laws was problematic as many children, especially those born abroad, did not have birth certificates, and parents would lie about the age of their children. Various states hired factory inspectors to check for underage workers. Pressure was put on schools to ensure that children leaving early and applying for work certificates were at least able to read and write. Florence Kelley and Julia Lathrop were frustrated by the poor compliance with the laws, allowing many unlettered children to leave school at an early age and enter the labor force.

At the start of the twentieth century, the forces in the United States for and against child labor were equally balanced. Manufacturers and their supporters in state government argued that the children of the poor and the working classes would be left idle and get up to mischief unless they were employed. Work taught character and responsibility. Child labor, they argued, helped support the family while lowering the price of goods and keeping companies in business. Mostly self-made men themselves, the leading manufacturers argued that work motivated children to success and entrepreneurship. The reformers, in contrast, considered childhood a period set aside for play and education, for children to learn to be productive and thoughtful citizens and to take part in the process of democracy. Education is uplifting while work dulls the mind and ruins the body, leaving these children without prospects. Early employment, the reformers believed, was an evil, a cancer on society. Socialists like Florence Kelley went further, arguing that child labor was the product of capitalistic monopoly, pulling down all wages and pushing adults out of work.

Each side marshaled its arguments through lobbying, influence peddling and studies to convince the public and persuade state and federal legislatures to support its view.

In Favor of Child Labor

Daniel Augustus Tompkins was a product of the Old South. He was born in 1851 in a plantation in Edgefield County, South Carolina. Too young and too frail for the Confederate Army, he attended the local academy before entering the University of South Carolina in 1867. After two years he traveled north to Troy, New York, to study civil engineering at the Rensselaer Institute. Early in his work career he traveled to Germany where he studied its textile industry that was fast surpassing Great Britain's. He was especially impressed by the German apprenticeship system and its textile schools to prepare the young for work in the mills. Florence Kelley was studying in Europe at the same time as Tompkins. The two Americans drew diametrically opposite conclusions about the role of children in the labor force.

Returning to the United States he founded D.A. Tompkins & Company, a construction company, which over the years built several hundred textile mills, playing a pivotal role in the industrial expansion of the New South. Tompkins owned three textile mills as well as several influential newspapers. In 1899, President William McKinley appointed Tompkins to the United States Industrial Commission. He joined the National Association of Manufacturers (NAM) and became its spokesman on issues regarding child labor. Just as Germany was supplanting Britain, as Tompkins correctly foresaw, the South would soon supplant New England in textile manufacture.

Founded in 1895, NAM responded vigorously to the accusation that manufacturers were exploiting children as cheap labor. In a 1906 speech, the chairman of the association, guided by Daniel Tompkins, accused the trade unions of instigating a socialist plot. "Socialism is slavery and not freedom," he said. Labor unionism "presents a peril which the National Association of Manufacturers is combating." The unions were against the apprenticeship system. "Every year in the United States the entire lives of hundreds of thousands of intelligent, ambitious boys is wrecked by the criminal stupidity of the labor unions." The vast majority of boys came from poor families and could not afford a college education. Instead "they look to apprenticeships in the trades as their principal chance of making a livelihood." By seeking to ban child labor, the union members were simply protecting their own jobs. "This labor union plot against the advancement and the happiness of the American boy ... is also a plot against industrial expansion and prosperity of the country." Since most children, boys and girls, were destined for factory work, a ban of child labor would deprive children of the chance to develop "good industrial habits."[1]

Daniel Tompkins "believed thoroughly in the early training of children for work and by means of actual work," using every occasion, in speeches and in the press, to make the case for early training. His own nephew Sterling Graydon started work in the cotton mill "at an early age," beginning at the bottom as an apprentice to learn all aspects of work in the mill. Sterling attended the state textile school and went on to serve as president of the Atherton Mills.

Addressing the Civic Federation in New York in December 1905, Tompkins laid out his views on child labor. He was willing to accept age fifteen as the starting age, banning night work and imposing a minimum wage, but all this should be done gradually, not "arbitrarily and not at once." He recommended to America the educational system he had observed in Germany where children are evaluated at age ten "to decide what [their] abilities and interests are." Those who are academically bright should be encouraged to receive a classical education. But, "those who will be engaged in industrial pursuits" should start their apprenticeship and manual training "not from 12 years of age, or 14, or 15 but from 10."[2]

In the apprenticeship plan Tompkins suggested, the child suited for manual work should begin his work in the mills at age 11, with three months in the mill and six months at school. The youngster should start his apprenticeship doing "light work," fetching and carrying for the trained workers. The older the child is, the more work he does and the less schooling he needs. By age 15, the child should do ten months working in the mill and two months at school.

Daniel Augustus Tompkins died in 1914 but others in the NAM, especially its chief counsel and lobbyist, James A. Emery, used their influence in state and federal government to block child labor legislation and the progress of the child labor amendment. In 1911, Emery co-authored a book on *Accident Prevention and Relief* to set nationwide standards for the NAM. Emery appeared frequently at government hearings to oppose "social legislation [that] involves the regulation of hours, wages and working conditions." Such legislation, he contended, is unconstitutional as it interferes with the "freedom of contract of an individual" without government restrictions. In 1924, Amery attacked the proposed Child Labor Amendment as "both socialistic and communistic." Child labor was not a federal affair. He made it known that "on the day Calvin Coolidge became President of the United States his 14-year-old son received $3.50 a week for his labor in a neighbor's tobacco field." In 1924, the Massachusetts referendum on the child labor amendment went down to a 3 to 1 defeat. The NAM used its rich resources to rally the Southern states also to oppose the amendment.

In 1926, the NAM presented its National Educational and Employment Program proposing a 48-hour workweek, no night work and offering age fourteen as the cut-off age for employment. These terms were not acceptable to Florence Kelley who insisted on age sixteen as the age to start work. The NAM failed to support any legislation to advance its program. James Emery continued for many years as principal lobbyist for the NAM. In 1937, he addressed the joint congressional hearings to block the proposed Fair Labor Standards Act.[3]

Stephen A. Knight offered his rags-to-riches story as proof that early labor is good. In 1836, aged six years, he began work as a bobbin boy in a cotton mill in the town of Coventry, Rhode Island. He earned forty-two cents a week, working fourteen hours a day, and six days a week. "Thus my pay," he wrote, "was at the rate of half a cent per hour." In the winter he started work in the dark at 5 o'clock in the morning and returned home, also in the dark, at 8 o'clock in the evening. 'There was little time for schooling and opportunities for education and recreation were very limited for all. My own first regular attendance at school was when I was about twenty years old."

Despite difficulties he remained for seventy years in the textile business, building B.B & R Knight, a textile conglomerate with eleven mills in Rhode Island. "I have seen," he wrote in 1906, "the hours of work reduced by 30 percent, wages increased some 200 percent, such child labor as was the unquestioned custom in those days (is now) prohibited by law and the increase for education and social advantage that we little dreamed of."[4]

The Committee on Industrial Education of the NAM regarded children going to work at age fourteen as the start of their apprenticeship. Almost all the children who entered the industries began at age 14, the committee reported in 1911. Fourteen years is the age when "the working people of this country" took their children out of school, "knowing from experience that if they stay in school until 16 they will have passed the psychological time when industry beckons." In Germany "the great body of her children shall enter the industries at 14" to start apprenticeships. Similarly, American children of fourteen "are grown up" and ready for work. American industry as a whole should follow the examples of General Electric, International Harvester and the Baldwin Locomotive Works, to establish two-year apprenticeships to prepare boys for worthwhile careers in industry.[5]

One of the investigators hired in 1907 by the Department of Commerce and Labor to investigate the conditions of child workers was Thomas Robinson Dawley, Jr., who was assigned to the Southern states. Born in 1862 in Connecticut, Dawley traveled to Central America and Cuba recording current and historical events. He wrote magazine articles about the war in Cuba in 1900, the history of coffee growing, archeology of Mexico and other exotic topics. For two years as a special investigator of the Bureau of Labor he traveled to the mountain farm districts of the South where he found the people "densely ignorant." He followed these farming families to their new homes and jobs at the cotton mills and found them much improved and able to take good advantage of their relative prosperity. Dawley sent his report to the Department of Commerce and Labor concluding that "child labor as he had seen it practiced, far from being an abomination, was a direct benefit to the little employees." Allegations that cotton mill owners and managers "have formed a trust for the oppression of their people" was not true. Rather, "The average condition of the cotton mill workers in the South is better than the average condition of the workers on the farms ... and that the cotton mill workers are living in a far better circumstance than before they went into the mills." Dawley asserted that because his findings contradicted the declared views of the Department of Commerce and Labor he was dismissed and his findings suppressed.[6]

In 1912, Dawley published *The Child That Toileth Not: The Story of a Government Investigation That Was Suppressed*. He claimed to have written a factual, even scientific account of what he had seen on the mountain farms and in the cotton mills. Rather than publishing the truth, Dawley "had seen the reports of good men and women suppressed, side-tracked or re-written to meet the requirements of the special interests that more or less controlled the administration of the Bureau of Labor under its regime." He believed that "the public has been fairly stuffed with lies respecting the employment of children." On the farms the poor children lived in tumbledown shacks, were fed a miserable diet of corn and pig fat, and walked about half-starved and dressed in filthy rags. By contrast, the cottages of the textile mills were built well, food was good, and the families prospered. The children who moved from farm to village "tasted the benefits accrued from light work in the cotton mill." For these impoverished Southern farm children the cotton mills were "the only means open to them for improving this condition." Paranoid or sane, Dawley accused the government of wasting money, and that Senator Beveridge, the National Child Labor Committee, the Bureau of Labor, "holier-than-thou" editors, reformers, and the newspapers were components of a huge conspiracy to suppress the "truth" that "the condition of children who get jobs in the cotton mills of the South are improved thereby." Dawley was "determined not to be suppressed; I kept on with dog-like persistency, seeking funds here and there with which to make my revelations, finally selling my farm in Connecticut, in order to do so."[7]

After his battle against the Progressive establishment, Thomas R. Dawley returned to journalism and served on the editorial board of the *Providence Journal*. During World War I, Dawley was employed in the Federal Bureau of War Risk Insurance. Once again, Dawley took on a federal agency, accusing the bureau of gross inefficiency and waste. His charges were investigated, but again he was dismissed "because of utter unfitness." He bounced back in 1920 as the editor of *Passing Show*, a Washington, D.C., journal that published reviews of current events and uses articles "of news interest, also jokes, humorous verse, photographs, etc." He died in 1930, a misguided and maligned fighter to the end.

David Clark of the Southern Textile Association gave testimony in 1916 before the United States Commission on Industrial Relations to refute NCLC charges of illegal child labor. He denied that North Carolina cotton mills had a high rate of accidents. "Very few people are hurt in the cotton mills," he claimed, "and, the machinery in the departments where women and children work is entirely harmless, and except through extreme careless-ness, it is almost impossible for anyone to be injured."[8] Clark used the columns of his *Bulletin* to refute the NCLC and to oppose the child labor amendment to the Constitution proposed by Congress in 1924. Industry brought out its biggest guns to oppose the Keat-ing-Owen Child Labor Bill. "The Southern cotton mill harpies," commented *Pearson's* mag-azine, "that fatten their dividends on the bodies and souls of the little children that work for them are here again in strength to defeat the anti-child labor bill."[9]

Clark, editor of the *Southern Textile Bulletin* published in Charlotte, North Carolina, organized the Southern mill owners by hiring as their legal counsel William Walton Kitchin to argue against Bill H.R. 8234 which sought to prevent interstate commerce in the products of child labor. W.W. Kitchin (1868–1924) was born in North Carolina and passed the bar examination at the tender age of nineteen years. He served six terms in the United States House of Representatives before returning to his home state to serve as governor. In 1912 he ran unsuccessfully for the United States Senate and settled down to a law practice. Kitchin argued against the bill "on the grounds that the textile industry of the South is new, and cannot grow under such rigid restrictions; that it would be detrimental to poor parents to be deprived of the support of their children; that the law would require a re-organization of factories and added machinery." Turning folksy, Kitchin insisted that "an arbitrary age limit for children cannot be fixed by law, any more than you can tell when a pig becomes a hog."[10]

James A. Emery used the states rights argument when he testified that the NAM "is not opposed to child labor restrictions by the States but fears the extension of federal reg-ulation to other industrial conditions." Stiff opposition to the Keating-Owen bill also came from Ellison A. Smyth, the owner of several textile mills and the chairman of the Cotton Manufacturers Association of South Carolina. Greenville, South Carolina, was a mill town with its young people so eager to work that they added a few years to their age in order to get a job. "It is impossible," Smyth argued, "to properly enforce the child-labor law unless there is a birth-certificate law." The people he employed were "pure, unadulterated, Anglo-Saxon stock." He knew several boys who grew up to be superintendents, earning up to $5,000 a year. Preventing children under sixteen years from working could drive from the mills a number who are "the main supports of widowed mothers." Smyth denied that children were prone to accidents. Work was good for them, their families and the town. "There was no tendency," he insisted, "towards race deterioration," an oft-expressed notion of the time. The mill owners of the South were willing to accept fourteen years as the starting age for work but insisted that age sixteen was too high. On closer questioning, Smyth admitted that his mills employed hundreds of boys and girls age twelve to fourteen years.[11] The Keating-Owen Act, backed by the National Child Labor Committee, passed by a vote of 243 to 46, and was signed into law in 1916 by President Woodrow Wilson, only to be ruled two years later as unconstitutional by the Supreme Court of the United States.

The 1924 issue of *Manufacturers' Record* reminded readers that 850,000 of the soldiers in the Union Army during the Civil War were under age eighteen years: "If they were old enough to fight for their country, they ought to be old enough to regulate the matter of their own employment." Passage of the child labor amendment, warned the writer, combining the Puritan ethic with the Red scare, "would mean the destruction of manhood and womanhood through the destruction of the boys and girls of the country. This proposed amendment is fathered by Socialists, Communists and Bolshevists ... aimed to nationalize the children of the land and bring about in this country the exact conditions that prevail in Russia. If adopted, the amendment would be the greatest thing ever done in America in behalf of the activities of hell. It will make millions of young people under eighteen years of age idlers in brain and body, and thus make them the devil's best workshop."[12]

On April 26, 1924, the House of Representatives gave its support to an amendment of the federal Constitution to "limit, regulate, and prohibit the labor of persons under eighteen years of age." The Senate added its approval on June 2, 1924, submitting the bill to the individual states for ratification. The National Association of Manufacturers strongly opposed the child labor amendment to the constitution. Its principal lobbyist and legal counsel, James A. Emery, issued a statement that the proposed amendment was "both socialistic and communistic ... unjustified and unnecessary [and] subversive to the principles of American life as well as an unjustifiable invasion of States' rights."

The powerful NAM put pressure on the state legislatures across the nation. It established the National Committee for Rejection of the 20th Amendment, under the leadership of Millard D. Brown, president of the Continental Mills, a large textile company in Philadelphia. With such opposition, the battle against child labor lost steam; from 1924 to 1932, only six states ratified the child labor amendment, while thirty-two others voted against or chose to pass their own child labor laws. Mississippi senator Hubert D. Stephens viewed the amendment as "part of a hellish scheme laid in foreign countries to destroy the Government." Textile interests — North and South — joined the National Association of Manufacturers and the American Farm Bureau Federation to fight attempts to ban child labor. By 1932, the amendment was considered lost. Granting votes to women had a speedier passage into law. Proposed on June 4, 1919, the 19th amendment to the U.S. Constitution was quickly ratified by the majority of the states and became law on August 4, 1920.

History is filled with rags-to-riches stories, boys with little formal education but blessed with big ideas and the intelligence and perseverance to see them through. Born in 1813 in Blantyre, near Glasgow, David Livingstone started work at age ten in a cotton mill. He began at six o'clock in the morning and finished at eight o'clock at night, after which he attended the company school for two hours, and then went home to read until midnight. Livingstone remained in the mill for twelve years, working up to being a spinner. Showing extraordinary determination he left the mill in his twenties and moved to Glasgow to become a medical missionary. Livingstone's travels through the jungles of Africa, to discover the Victoria Falls, and seek the source of the Nile River, caught the imagination of the world.

Another Scot, William Carnegie, earned a decent living weaving damask linen. His wife, Margaret, wound the bobbins while he worked the hand-operated loom. Their town, Dunfermline, was famous in Scotland as a center of weaving and was "for a large part composed of men who were small manufacturers each owning his own loom or looms." The town lay on a hill three miles north of the Firth of Forth "overlooking the sea, with Edinburgh in sight to the south." The Carnegie family occupied a traditional weaver's cottage, where William kept his handlooms. Early in the nineteenth century the power machines of the British industrial revolution destroyed this pattern of life. "The change from handloom to steam-loom," remembered Andrew Carnegie in his autobiography written shortly before he died in 1919, "was disastrous to our family." Mother Margaret's efforts to keep the family afloat by mending shoes did not succeed and in 1848 the Carnegie family left Scotland to settle in the New World, choosing Allegheny City, Pennsylvania, where they had relatives. To pay for their passage the Carnegie family sold their possessions including the redundant looms, which "brought hardly anything," requiring them to borrow twenty pounds.

William Carnegie was forty-three, his wife, Margaret, thirty-three and son Andrew thirteen years of age when the family arrived in America. "The great question," Andrew recalled, "now was, what could be found for me to do. I had just completed my thirteenth year, and I fairly panted to get to work that I might help the family to start in the new land." William found work in a cotton factory and also for Andrew as a bobbin boy earning a dollar and twenty cents per week. Andrew recalled: "It was a hard life. In the winter, father and I had to rise and breakfast in the darkness, reach the factory before it was daylight, and, with a short interval for lunch, work till after dark." Young Andrew took no pleasure from the work but "the cloud had a silver lining, as it gave me the feeling that I was doing something for my world (and) I was a helper of the family, a breadwinner, and no longer a total charge upon my parents."

From bobbin boy in a textile mill, Andrew Carnegie found work at two dollars a week running the steam engine in a factory making bobbins. Next he took a job bathing the newly made spools in oil while suffering "the nausea produced by the smell of oil." The ever-ambitious youth was not ground down by the repetitive and foul-smelling work but found the time to study double-entry bookkeeping, to move from factory floor to the office. At age fifteen Andrew started work as a messenger boy in a telegraph office. While his father still labored in the mill, Andrew sensed that he now had his foot "upon the ladder and that I was bound to climb." The telegraph office was "an excellent school for a young man" and as a messenger boy Andrew met some of the leading men of Pittsburgh. Climb he did to own steel mills and become one of the richest men in America.

Philip Danforth Armor left home a mere youngster to trek across the continent to the gold fields of California. He earned his fortune as a Chicago meatpacker. So did Gustavus Swift who butchered meat on Cape Cod before making his way to Chicago as another of the great meat cutters. William L. Douglas was bound-out at age seven as a shoemaker and went on to own one of the nation's largest shoe companies and was elected governor of Massachusetts. George Eastman overcame the odds to grow rich on the Kodak camera. Henry Ford did not see the value in education and made his way to Detroit to work on power engines. Cyrus Hall McCormick overcame poverty to invent and market the mechanical reaper.

The Washburn brothers of the village of Livermore in Androscoggin County, Maine, rose to greatness despite the struggle against poverty after their father became bankrupt. As a boy of twelve, Elihu was sent to work as a farmhand. In adult life brothers Israel, Elihu and Cadwallader served in the United States Congress at the same time, while brother William was a member of the United States Senate. Israel was governor of Maine and Cadwallader governor of Wisconsin. Elihu was a close friend of Abraham Lincoln and Ulysses S. Grant and served as secretary of state and was ambassador to France from 1869 to 1877, serving in Paris during the Franco-German War and the insurrection of the Commune. Cadwallader founded the Washburn-Crosby Milling Company that became General Mills.

These true-life stories of children who rise up in life have been used by the proponents of early labor as the spur to ambition and success.

The Fight Against Child Labor

From her office at 108 East Twenty-Second Street, New York, Florence Kelley, executive secretary of the National Consumers League, continued the arduous task of assembling evidence to show how children and women were exploited, even abused, at work. Armed with a law degree from Northwestern University, Kelley was ready for the long struggle to persuade state and federal legislatures to ban outright the employment of children under the age of fourteen years and outlaw night work and long hours of work for children age fifteen and sixteen years. While a student in Switzerland, she viewed child labor from a Marxist perspective, to be eliminated by the revolutionary action of the workers' state. In Chicago she used the law to combat child labor. Now in New York, she skillfully wove socialism, women's suffrage and the rights of children into one great cause. In a 1905 speech before the National American Women Suffrage Association she criticized men voters and all-male legislatures for permitting child labor. "Until the mothers in the great industrial States are enfranchised," Kelley explained, "we shall none of us be able to free our consciences from participation in this great evil. We prefer our work done by men and women." Women's organizations should vociferously demand the vote and "enlist the workingmen voters, with us, in the task of freeing children from toil." Without the vote women were "almost powerless."[13]

The aim of the National Consumers League was to bring together people "who strive to do their buying in such ways as to further the welfare of those who make or distribute the things bought." The league urged its members "to demand the label" when buying clothing. Kelley and her staff awarded the coveted white label to those companies which did not employ child labor or sweatshop methods of production. Consumers League branches from New England to Wisconsin sought to influence legislators, the press and manufacturers to show that the abolition of child labor was "not detrimental to their business."

Borrowing from the ideas of Felix Adler, in 1905, Florence Kelley published *Some Ethical Gains Through Legislation*. Children by right should receive "fourteen free years for school and wholesome growth before children enter upon the life of steady work. There should be no reason for a child under fourteen to work; not even if he were an orphan, the child of disabled parents, the child of a single mother or even if his parents were poor."

Child labor stunts growth and leads to illiteracy, "degeneracy and delinquency." Child labor is due to "the greed of employers for cheap labor and it drags down the wages paid to adults." The withdrawal of the working child from competition with adult worker contributes to the adult's ability to fix his own terms for wages, enough to support his family.

If child labor is tolerated, Kelley writes, "the ethical standards of the community are bad." Who then is responsible to support a child and a family? Florence Kelley bluntly responds, "The responsibility is placed, where it belongs, upon the parents or upon the community." Child labor is not only a local issue but also should be addressed at the federal level with a single set of laws protecting all children across the land. The ideas in Kelley's book helped set the agenda for the United States Children's Bureau, established in 1912.[14]

In his fourth annual message to Congress, December 6, 1904, President Theodore Roosevelt called for a nationwide investigation of child labor. He repeated this request on December 3, 1906. "The horrors incident to the employment of young children in the factories or at work anywhere," he said to Congress, "are a blot to our civilization." Roosevelt noted that each state "must ultimately settle the question in its own way," but in such a manner to secure "unity of State action." If this failed, Roosevelt hinted at a federal response. In his message to the sixtieth Congress, December 3, 1907, Roosevelt was more explicit, describing child labor as an evil: "If the States will correct their evils, well and good, but the Nation must stand ready to aid them." His efforts to enact a federal child labor law were opposed by industry, the pro-business power brokers of his own party and by conservative Southern Democrats. In his March 25, 1908, message to Congress, President Roosevelt again demanded that "child labor should be prohibited throughout the nation," but he succeeded only in getting a child labor bill for the District of Columbia. In his autobiography, Roosevelt wrote:

> It is not always easy to avoid feeling very deep anger with the selfishness and short-sightedness shown both by representatives of certain employers' organizations and by certain great labor federations or unions. One such employers' association was called the National Association of Manufacturers. Extreme though the attacks sometimes made upon me by the extreme labor organizations were, they were not quite as extreme as the attacks made upon me by the head of the National Association of Manufacturers.... The opposition of the National Association of Manufacturers to every rational and moderate measure for benefitting workingmen, such as measures abolishing child labor or securing workmen's compensation, caused me real and grave concern.[15]

The first federal action against child labor came in January 1907, when the reformist Senator Albert J. Beveridge of Indiana addressed the United States Senate with a plea for support of his bill prohibiting interstate commerce of products made by children. Using the writings of John Spargo, Florence Kelley and the National Child Labor Committee, Beveridge outlined the horrendous conditions of work in the mills, mines and sweatshops, in which "child slaves" were crushed by the greed of the owners. A federal response was needed, he argued, because the states were too weak to enact their own child labor laws. Beveridge extended the argument against child labor by evoking the eugenics theories of his day. When working children "grow into manhood and womanhood, they become enemies of society," he thundered.

> I do not blame them. They know that they are not equal to their fellows in body, mind or soul; that their bodies are dwarfed, crooked and weak; their minds dull and clouded; their souls darkened

and vicious.... Physicians testify that nervous exhaustion, provided by child labor in factories, sweatshops and mines, not only stunts growth, but produces nervous irritation which calls for liquor and tobacco and causes still another vice worse than others.

The children ... become the parents of offspring inheriting their degeneracy, and these children in turn grow up to produce their own children still more degenerate. This ruin of American citizenship ... is too high a price to pay for making still richer a few men who are already too rich.[16]

Swayed by Roosevelt and by Beveridge's passionate plea, the House and Senate allocated $300,000 and authorized the Department of Commerce and Labor to investigate the industrial, social, moral, educational and physical conditions of women and child workers. The department hired a team of investigators resulting in an exhaustive nineteen volume-report.

In 1908, in his introduction to Mrs. John Van Vorst's book *The Cry of the Children: A Study of Child Labor*, Senator Albert Beveridge wrote:

The truth is that an army of American children greater in number than the army of soldiers with which either Russia or Japan flooded Manchuria are daily marched to the mills, factories, and sweatshops here in America and either killed outright or forever ruined. The combined losses of both Russia and Japan in the battles of the Russo-Japanese war were not so great as the number of American children who are worked to death or made degenerates every year in the mills, mines and sweatshops of our own country ... child-labor brings manhood wages down to the level of childhood wages.[17]

Beveridge was inspired during his visit to Russia in 1901 by meeting Leo Tolstoy. He railed against the "legal jugglers" who stood in the way of "every reform that looks to the betterment and upliftment of the American people." Beveridge lost his senate seat in 1911 and, despite several attempts, was not elected again to high public office. Beveridge won the Pulitzer Prize for his scholarly four-volume *The Life of John Marshall*. At his death in 1927, he left unfinished his two-volume account of the life of Abraham Lincoln.

Florence Kelley measured the progress and setbacks in efforts to prevent young children from leaving school to go to work. Schooling until age sixteen and beyond ensured that children would be able to read or write, and also capable of abstract and critical thought, necessary to be responsible consumers and responsible citizens in a democracy. Progressive organizations like the National Child Labor Committee and the National Consumers' League, Kelley urged, should strive to prevent children dropping out of school to work in dead-end jobs such as picking cotton, tobacco, sugar beets or fruit, working in the mines, the cotton mills, glassworks or sweatshops.

Josephine Clare Goldmark (1877–1950) was born in Brooklyn, New York, the youngest of the ten children of the Jewish-Austrian family. Her father died when she was only four years old and she was deeply influenced by her brother-in-law Felix Adler, chairman of the NCLC. Josephine graduated from Bryn Mawr College and returned to New York to do graduate work at Barnard. Fired with reformist zeal, she volunteered at the National Consumers' League and became a disciple of the league's director, Florence Kelley. Josephine introduced Florence Kelley to her two illustrious brothers-in-law, Felix Adler and Louis D. Brandeis, who would soon play major roles protecting women and children in the workplace. Adler and Kelley were of the same generation and both were influenced by social reformist ideas while graduate students in Europe.

Progress was being made, reported Kelley in 1914. "Forty states now forbid employment of children before the fourteenth birthday." New York State jumped to the lead in protecting children. From 1909 to 1912, that state conducted 26,148 workplace inspections, finding 9,339 children less than sixteen illegally employed. In 1911 alone, a total of 555 cases for prosecution were cited. But, change was thwarted in the Carolinas, Georgia and Alabama where the "cotton mill interest has hitherto succeeded in preventing the adoption of the fourteenth birthday as the lowest limit of children beginning work." In West Virginia and Pennsylvania the glass companies defeated child labor legislation, allowing fourteen-year-old boys to work the night shift. Florence Kelley abhorred "the monstrous spectacle ... of wholesale poverty in the midst of riches." Kelley was moving beyond the issues of child labor and compulsory education to age sixteen to advocate for universal suffrage, minimum wage levels, workmen's compensation and old-age pensions.[18]

The settlement houses in New York, Chicago and other cities attracted many idealistic young women (and some men) eager to help the impoverished immigrants and their children. Anna Eleanor Roosevelt came from the highest ranks of New York society and was a niece of President Theodore Roosevelt. Still in her teens, she volunteered at the University Settlement House at 184 Eldridge Street in New York's Lower East Side. At age twenty she married her cousin Franklin Delano Roosevelt. The experience of the settlement house greatly moved her as she imbibed the ideas and values propagated by Florence Kelley and other reformers. In June 1940, Eleanor, as the first lady of the United States, wrote:

> That sense of obligation to smaller and weaker children remained with me through my school years and gained great impetus through my five years of teaching some classes of small girls in a New York settlement house.... All children, it seems to me, have the right of food, shelter and equal opportunity for education and an equal chance to come into the world healthy and to get the care they need through their early years to keep them well and happy. Child labor has frequently flourished in underprivileged groups. Child labor ... is a menace, not only to other young children but to all workers.... There is much child labor in this country which we should make every effort to control.... We should follow them through every step of their development until the children are firmly on their feet and starting in life as citizens of a democracy.[19]

The seeds of concern over child labor, derived from the passion of Florence Kelley that were planted in the conscience of the young Eleanor Roosevelt, grew to a mighty force as she influenced her husband during the years of the Great Depression. Children were no longer regarded as cheap labor to make adult workers redundant, but had rights to health, education and happiness upon which democracy could grow.

During the sixty-fourth Congress, Edward Keating of Colorado and Robert Latham Owen Jr. of Oklahoma submitted their Child Labor Act of 1916 to prevent the shipment from one state to another of products made where "children under the age of sixteen years have been employed or permitted to work," or where children 14 to 16 years worked more than eight hours a day, six days a week; or where children worked at night. These restrictions included any mill, cannery, workshop, factory or manufacturing establishment situated in the United States.

In February 1916, the Committee of Interstate Commerce conducted hearings into the Keating-Owen bill. Julia Lathrop, chief of the Children's Bureau, endorsed the proposed bill. "To be a man too soon," she said, "is to be a small man. It is a shame for a nation to make young girls weary." With the support of President Woodrow Wilson, Florence Kelley and the NCLC, the Keating-Owen Act was overwhelmingly approved on September 1, 1916. The House voted 357 to 46 in favor and the Senate 52 to 12. The victory, alas, was short-lived. Roland Dagenhart from Charlotte, North Carolina, with his sons Reuben, then aged 13, and John, aged 15, working in textile mills, chose to sue. A federal judge sitting in North Carolina declared the law unconstitutional. U.S. attorney W.C. Hammer for the western district of North Carolina appealed to the Supreme Court. In *Hammer v. Dagenhart*, 247 U.S. 251 (1918), also known as the Child Labor Decision, the United States Supreme Court heard the arguments for and against the law. Opponents of the national Child Labor Act argued that with the doughboys fighting in France, there was a labor shortage at home, and child labor was cheap, necessary and readily available. Furthermore, the earnings of children helped support the family. The Supreme Court ruled five to four that the Child Labor Act was unconstitutional. The majority determined that Congress lacked the authority to regulate the commerce of goods made by children. Justice Oliver Wendell Holmes Jr. together with Justices McKenna, Brandeis and Clarke dissented. Justice Holmes issued a strong rebuttal against the majority opinion. "It seems to me," said Justice Holmes, "entirely constitutional for Congress to enforce its understanding [of the nation's welfare] by all means at its disposal." *Hammer v. Dagenhart*, a landmark decision, represented a shift away from progressive thinking and for many years to come inhibited social legislation.

Despite these major setbacks, the progressives kept up the battle. On February 24, 1919, Congress passed the Child Labor Tax Law, imposing a 10 percent excise tax on the net profits of any company that employed children "under the age of sixteen in any mine or quarry, and under the age of fourteen in any mill, cannery, workshop, factory or manufacturing establishment." Taxes could also be levied on any company hiring children aged fourteen to sixteen for more than eight hours of work a day, more than six days a week or for work at night.

On September 21, 1921, the Bureau of Internal Revenue determined that Drexel Furniture Company of North Carolina employed a child under fourteen and assessed the company $6,312.79 in excise taxes. Drexel appealed and the case reached the U.S. Supreme Court arguing that the tax was unconstitutional and an attempt to regulate manufacturing (259 US.20, 1922). Chief Justice William H. Taft, supported by Justices Oliver W. Holmes Jr. and Louis Brandeis, voted eight to one in favor of the company, reasoning that the child labor law was indeed an unconstitutional penalty on business, and was an attempt to interfere with the exclusive functions of the states, as outlined in the Constitution and the Tenth Amendment. In his summation Justice Taft said: "The so-called tax is imposed to stop the employment of children within the age limits." Such restrictions should be left "to the control of the States." The Supreme Court must follow the law "even though it require us to refuse to give effect to legislation designed to provide the highest good."[20]

Technology and the Law

From the earliest days of the Republic, the American laborer, including children, worked with power machinery. Water-powered and then steam-powering spinning and weaving machines built the great industrial city of Lowell and many other American industrial towns. On the farm, horse-powered plows and harvesters were plentiful after the Civil War. Martin Brown and his colleagues, Jens Christiansen and Peter Philips, advanced economic and technologic reasons for the decline in child labor, especially in the canning industry. In San Francisco, the Cutting Packing Company used new technologies to can fruits, vegetables, meats, fish, and jams, year round. More mechanization required higher skills than little children could offer. The Shriver's Kettle, a large super-heated pressure cooker, began in 1874 to replace the stovetop to cook fruits and vegetables. The Shriver's Kettle, invented by A.K. Shriver of Baltimore, not only saved fuel to operate, but could "process 10,000 cans a day at any desired degree of heat." Next came the corn steamer (1878), the pea huller (1884), pulp machines for tomato catsup, string bean cutter (1900), apple and pear-parer (1900), tomato skinning machines, and the conveyer belt. Similarly, the spread of the telephone early in the twentieth century menaced the jobs of the telegraph boys. These and other machines were fast taking away the jobs previously done by children.

The American bottle industry once employed thousands of boys, working the day and night shift, as helpers to the glassblowers. Michael Joseph Owens (1859–1923), born in Mason County, West Virginia, began his work life at age ten in this wretched job. In adult life he moved to Toledo, Ohio, to work for the Libbey Glass Company where he invented the revolutionary Owens Automatic Glass-Blowing Machine. His Owens Bottle Machine Company, established in 1903, in one fell swoop eliminated child (and most adult) labor from the nation's glassworks.

Innovation was changing the jobs in department stores. Helene Hoerle and Florence Saltzberg wrote in 1919 that "department stores today do not employ as many young girls as formerly — pneumatic tubes are almost universally used, thus eliminating the once familiar cash girls who hurried to and fro from early morning until the store closed at night."[21] Complex machines of the twentieth century, powered by gasoline or electricity, required greater skills to operate than small children could muster. A child had to be sixteen or older to drive a motorcycle or automobile. More and more, technology was keeping children out of the workplace.

By the 1910s, state laws restricting child labor were taking effect. Companies caught hiring underage workers were subject to stiff fines, even triple fines and to public embarrassment. Children injured at work received large court-ordered settlements. The cost of child labor became too great and companies were less willing to hire the young. By the 1920s, expensive court cases and settlements of $10,000 or more were taking the profit out of child labor.

In 1945 the industrial commission of New York reported "nine out of ten youngsters working as pin-boys in bowling alleys up–State and 54 percent of those in New York City were employed in violation of the child labor laws." Boys as young as nine years were found "working until midnight on school nights and until 3 A.M. or 4 A.M. on Sundays." The commissioner understood that the bowling alley owners were "hard-pressed because of the manpower shortages" during the war. Nonetheless he had to take action. The children were falling asleep in school or playing truant, and flying pins or bowling balls injured a number of them.[22] The solution came not from law enforcement but from technology. The Brunswick Company and the American Machine & Foundry Company introduced electrically operated pin setting and ball return machines, making the pin boys redundant.

18

Frances Perkins and the New Deal

I came to work for God, F.D.R., and the millions of forgotten, plain, common working men.

— Frances Perkins, letter to Justice Felix
Frankfurter, June 7, 1945, soon after
her retirement as secretary of labor

As a radical in the Progressive Era, Florence Kelley was much in demand as a public speaker and found an especially appreciative audience at the Seven Sisters — the new women's colleges. On February 20, 1902, she spoke to a group of eager students of Mt. Holyoke College in Massachusetts, where her message had a profound influence on Fannie Coralie Perkins of Boston. In 1908, Kelley spoke at Barnard College on the issue of votes for women.[1] In 1913 she spoke at Wellesley College. "Mrs. Kelley's speech was a masterly historical and critical study of the minimum wage question.[2] The Mt. Holyoke speech, wrote Perkins to a friend, "first opened my mind to the necessity for and the possibility of the work which became my vocation ... [Kelley] took a whole group of young people, formless in their aspirations, and molded their aspirations for social justice into a program that had meaning and that had experience and that had practicality back of it."

Her father, Frederick Perkins, came from a Maine family that once prospered making bricks. Down on his luck, he moved to Boston to work as a clerk in a retail store. On April 10, 1882, in a house on Joy Street on Beacon Hill, overlooking Boston Common, Fannie was born. Two years later, Frederick moved his family to the industrial town of Worcester, forty miles west of Boston, where he opened a stationery and office supply store. The business succeeded and Fannie grew up in a comfortable, middle-class suburb where she attended high school, before enrolling in the nearby Mt. Holyoke College to study physics and chemistry. She later changed her name to Frances Perkins.

After graduating from college, Frances worked as a teacher before gravitating to Chicago to enter Hull-House, as Florence Kelley had done fifteen years earlier. In that setting she met Clarence Darrow, Frank Lloyd Wright and the author Upton Sinclair, whose novel *The Jungle*, on the inhumane conditions in the meat packing industry, was released in 1906. From Chicago she moved to Pennsylvania to study economics at the conservative Wharton School of Finance and Commerce. Her political views were moving in a different direction as she imbibed the views of Florence Kelley to become a committed socialist. In 1909, Frances moved to New York to study at Columbia University, graduating the following year with a master's degree in political science, writing her thesis on *Some Facts Concerning Certain Undernourished Children*. Now thirty years old, she was ready to start work.

She was hired as executive secretary by the New York City branch of the National Consumers League at a salary of $1,000 a year, working under the guidance of her mentor, Florence Kelley. She shifted theory into action by endorsing Florence Kelley's beliefs that the low wages and deplorable working conditions of male workers were due to the use of cheaper child and women's labor. Only by abolishing the competition of cheap child labor could adults receive decent pay, working no more than fifty-four hours a week. Research, influence and legislation were the tools needed to abolish child labor and improve working conditions for adult workers.

On March 25, 1911, Frances Perkins was in New York when the fire at the Triangle Shirtwaist Factory took the lives of one hundred and forty-six garment workers, mostly female and many of them young. She rushed to Washington Place and saw the tragedy unfolding before her eyes. "People had just begun to jump as we got there," Frances recalled, "They had been holding on until that time, standing in the windowsills, being crowded by others behind them, the fire pressing closer and closer, the smoke closer and closer." People cried out: "Don't jump." But the fire brigade ladders were too short and the safety nets too flimsy to be of help. They could not hold on any longer. One by one, the desperate people lost their grip and fell to their deaths. On that day, Frances Perkins tells, the New Deal was born.

Frances Perkins made herself an expert in fire safety and prevention and was appointed executive secretary to the Committee on Safety of the City of New York. In 1912 a slipper manufacturer admitted that children "from 10 to 12 years of age did the work for 30 cents a dozen." Work at home, he expanded, was a good thing because it kept young girls off the streets. Frances Perkins offered a different picture. "She declared home work was a menace to the community, to health and to the workers." One community worker "had seen thousands of children under seven at work. She had witnessed children whipped for not working as rapidly as the mother thought they ought to, and for crying because they could not go to bed."[3] In her capacity as secretary of the Committee on Safety, Frances was involved with the State of New York Factory Investigative Committee, headed by the up-and-coming politician Al Smith. Frances Perkins allied herself with Smith when he became governor of New York in 1918, and he appointed her a member of the state's industrial commission at a salary of $8,000 a year. Florence Kelley was delighted "that someone that we had trained and who knew industrial conditions," and who shared her agenda, was placed in a high state government position. In 1929, Perkins was appointed chairperson of the New York Industrial Commission and played a key role implementing the state's worker's compensation program and investigating the harm done by dangerous chemicals used in industry. Her star rose higher under Governor Franklin Delano Roosevelt, allowing her to implement the forty-eight hour maximum workweek and minimum wages.

Florence Kelley congratulated Perkins on her appointment, writing, "There will be less, death, misery and poverty because you are at the helm." An appreciative Perkins wrote back, "Darling Mrs. Kelley, It is a shame that you weren't here on my induction into office. You were the only person whom I particularly wanted to be here.... I would have given a great deal to have you here for I regard you as the head of the family in this enterprise, which binds us all together."

"Thank you for believing that I shall accomplish something," continued Perkins in her letter to Kelley, pupil to teacher. "To the very last of my ability I shall try to do what you expect of me, and partly shall try because it is you who is expecting so much. Your demand for good work and results has always been an inspiration, quite as much of an inspiration, I think, as your continual stream of new ideas."[4]

The stock market crash of 1929 precipitated the Great Depression. Franklin D. Roosevelt was elected president of the United States in 1932 supported by Democratic majorities in both houses of government. The president was subject to intense lobbying to appoint a secretary of labor who was capable of carrying out his social and economic plans to rescue the nation from the Great Depression. Felix Frankfurter, Louis Brandeis, Molly Dewson, Jane Addams and many others recommended Frances Perkins. "She is," wrote Lincoln Filene of Filene's department store, "the best equipped man for the job that I know of." In the middle of the Great Depression in 1933 Frances Perkins was appointed by President Franklin D. Roosevelt as the 4th United States secretary of labor, and the first female cabinet member in the history of the United States.

In a course of lectures at Teachers' College, Columbia University, in 1913, Florence Kelley enumerated her requirements for a more humane and civilized America. She called for laws "to keep all the children in school, at least to the 16th birthday," and the absolute banning of child labor before that age, abolition of the sweating system, workmen's compensation, minimum level of wages, mothers' pensions, a shorter workweek, and equal suffrage. Toward the close of her life, Florence Kelley, in 1926 and 1927, wrote a series of articles, *Notes of Sixty Years*, describing the ups and downs of her life. She concluded with fighting words against "the suffering inflicted by our class-rule," and continued to cast her lot "with the workers [and] to spread enlightenment among the men and women destined to contribute to the change to a higher social order, to hasten the day when all good things of society shall be the goods of all the children of men, and our petty philanthropy of today superfluous." Florence Kelley died in 1932 at age seventy-four years, tantalizingly close but unable to achieve her goals. The task of proposing and implementing these and other New Deal policies fell to her protégée, Secretary of Labor Frances Perkins.

According to Kristin Downey, biographer of Frances Perkins, she "felt deeply responsible to Kelley's legacy." To be an effective secretary of labor was "the best way to honor Kelley's memory." Perkins served as secretary of labor for twelve years. One of her first goals was to seek progress in the amendment to the Constitution to ban child labor. Since 1924, when the Child Labor Amendment was sent to the state legislatures, twenty-four states had voted for ratification. In 1933 the Roosevelt administration introduced the National Recovery Administration (NRA), headed by Hugh Samuel Johnson, a retired army general, which aimed to end fierce competition by cutting production, improving working conditions, instituting a minimum wage and prohibiting the employment of children less than sixteen years old.

An editorial dated June 11, 1933, asked of the NRA: "Is it necessary?"[5] Two days later Secretary Perkins gave her response. "It is quite true," she wrote, "that census figures show a great decline in the number of minors employed between 1920 and 1930 ... but there has been an actual increase in the employment rate of fourteen and fifteen year old children in 1931 over 1930.... Child employment has increased in some industries, even during the depression.... There has been a mushroom growth of sweated industries throughout the industrial east." Children faced the responsibility of helping the family survive. Many found part-time jobs or even left school to earn a little money selling newspapers, working in fac-

During the Great Depression adult workers were dismissed and children hired to work long hours for little pay. In 1933, Allentown, Pennsylvania, experienced a children's strike against the sweatshop system, seeking shorter hours and the establishment of a minimum wage.

tories, delivering goods or selling goods on street corners. Other children felt they were a burden to their families and left home to travel the railroads in boxcars, finding work here and there.[6] Between July and December 1933 over 100,000 children under 16 years were removed from industry and a further 50,000 were let go from hazardous jobs such as mining, and logging. The most vocal complainer against the NRA was the American Publishers Association, whose members depended on the newsboys to distribute the papers.

In his fireside chat to the American people on July 24, 1933, President Franklin D, Roosevelt said that the NRA, by abolishing child labor, "makes me personally happier than any other one thing with which I have been connected since I came to Washington.... Child labor was an old evil. But no employer acting alone was able to wipe it out. If one employer tried it, or if one state tried it, the cost of operation rose so high that it was impossible to compete with the employers or states, which had failed to act. The moment the Recovery Act was passed, this monstrous thing ... went out in a flash."[7]

On September 3, 1934, in the depths of the Depression, Perkins, in a radio broadcast, laid out the bold goals of the Department of Labor. "Child labor has been practically abolished under the NRA codes." Future legislation, she said, would include job and income insurance and old-age benefits. Unemployment insurance is vital to workers as it "will keep them from real poverty during brief periods when they are unemployed through no fault of their own." Her greatest achievement came in 1934 as chairperson of the president's committee on social security, leading to the momentous Social Security Act of 1935.

President Roosevelt congratulated Congress on the passage in June 1933 of the National Industrial Recovery Act, which had given employment to millions. "In our progress under the act," the president said, "the age-long curse of child labor has been lifted, the sweatshops outlawed, millions of wage earners have been released from starvation wages and excessive hours of labor." Empowered by these acts, workers' wages rose to a minimum of $13 a week and the workweek was reduced to between 35 and 40 hours. Pictures of gaunt, forlorn men, family men shuffling patiently in long bread lines, rankled the public who knew that many children were still working in factories. The child labor amendments stopped children under sixteen from working, rising to age eighteen in hazardous jobs, such as mining and in saw mills. In 1935, Rose C. Feld stated bluntly: "Child labor is cheap labor." As a result of the new laws, "100,000 children marched out of mills, factories, commercial establishments and trades and made place for adults hitherto unemployed because they could not compete against the wages at which the children were hired."[8]

The hopes of the reformers were short-lived. In 1935, the United States Supreme Court declared the NRA unconstitutional leading to a dramatic shift in hiring practices. In the midst of the Great Depression millions of adult jobs were lost, while 850,000 children were put to work. Those lucky enough still to be working had their wages cut, creating bad economic conditions similar to a half-century earlier. Cheap child labor returned as adult jobs and adult pay fell. Rose C. Feld reported, "Children have found work while their elders have gone to the bread lines or the relief agencies.... In the tobacco lands in harvest time, little boys of 8 put in ten and twelve hours a day moving on their hands and knees, gathering the lower leaves." In factories children are "working shoulder to shoulder with adults." Migrant child labor returned to the fields. It is, she wrote, "the same vicious cycle of unbalance ... children working in order to add to the adult earnings of the family."

Applications for employment certificates for children aged fourteen and fifteen rose nationwide by 58 percent. In New York City there was an increase "of almost 400 percent in employment certificates" compared with the year before, meaning "that adults and older children are being displaced by younger and cheaper laborers." The U.S. Department of Labor told of "fly-by-night textile sweatshops, which set up in an abandoned barn or factory, works its employees mercilessly for a few weeks, and then moves secretly at night without paying even the meager wages promised." Child labor was again increasing in the anthracite mines and in agriculture. Towns and cities witnessed the re-appearance of news and messenger boys, peddlers, and boys shining shoes.[9] Anita P. Davis writes that in the Carolinas during the Great Depression, children went to work with cardboard in their worn-out shoes and flour sacks for clothing. Jobs for children increased dramatically while jobs for adults decreased. Factories and farms looked for "laborers who would work for low wages and for long hours without complaint."

Considered moribund, the 1924 child labor amendment suddenly showed signs of life as more and more states ratified it. In 1936 Roosevelt was resoundingly re-elected and saw his victory as a mandate to overcome court opposition to his New Deal legislation. On January 7, 1937, President Roosevelt sent a letter to the governors of uncommitted states urging them to ratify the child labor amendment and "place it in the Constitution [so] that child labor should be permanently abolished." The Sugar Beet Act of 1937 made growers ineligible for subsidy payments if they employed children younger than sixteen.

Frances Perkins worked feverishly to re-craft legislation to overcome the objections of the Supreme Court. The president wanted a bill that would cover child labor and low wages as well as long hours of work. It was submitted to Congress in May 1937. The bill was vigorously opposed by the National Association of Manufacturers and by conservative congressmen. To satisfy them, the minimum wage was set low at 25 cents an hour, with 5-cent increases for five years to reach 40 cents an hour, still subsistence wages. The workweek would be forty-four hours for the first year and reduced to forty hours by the third year. Frances Perkins addressed the joint hearings on the Fair Labor Standards Act of 1937. "Child labor," she said emphatically, "must be eliminated from all industries and commercial employment, whether interstate or intrastate in character." This bill would bar employment to all children under the age of sixteen and to all those under eighteen for "occupations deemed to be particularly hazardous to the employment of children or detrimental to their health or well-being."[10] In his May 24, 1937, message to Congress, President Roosevelt urged the passage of the act, saying, "The time has arrived for us to take further action to extend the frontiers of social progress.... A self-supporting and self-respecting democracy can place no justification for the existence of child labor, no economic reason for chiseling workers' wages or stretching workers' hours. [The] government must have some control over maximum hours, minimum wages, the evil of child labor and the exploitation of unorganized labor."[11]

On June 14, 1938, the Fair Labor Standards Act passed by a voice vote of the Senate and by 291 to 89 votes in the House of Representatives. Section 212 of the act defines "oppressive child labor" as the employment of "any employee under the age of sixteen.... No producer, manufacturer, or provider shall ship or deliver for shipment in commerce any goods produced by an establishment situated in the United States [in which] oppressive child labor has been employed." The act empowered the secretary of labor to investigate and inspect places of work and to obtain proof of age of employees to ensure that it was

Frances Perkins, secretary of labor from 1933 to 1945, the first woman appointed to a presidential cabinet. She was a strong proponent of the New Deal legislation of the Franklin Roosevelt administration. As a disciple of Florence Kelley, she helped craft the laws against child labor embodied in the Fair Labor Standard Act of 1938. She is seen here in 1936, getting ready to address a conference on Industry and Labor on the subject of the occupational lung disease, silicosis.

faithfully enforced. President Roosevelt signed it into law on June 25, 1938. With the Fair Labor Standards Act "oppressive child labor" in the United States finally ended. A more quiescent Supreme Court did not oppose the law. From Florence Kelley to Frances Perkins, the American welfare state moved from ideal to reality.

There was stiff opposition to the New Deal, with accusations of erosion of states' rights and creeping socialism. Clinton L. Bardo, a railroad and shipbuilding man, was president from 1934 to 1935 of the National Association of Manufacturers and was a bitter opponent of President Roosevelt. In 1935, the NAM announced that it was entering politics to rid the nation of the New Deal. Bardo claimed that these programs indicated the "substitution of socialism for American ideas." The NAM "was out to end the New Deal."[12] Like her mentor, Florence Kelley, Frances Perkins was personally accused of being a communist, an impostor and a spy. Her critics latched on her reluctance to deport aliens charged with being communists and for her sympathy to refugees fleeing Nazi Germany. The whispering campaign against her culminated in 1939, when Congressman J. Parnell Thomas of New Jersey introduced a charge of impeachment, accusing Perkins of "conspiring against the best interests of the United States." After Perkins voluntarily testified before the congressional committee, the United States House of Representatives voted to proceed no further on the Thomas resolution.

As the Depression eased adult jobs returned. The 1940 census showed a profound drop in child labor with only a quarter-million children 14 or 15 years old in the labor force. As the Second World War ratcheted up, children once more went to work. The NCLC in 1943 issued a statement that "the chief contribution a child can make to his country in the present crisis is to remain in school and prepare himself for the future responsibilities of citizenship." Despite this plea, the expanding war economy proved too great an allure for many youngsters, three million of whom aged 14 to 17 years, joined the work force. In January 1944, the NCLC tried again. "The demands of war production and essential civilian services," the committee insisted, "can be met without exploiting children." At war's end, the troops came home and fewer children stayed at work.

Eleanor Roosevelt, niece of President Theodore Roosevelt and a wealthy debutant, was a member of the Junior League. Her wish "to be useful" took her from the comforts of Midtown to the squalor of the Lower East Side's Rivington Street settlement house to teach calisthenics and dance to the children of the immigrants. Eleanor was much influenced by the child labor stance of Florence Kelley and the National Consumers' League. In 1903, the eighteen-year-old Eleanor joined the Consumers' League. The memory of her time spent among the poor immigrants stayed with her.

> One of the things they asked me to do was to investigate the sweatshops in which artificial feathers and flowers were being made. I was appalled. In those days, these people often worked at home.... I entered my first sweatshop and walked up the steps of my first tenement.... I saw little children of four or five sitting at tables until they dropped with fatigue, and earning tragically little a week.

During fall of that year she took Franklin D. Roosevelt, then a senior at Harvard, to visit the Lower East Side. "He was absolutely shaken when he saw the cold water tenement," Eleanor later recalled, "and kept saying he could not believe human beings really lived that way." When Franklin "got out on the street afterward he drew a long breath of air."[13] Eleanor had awakened Franklin's social conscience. On November 22, 1903, the day after the Harvard-Yale football game in Cambridge, Franklin proposed marriage and Eleanor accepted.

In *Collier's* magazine, June 15, 1940, Eleanor wrote:

> Child labor has frequently flourished in underprivileged groups. Child labor, of course, is a menace, not only to other young people but to all workers.... We are concerned about children before they are born but we should follow them through every step of their development until the children are firmly on their feet and started in life as citizens of a democracy.[14]

In her statement before the Senate Subcommittee on Labor and Public Welfare on May 14, 1959, Eleanor Roosevelt again acknowledged her debt to the National Consumers' League, in which she served for "many, many years" as vice president.

> I was 18 years old when I first went with the Consumers' League into sweatshops in New York City. For the first time in my life I saw conditions I would not have believed existed, women and children working in dark, crowded quarters, toiling, I was told, all day long and way into the night to earn a few pennies.
>
> These conditions I can never forget. So when some twenty years ago the Congress passed and my husband signed the Fair Labor Standards Act, I rejoiced.

Eleanor could have added that the Fair Labor Standards Act of 1938 was revisited in 1941 when the Darby Lumber Company of Georgia illegally shipped goods out of state, leading to the arrest of its owner. In *United States v. Darby Lumber Company*, 312 U.S. 100 (1941) the Supreme Court upheld the Fair Labor Standards Act ruling that Congress has the power to regulate conditions of employment. In so doing, the court unanimously reversed *Hammer v. Dagenhart* of 1918 as "a departure from the principles which have prevailed in the interpretation of the commerce clause.... It should now be overruled." The *Darby* decision vindicated the dissent of Justice Oliver Wendell Holmes. The Fair Labor Standards Act is still in force to this day.

Frances Perkins remained secretary of labor through the twelve years of the Franklin D. Roosevelt administration, covering the Great Depression and the Second World War. After Roosevelt died, she briefly held the same post under President Harry Truman, until she resigned in 1945. Truman appointed her to the Civil Service Commission, a position she held until 1953. She was appointed professor at Cornell University. Eleanor Roosevelt and Frances Perkins were of the same generation and shared the same values. They were two of America's most remarkable women. Eleanor died on November 7, 1962. In a tribute to her long-time friend, Frances Perkins described Eleanor as "a symbol of the rightness of the American ideals of democracy. " Eleanor Roosevelt believed in the equality of all people and worked to give greater opportunities to the young. Eleanor personified "the freedom of individuals to be themselves, to do what they think is right, to choose their own path."[15] Frances Perkins died on May 14, 1965, aged eighty-three years. Her term of office as secretary of labor coincided "with the greatest period of labor unrest and economical upheaval in American history." Despite repeated personal attacks against her, she presided over her office with "efficiency and with restraint." There are some who said: "The entire New Deal relief program was nothing more than an expanded version of the Consumers' League platform."[16]

19

Child Labor Today

Child labor declines very rapidly as families become richer and their dependence on the income of children decreases.... Economic development that raises the incomes of the poor is the best way to reduce child labor around the world. But this process may take a long time.
— Eric V. Edmonds and Nina Pavcnik,
Child Labor in the Global Economy, 2005

The period from the end of the Civil War to 1900 heralded the explosive industrial growth of the United States coupled with the expansion of child labor. America beckoned as a beacon of opportunity. Indeed, the great expansion to the West and the rapid growth of industry offered the chance of finding work. Immigration from Europe brought in tens of millions dislodged by economic and political upheavals. The America they came to was still raw, with only a flimsy safety net in case of hardship, injury or death. For most immigrants, conditions during their early years in the United States were not much better than the life they left behind.

Solomon Gompers was a cigar maker in London. His earnings "were too small to afford anything but the most meager living for his family. [He was] scarcely able to keep the wolf from the door." To add to the family income, Solomon was compelled to take his children out of school early and put them to work. His oldest son, Samuel, at age ten, became an apprentice cigar maker and "contributed his bit, too, but it was all too pitiful." In 1863, hoping for a better life, Solomon gathered his family and moved to the United States. Trading the East End of London for New York's Lower East Side slowly brought the family a better life and advanced Samuel Gompers to leadership positions in the American trade union movement.[1]

Children dropped out of school early and went to work because the wage of their father was too meager to support the family. In many cases one or both of the parents were disabled or missing. During the first half of the twentieth century, legislation by the states and the federal government, combined with the improved earnings of adults and technological advances, gradually reduced the need for children to work. In 1900, only 6.3 percent of the adult population in America had completed high school. By 1940 only 40 percent but by 2010, 90 percent of native-born Americans stayed in school until age seventeen or eighteen to complete high school. In 1940 only 5 percent of the adult population had a bachelor's degree. Now, 28 percent have a bachelor's degree.

Child labor was endemic across the world. During the twentieth century wealthy countries banned child labor, declaring schooling, play and leisure as the preferred activities for children. The United States, Canada, and the countries of Western Europe with porous borders attracted millions of illegal aliens willing to work at the lowest pay scales and in the worst jobs. These undocumented aliens, and their children, continue to work on farms, pick fruits and vegetables, cut grass or clean dishes in restaurants. Lacking legal status and being unfamiliar with the language and the way of life, they are afraid to complain about their wages and conditions of work.

Child labor is tenacious and re-emerges in altered forms. Soon after its passage in 1938, loopholes were found to get around the Fair Labor Standards Act. Secretary of Labor Frances Perkins "stirred up a hornet's nest" by recommending the Social Security Act be extended to cover migrant farm laborers.[2] In 1950, there were 50,000 migrant laborers, of whom 10,000 were children, laboring in the farms of the Middle Atlantic States. With their parents, the children of migratory labor "follow the crops from early spring to late fall." It was "almost impossible to determine the ages of many migrant children," because they lacked birth certificates, but many were below the legal working age of fourteen years.[3] In Colorado the "migrant laborers were chiefly Spanish-speaking and the use of child labor in the sugar beet fields constituted one of the most vicious aspects of migrant agricultural labor."[4] By the 1960s, nationwide, there were some 100,000 children of migrant laborers "who accompany their parents from community to community, and state to state each year in search of agricultural employment." The children move from school to school and drop out early with little education. They gain no work skills and "wind up on welfare rolls or become involved in crime and delinquency."[5]

Cassandra Stockburger of the National Committee on the Education of Migrant Children described the plight of migrant children in the 1970s. She quoted from the 1971 report of the United States Department of Labor that "more than one-fourth of the country's seasonal farm work force — roughly 800,000 out of 3.1 million — was children under age sixteen.... Of these almost half were between ten and thirteen." Children helped bring in Maine's potato crop and Louisiana's strawberries as well as Colorado's sugar beet crop. The supporters of child labor, said Stockburger, use the old arguments that farm work is wholesome, teaches children good work habits and the value of money. Stockburger insists that farm work, especially exposure to pesticides and machinery, is hazardous. The children who work on farms perform below grade level and suffer from exhaustion and heat stroke. Migrant children, she emphasizes, are "a truly victimized group of American children."[6]

Child labor followed the United States into the twenty-first century. Driven by poverty and using fake identification papers, the children of migrant workers pick tomatoes, apples and strawberries, working twelve-hour days. "Amelia, Jose and Daniel are among hundreds of child farm workers in Virginia's Eastern Shore, part of an estimated 150,000 children 16 years or younger who work on the nation's farms, picking fruits and vegetables."[7]

Picking machines have taken many of the jobs once done by children. Enforcement of child labor laws was poor. Of the nearly two million farms in the United States in 1999, only forty-six were found to have violations involving the hiring of 102 minors. Spanish-speaking migrants and their children have for decades picked the blueberry crop of North Carolina. "I picked blueberries last year," explained 12-year-old Manuel, who supports two younger siblings: "I need to help pay our own way."[8] The proposal, made in April 2012, by the United States Department of Labor to stop children under age sixteen from hazardous occupations such as distributing pesticides, operating heavy equipment or cutting timber, met with the full wrath of the farming interests who saw this as further government intrusion into "the relationship between parents and children on their own family farms."[9]

Based on visits to hospital emergency rooms, the U.S. Public Health Service calculated that the rate of occupational injuries among those 15 to 17 years old was three times as high as among those older than 25. The U.S. Department of Labor, located at the Frances Perkins Building in Washington, D.C., has for many years monitored child labor violations across the United States. For the year 2001, there were 2,103 cases with child labor violations, involving a total of 9,918 children. Among these were 876 cases with hazardous occupations violations, involving 2,060 children. Over the next decade there was a steady decline in violations. For the year 2011, there were only 729 cases with child labor violations, involving 1,873 children; among these were only 368 cases with hazardous occupations violations, involving 949 children. Included in the recent cases was a Texas agricultural company fined $14,000 for allowing a 10-year-old boy to harvest onions. A Pennsylvania company was fined $15,000 for endangering the well-being of minors by requiring them to perform prohibited hazardous jobs. A restaurant in Ohio was found guilty for failure to pay 33 employees the minimum wage and overtime. Three of these employees were 14 or 15-year old, working late hours. A group of Connecticut restaurants agreed to pay back wages to 53 workers. The investigation found a 15-year-old dishwasher operating a meat slicer and another youngster operating a meat chopper. A Pennsylvania company was fined $50,000 for putting the health and well-being of minors at risk by requiring them to perform hazardous jobs. One more example was a group of restaurants in Alabama fined for 180 child labor violations for "consistently exceeding the time and work hour limitations established for 14- and 15-year old employees."[10]

There is a correlation between a nation's economic, social and political development and the proportion of children in its workforce. Child labor is much more likely in poor countries than in the rich. As nations gain wealth, child labor declines. "Child labor in China is universal," declared *The Weekly Review of the Far East*, printed in Shanghai in March 1922. "Its abolition is a matter of education, of providing a higher standard of living in order that one or two instead of all of the members of the family may be employed." *The Review*, in May 1922, reported from Shanghai, "The child labor problem with its heavy toll on the minds and bodies of China's future citizens, is at its worst here. Thousands of children from six years of age up are employed on both day and night shifts from twelve to sixteen hours." Gail Hershatter described the China of the 1920s, when children made up more than one-quarter of its cotton mill hands and its artisans. These children were paid a mere pittance beyond room and food. While children lacked the strength of adults, they came "cheap, they were young, they were pretty honest and they don't try to shirk the job."[11]

In a 1926 report, *Child Laborers Flood Shanghai*, children as young as six were sold by their impoverished parents to work in the textile mills of Shanghai. "More than 22,000 Chinese children under 12 years of age have been farmed out to toil twelve hours a day for contractors, with whom the children's parents share the profits." There were 50,000 children aged 12 to 16 also working under "slave-like" conditions, standing all day, with only an hour off for lunch, with only one day off every two weeks. The situation of the children, noted one British observer, resembled the "conditions that existed in England 100 years ago." For this backbreaking labor the children were paid 10 cents a day "in American money."[12]

According to the International Labor Organization (ILO), in 1996, China had over three and one-half million textile workers of whom 30 percent were children. Entering the twenty-first century, with its economy booming, China was close to eliminating child labor.[13] The national child labor laws of China, issued July 6, 1994, state that children younger than sixteen are not permitted to work. Companies are subject to heavy monthly fines for every under-aged worker found in their employ. Education in China is compulsory up to age sixteen.

Pockets of child labor in China still exist. In 2007, the *China Labour Bulletin* of Hong Kong published "Small Hands, A Survey Report on Child Labour in China." "Child workers are most typically found in low-level service positions or in labour-intensive industries such as textiles, clothing, shoe, luggage and toy manufacturers, and the food and beverage industries," noted the report. "Most employers are either individual workshop owners or the owners of small private enterprises." Why do companies hire children despite the risk of prosecution? The "demand for child labour," continues the *China Labour Bulletin*, "can best be explained by the relatively low cost of child labour.... Child workers tend to be more docile and compliant," and work long hours. Poverty, especially in rural areas, drives children to leave school before age sixteen. Some parents who cannot afford the school fees will lie about the age of their children to get them into jobs.[14]

The more egregious cases of child exploitation in China have found their way into the international press. In 2007 the Shanxi brickyard scandal was exposed. A group of parents from Zhengzhou in Henan told the authorities that their children had disappeared. Over one hundred children, as young as eight years, were abducted and sold into slavery to work in the brickyards of nearby Shanxi. Factories in China making shoes and sneakers for the United States market were found to employ child labor. Factory owners in the province of Hebel worked children twelve hours a day, withheld their wages and gave only food and accommodation.[15] In 2008 a child labor ring was exposed in the city of Dongguan in Guangdong Province involving children age 13 to 15 kidnapped from impoverished parts of Sichuan Province and made to work in "almost slave-like conditions for minimal pay." The children were threatened with death if they tried to escape. These illegal practices were explained by the poverty of the hinterland of China compared with the boom along the eastern and southern parts of China, creating a vast demand for labor.[16] Not only textiles and shoes used child labor. In 2012, even the computers, telephones, tablets, games and other electronics gadgets, much in demand in the West, were manufactured in China by companies using in their workforce a small number underage workers.[17]

The United States has long been concerned about child labor abroad. The Tariff Act of 1930 (known as the Smoot-Hawley Tariff) prohibits the importation of goods made by "forced or indentured labor." This bill was modified in 1997 by the representative from Vermont Bernard Sanders, by excluding goods made by "forced and indentured child labor." The International Child Labor Elimination Act of 1997 (H.R 2678) would impose sanctions on countries with a high incidence of child labor. In 1995, the United States Department of Labor, in a reported titled "By the Sweat & Toil of Children," declared: "The use of illegal child labor is widespread." In many parts of the world little children were used as cheap labor in agriculture, carpet-making, stone quarries, brick-making and in glassworks.[18]

The International Labor Organization was founded in 1919 after the devastating First World War. Its purpose was to bring management and labor together to amicably work out their differences, promote workers' rights and foster social justice. The end of child labor was another of its goals. In 1946 the ILO became an agency of the United Nations. In 1995, the ILO estimated that worldwide up to 250 million children younger than fifteen were put to work, many of them in hazardous jobs. Asia and Africa had the highest number of working children. By 2002, the world still held 248 million child laborers. Three years later there was a reduction to 218 million child laborers, aged five to fourteen. The World Bank, in its 2011 report, gave nation-by-nation figures of children aged seven to fourteen in employment. Sub-Saharan Africa had the greatest percentage of children in its workforce, led by the Central African Republic with 67 percent, Ghana with 46 percent, Angola with 30 percent, Kenya with 37 percent and Zambia with 34 percent. In Asia, underdeveloped Cambodia with 43 percent of its children in the workforce had the poorest record, while Bangladesh fared better with 10 percent. Child labor was still pervasive in the highly populated India (12.4 million children, being 4.2 percent of all children between 5 and 14 years). Peru with 42 percent of its little children working had the poorest record in South America, while in Europe Albania, with 25 percent, had the largest proportion of children working. Rumania, Turkey and Portugal were close to eliminating child labor.

Article 24 of the Constitution of India, 1919, prohibits children younger than 14 from working in factories or mines or engaging in any other hazardous employment. Despite this and other laws, child labor persists in India. According to Usha Sharma, writing in 2006, most of India's child labor is hidden in rural areas, where children work on the small family farms or businesses. As in other places, children are put to work because their families are poor. Indian children still work in glass factories, potteries, brass works, gem polishing, traditional crafts and carpet weaving.[19] These children receive little education and their health suffers from heavy labor.[20]

Worldwide, 69 percent of the children at work are engaged in agriculture, mostly on small family farms, working by the side of parents, receiving shelter and food but little income. Cuts, abrasions and fractures were common. One-quarter of the working children are employed in services, such as domestic work, restaurant and hotel work, for which they receive little payment. Girls in domestic service are at risk of physical and sexual abuse. Only 7 percent of the child workers are employed in industry.[21]

Eric Edmonds and Nina Pavcnik have written extensively on the role of child labor in the world economy. Most of the children who work are assisting their parents in the home, farm or meager family business. In underdeveloped countries, girls have the added responsibility of cleaning, cooking, looking after younger siblings and shopping. Children walk long distances to collect firewood and water and carry them back to the home. Despite the many chores and responsibilities poor families place on their children, most still manage to some extent, to attend school. Child labor declines rapidly with improved household living standards. Electricity, which powers washing machines, vacuum cleaners and dishwashers, takes much of the grunt work out of running a household. Power pumps to draw water, gasoline-powered tractors, plows, reapers and milking machines greatly ease the burden of farm work.

Working children in poor countries are not engaged in high skill manufacturing work and contribute little to international trade or to the gross national product. The illness or disability of a parent can easily push a child to quit school for work. The younger the child who goes to work the more likely he is to be injured. The lack of social services and the high cost of education are barriers to progress and keep children at work. Without economic progress, a ban on child labor and the requirement for children to attend school, will not work.[22]

The ILO estimated that in 2005, South Asia held over twenty-one million child workers; India had half that number, Nepal 1.66 million, Bangladesh 5.05 million, and Pakistan 5 million. In these countries, child labor is linked closely with underdevelopment, poverty and illiteracy. "Child labor also depresses adult wages and keeps adults unemployed."[23]

Africa and Asia face the worst forms of child labor, in particular, kidnapping children and selling them into serfdom or slavery. Desperately poor parents sometimes sell their children into pornography, prostitution or hazardous work. Many children are forced by poverty to scour the garbage dumps for salvageable items such as rags, cans, toys or food. Palates, the dump outside Manila, La Chureca, near Managua, Nicaragua, and Rach Gia, near Hanoi, Vietnam, all have colonies of children who live and work among the mountains of trash. Other children work as porters carrying heavy loads. For centuries girls with dexterous fingers tied the knots to make intricate silk and woolen carpets in Turkey, Iran, Uzbekistan, India and China. An 1890 report from Nanking says "there are seven or eight thousand looms employed in weaving silk and satin.... The silk and satin embroiderers of China are brilliant and beautiful. They are made by women and young girls."[24]

Joseph Kong's Lords Resistance Army abducted thousands of boys and trained them to fight and kill in a war that brought chaos to northern Uganda. In the Iran-Iraq War (1980–1988) tens of thousands of boys on both sides fought and died. Boys have been forcibly conscripted and trained as soldiers in wars in Burundi, Rwanda, the Central African Republic, Chad, the Democratic Republic of the Congo, Sudan, Nepal and in many other wars. Young girls have been abducted from their families to be the servants and sex slaves of army commanders.

In 2012 the screams of a thirteen-year-old girl were heard from a balcony of an upscale residential section of New Delhi. The girl was working as a maid for a well-to-do couple who locked her in the apartment, with little food, while they went away on vacation.[25] India's rising middle class has created a demand for live-in domestic help, even buying little children for the jobs.

Cotton textiles started the American Industrial Revolution early in the nineteenth century. By the close of that century, the South, with its cheap child labor, was supplanting New England as the textile region of America. As mills closed down in Massachusetts and Rhode Island they opened in North and South Carolina and Georgia. The Bureau of Labor Statistics showed a rise in manufacturing jobs in the United States from the end of the Great Depression until the 1980s. Industrial employment remained flat until 1999 when many of these jobs started to disappear. From 1999 to 2009 the United States shed one of every three manufacturing jobs, a loss of six million workers. America's once great domestic shoe, textile, clothing and tool-making industries have largely disappeared, shutting factories and putting people on the unemployment lines. The jobs lost at home were transferred abroad. Instead of the manufacture of textiles, shoes, television sets, radios and furniture at home, these goods were made in other countries, using their cheaper labor.

Concerns about child labor followed the transfer of production abroad. As South Korea, China, Singapore and Hong Kong have flourished, these nations, like the West, have largely shed their historic image as centers of child labor. Child labor has wilted under the assault of reformers, raised living standards, civil rights, legislation, education and technology. But, like a chronic disease, child labor is prone to return and needs continual surveillance to keep it in check. The tools of change, especially economic progress, are needed to rid the world of child labor.

Chapter Notes

Introduction

1. Chaim M. Rosenberg, *The Life and Times of Francis Cabot Lowell, 1775–1817* (Lanham, MD: Lexington Books, 2011).

2. Daniel Roberdeau (1727–1795) was a Philadelphia merchant interested in domestic textile manufacture. He represented Pennsylvania from 1777 to 1779 in the Continental Congress.

3. George Washington, October 28, 1789, *The Diaries of George Washington, 1748–1799*, edited by John C. Fitzpatrick (Boston: Houghton Mifflin, 1925), Vol. 4, pp. 37–38.

4. Washington, January 22, 1790, *The Diaries of George Washington*.

5. Alexander Hamilton, *Report on Manufactures*, December 5, 1791, *The Works of Alexander Hamilton*, edited by John C. Hamilton (New York: Trow, 1850), Vol. 3, pp. 207–208.

6. Tench Coxe, *A View of the United States of America* (Philadelphia: Hall, 1794), p. 55.

7. Walter Licht, *Getting Work: Philadelphia, 1840–1940* (Philadelphia: University of Pennsylvania Press, 2000).

Chapter 1

1. Uria Bonnell Phillips, *American Negro Slavery* (New York: Appleton, 1918), p. 306.

2. American Anti-Slavery Society, *American Slavery as It Is: Testimony of a Thousand Witnesses* (New York: American Anti-Slavery Society, 1839), p. 40.

3. *Report of the United States Industrial Commission on Agriculture and Agricultural Labor*, Vol. 10 (Washington, DC: Government Printing Office, 1901), p. 439.

4. Edwin Markham, Benjamin Lindsay, and George Creel, *Children in Bondage* (New York: Herbst, 1914).

5. George Savage White, *Memoir of Samuel Slater* (Philadelphia: 1836). John L. Bishop, Edwin T. Freedley, and Edward Young record the purchase of farmland to employ the parents of child workers in *A History of American Manufactures from 1608 to 1860* (Philadelphia: Young, 1864).

6. Henry Wansey, *An Excursion to the United States of America in the Summer of 1794* (London: Easton, 1798).

7. Josiah Quincy, "Journey of Josiah Quincy through Southern Parts of New England, 1801," *Massachusetts Historical Society Proceedings* 4 (1887–1889), p. 124.

8. Committee of Commerce and Manufacturers, in a report to the House of Representatives of the United States, February 13, 1816. See also Bishop, Freedley, and Young, *A History of American Manufactures from 1608 to 1860*, pp. 213–214.

9. Harriet Hanson Robinson, *Loom and Spindle, or Life Among the Early Mill Girls* (New York: Crowell, 1898).

10. Massachusetts General Laws 1836, Chapter 245.

11. Henry F. Bedford, *Their Lives & Numbers: The Condition of Working People in Massachusetts, 1870–1900* (Ithaca, NY: Cornell University Press, 1995).

12. *The New York Times*, February 15, 1898.

13. *The New York Times*, March 20, 1898.

14. Article by Elbert Hubbard in the April 1905 issue of the *American Federationist*, a trade union magazine.

15. Muckraking article by Irene Ashby published in the journal *Public Policy*, August 9, 1902.

16. United States Industrial Commission, Vol. 19 (Washington DC: Government Printing Office, 1902), p. 917.

17. Mary Harris Jones, *Autobiography of Mother Jones* (Chicago: Kerr, 1925).

18. U.S. Congress, House, Committee of Rules of the House of Representatives, *The Strike at Lawrence, Mass. Hearings before the Committee of Rules of the House of Representatives*. 62nd Cong., 2nd sess., March 2–7, 1912.

Chapter 2

1. Benjamin Franklin, *Autobiography of Benjamin Franklin, edited from his Manuscript, with Notes and Introduction by John Bigelow* (Philadelphia: Lippincott, 1861).

2. Samuel Sewall, *The Diary and Life of Samuel Sewall*, ed. Mel Yazawa (Boston: Bedford/St. Martin's, 1998), p. 145.

3. Lorenzo Sears, *John Hancock: The Picturesque Patriot* (Boston: Little, Brown, 1923).

4. Abbot E. Smith, *Colonists in Bondage: White Servitude and Convict Labor in America, 1607–1776* (Gloucester, MA: Smith, 1965).

5. William D.P. Bliss, *The Encyclopedia of Social Reform* (New York: Funk & Wagnalls, 1897), p. 234.

6. Charles Dickens, *Oliver Twist* (Boston: Ticknor & Fields, 1866).

7. Charles Dickens, *David Copperfield* (New York: Sheldon, 1863).

8. Charles Dickens, *Great Expectations* (Leipzig: Tauchnitz, 1861).

9. Samuel Kydd, *The History of the Factory Movement* (London: Simpkin, Marshall, 1857). Also Jane Humphries, *Childhood and Child Labour in the British Industrial Revolution* (New York, Cambridge, 2010). Based on 600 autobiographical accounts from the eighteenth and nineteenth centuries, *Childhood and Child Labour* is an outstanding British history of child labor.

10. John Spargo, *A Bitter Cry of the Children* (London: Macmillan, 1909).

11. Katarina Honeyman, *Child Workers in England, 1780–1820* (Aldershot, England: Ashgate, 2007).

12. Office of the Mayor of the City of Philadelphia, *Record of Indentures of Individuals Bound Out as Apprentices, Servants etc. and of German and other redemptioners in the Office of the Mayor of the City of Philadelphia, October 3, 1771, to October 5, 1773* (Lancaster, PA: American Philosophical Society, 1902).

13. Rurg W. Herndon and John E. Murray, eds., *Children Bound to Labor: The Pauper Apprentice System in Early America* (Ithaca, NY: Cornell University Press, 2009).

Chapter 3

1. Felix Frankfurter was born in Vienna and grew up in New York's Lower East Side. His leftist and liberal values were close to those of Florence Kelley. He was a professor at Harvard Law School before being appointed associate justice to the United States Supreme Court. He wrote these comments about Florence Kelley in the Foreword to Josephine Goldmark's book *Impatient Crusader: Florence Kelley's Life Story* (Urbana: University of Illinois Press, 1953). L. P. Brockett's *Men of Our Day* (Philadelphia: Zeigler, McCurdy, 1868) gives a sketch of the early life of William D. Kelley, pp. 566–474.

2. Her Cornell thesis, "On Some Changes in the Legal Status of the Child Since Blackstone," was published in the *International Review* in 1882.

3. Engels to Kelley, February 10, 1885.

4. Engels to Kelley, June 3, 1886.

5. Kelley to Engels, June 16, 1887.

6. Kelley to Engels, August 28, 1887.

7. *The Need for Theoretical Preparation for Philanthropic Work: The Autobiography of Florence Kelley* (Chicago: Kerr, 1986).

8. Kelley to Engels, December 29, 1887.

9. Engels to Kelley, December 28, 1886.

10. Kelley to Engels, March 19, 1888.

11. Kelley to Engels, November 21, 1893.

12. Kelley reported to Henry D. Lloyd, January 31, 1899.

13. Kelley to John A. Fitch, March 26, 1925.

14. Kelley to Anthony F. Dirksen of the Chicago Candy Association.

15. *New York Times*, December 21, 1932.

16. *New York Times*, December 22, 1932

Chapter 4

1. *New York Times*, August 3, 1879.

2. *New York Times*, April 1, 1882.

3. *New York Times*, December 26, 1882.

4. In 1904, when the National Child Labor Committee was formed, Anita's brother, Princeton-educated Stanley Robert McCormick of International Harvester fame, was elected to the board of trustees. The McCormick Harvester Machine Company in 1886 was the scene of intense worker unrest leading to the Haymarket Massacre on May 4. The experience had a profound effect on Anita and her younger brother Stanley, who became active in efforts to end child labor.

5. Jane Addams, address at the Chautauqua Assembly, July 9, 1902, in *Writing on Peace* (New York: Continuum International, 2006).

6. *New York Times*, March 10, 1905.

Chapter 5

1. Julia A. Holmes, "Children at Work," *Scribner's Monthly* 1 (1871), 607–615. Julia grew up in Massachusetts and moved with her family to Kansas in the hope of keeping it a slave-free state. There she met the dashing New Yorker James Holmes. They married in 1857 and set out for Colorado in the hope of making their fortune discovering gold. On the way to the goldfields, they climbed the 14,115-foot Pikes Peak. Wearing bloomers (short skirt and long trousers) and moccasins, Julia was the first woman to scale the mountain. Julia and James did not find gold. They returned to the East where Julia fashioned a reputation as an early reformer, campaigner for the freedom of slaves and the rights of women and children. She held various federal jobs in Washington, D.C, and attended the first women's suffrage convention in 1869. She conducted her research into child labor on behalf of the federal government. Julia Holmes died in 1887.

2. The plea to abolish child labor in New York was published in the *New York Times*, October 1, 1871. The activities of Charles F. Peck are described in the *Second Annual Report of the Bureau of Statistics of the State of New York* (Albany: Parsons, 1886), and in Jeremy P. Felt's book *Hostages of Fortune: Child Labor Reform in New York State* (Syracuse, NY: Syracuse University Press, 1965). *New York Times*, March 24, 1874, describes the opposition to legislation to curtail child labor.

3. Henry George, *The Condition of Labor* (London: Swan, Sonnenschein, 1898).

4. American Federation of Labor, convention in St. Louis, December 1888. At this convention, the AFL officially recognized May 1 as the international workers solidarity day.

5. Resolution 99 at the 22nd annual conference of the AFL, held in New Orleans, November 1902.

6. Robert La Follette, "Child Labor and the Federal Courts" (speech before the American Federation of Labor convention, held in Cincinnati, June 14, 1922). Printed in the *American Federationist* 29, no. 7 (July 1922), pp. 468–486.

7. Richard T. Ely, *The Strength and Weakness of Socialism* (New York: Chautauqua Press, 1894), p. 262.

8. First Annual Report of the New York State Department of Labor, 1902.

9. Edwin Markham, "The Hoe-Man in the Making," *Cosmopolitan* 41 (1906), pp. 567–574.

10. Ibid.

11. Bessie van Vorst and her sister-in-law Marie published *The Woman who Toils: Being the Experiences of Two Ladies as Factory Workers* (New York: Doubleday, 1903). As Mrs. John van Vorst, Bessie wrote *The Cry of the Children: A Study of Child-Labor* (New York: Moffat, Yard, 1908). Moving to France, Bessie wrote *France: Our Ally* (New York: Association Press, 1918).

12. Florence Sanville's articles were published in *Harper's Magazine* in 1909 and 1910. "Women in the Pennsylvania Silk Mills" appeared in vol. 120 (April 1910), pp. 651–662.

13. An account of Florence Sanville's investigation of the silk mills appeared in the *New York Times*, January 20, 1909.

14. Theodore Roosevelt, "The Conservation of Childhood" (speech before the 7th annual conference of the National Child Labor Committee, Birmingham, March 1911).

15. Rheta Childe Dorr, "The Child who Toils at Home," *Hampton Magazine* 28 (April 1912), pp. 183–188 and 221–223.

16. Katharine DuPre Lumpkin and Dorothy V. Douglas, *Child Workers in America* (New York: McBride, 1937).

17. Charles P. Neill, "Child Labor in the National Capital" (part of a 1906 symposium on Child Labor: A Menace to Industry, Education and Good Citizenship). Published in the *American Academy of Political and Social Sciences* 28, no 2 (March 1906), pp. 270–280.

18. Royal Meeker on educational reform, *New York Times*, April 6, 1913.

Chapter 6

1. Suzanne McIntire, *American Heritage Book of Great American Speeches for Young People* (New York: Wiley, 2001), p. 116.

2. Sadie Frowne, "Story of a Sweatshop Girl," *Independent Magazine*, September 25, 1902.

3. United States Bureau of Labor, *Report on the Condition of Women and Child Wage Earners in the United States*, vol. 11 (Washington, DC: Government Printing Office, 1911), p. 26.

4. *New York Times*, March 28, 1911.

5. *New York Times*, January 22, 1913.

6. *New York Times*, May 25, 1893.

7. *New York Times*, May 19, 1895.

8. *New York Times*, April 5, 1904.

9. *New York Times*, November 16, 1913.

Chapter 7

1. Owen R. Lovejoy, "The Coal Mines of Pennsylvania," *Annals of the American Academy of Political and Social Science* 28 (1911), pp. 133–137.

2. Mary Harris Jones, *Autobiography of Mother Jones* (Chicago: Kerr, 1925).

3. Death of Corey Downs recorded by the Pennsylvania Inspectors of Mines, *Report of the Inspectors of Coal Mines in the Anthracite Coal Region of Pennsylvania for the Year 1871* (Harrisburg, PA: State Printer, 1872).

4. Pennsylvania Inspectors of Mines, *Report for the Year 1871*, p. 259.

5. Craig Phelan, *Divided Loyalties: The Public and Private Lives of Labor Leader John Mitchell* (Albany: State University of New York, 1994).

6. Francis H. Nichols, "Children of the Coal Shadow," *McClure's Magazine* 20 (February 20, 1903), pp. 435–444.

7. Clarence Darrow, "Johnny McCaffery — The Breaker Boy," *Hearst's Magazine*, 1903.

8. *New York Times*, April 12, 1898.

9. U.S. Congress, House, Committee on Mines and Mining, *Conditions in the Copper Mines of Michigan: Hearings before the Committee on Mines and Mining*, 63rd Cong., 2nd sess., February 16–21, 1914.

Chapter 8

1. Daniel Vickers, *Farmers and Fishermen: Two Centuries of Work in Essex County, Massachusetts, 1650–1850* (Chapel Hill: University of North Carolina Press, 1994).

2. Arthur Wallace Calhoun, *A Social History of the American Family from Colonial Times to the Present*, Vol. 1 (Cleveland: Clark, 1917).

3. Edmund Morris, *Farming for Boys* (Boston: Lathrop, 1881).

4. Senator Albert Beveridge, speeches to the United States Senate on January 23, 28 and 29, 1907.

5. *New York Times*, October 27, 1910.

6. Ulrich Bonnell Phillips, *Life and Labor in the Old South* (Boston: Little, Brown, 1929).

7. Robert William Fogel, *Without Consent or Contract: The Rise and Fall of American Slavery* (New York: Norton, 1989), p. 54. Wilma A. Dunaway, *The African-American Family in Slavery and Emancipation* (New York: Cambridge University Press, 2003).

8. Joseph Fourier is quoted in *The Primitive Expounder*, edited by R. Thornton and J. Billings, Ann Arbor: 1843.

9. United States Immigration Commission (1907–1910), *Immigration in Industry, Part 24: Recent Immigrants in Agriculture* (Washington, DC: Government Printing Office, 1911).

10. Robert Grimshaw and Lewis S. Ware, "Suggestions Worth Considering of Interest to Farmers and Agronimists," *The Sugar Beet* Vol. 27 (1906).

11. United States Bureau of Labor Statistics, *Labor Laws and Their Administration in the Pacific States*, no. 211 (Washington, DC: Government Printing Office, 1917), pp. 15–16 and 53–65.

12. "Canning Industry," *Appleton's Annual Cyclopedia for 1897* (New York: Appleton, 1898), p. 197.

13. Bulletin of the Bureau of Labor, Vol 23 (Washington, DC: Government Printing Office, 1912) , pp. 468–487.

14. *New York Times*, April 7, 1874.

15. *New York Times*, December 7, 1902.

16. Martin Brown, Lars Christiansen, and Peter

Philips, "The Decline of Child Labor in the U.S. Fruit and Vegetable Canning Industry: Law or Economics?" *Business History Review* 68 (Winter 1992), pp. 721–770.

17. *New York Times*, March 24, 1935.
18. *New York Times*, September 4, 1972.
19. *New York Times*, June 18, 2010.
20. *New York Times*, May 7, 2012.

Chapter 9

1. *New York Times*, December 28, 1882.
2. William F. Cody, *The Life of the Hon. William F. Cody, known as Buffalo Bill* (Hartford, CT: Bliss, 1879).
3. Horatio Alger Jr., *The Telegraph Boy* (Chicago: Winston, 1878).
4. Horatio Alger Jr., *Mark Mason's Victory: The Trials and Triumphs of a Telegraph Boy* (New York: Burt, 1899).
5. *New York Times*, July 22–26, 1899.
6. *New York Times*, October 4, 1913.
7. Edward N. Clopper, "The Night Messenger Boy," in Proceedings of the 7th Annual Conference of the National Child Labor Committee, Birmingham, Alabama, March 9–12, 1911, p. 103.
8. *New York Times*, February 17, 1910.
9. *New York Times*, March 12, 1853.
10. Edward Winslow Martin, *The Secrets of a Great City* (Philadelphia: Jones Brothers, 1868), p. 263.
11. *New York Times*, October 13, 1884.
12. *New York Times*, August 13, 1889.
13. *New York Times*, April 22, 1894.
14. *New York Times*, February 22, 1903.

Chapter 10

1. Laurence A. Glasco, *Ethnicity and Social Structure* (New York: Arno, 1980).
2. Francis Amasa Walker, "Our Domestic Service," *Scribner's Magazine*, December 1876, pp. 273–278.
3. Emily Blackwell, "The Industrial Position of Women," *Popular Science Monthly* 23 (July 1883), pp. 388–89.
4. Alexander Hamilton Institute, *Modern Business* (New York: Alexander Hamilton Institute, 1919), pp. 181–182.
5. Helen Christine Hoerle and Florence S. Salzberg, *The Girl and the Job* (New York: Holt, 1919), p. 6.
6. *Charity Magazine* 15 (1905), p. 708.
7. Ann Ruggles Gere, *Intimate Practices: Literacy and Cultural Work in U.S. Women's Clubs, 1880–1920* (Champaign: University of Illinois Press, 1997).
8. Edith Abbott, *Women in Industry: A Study of American Economic History* (New York: Appleton, 1918), p. 110.
9. E.W. Weaver, *Profitable Vocations for Girls* (New York: Barnes, 1918). Also William Drysdale's *Help for Ambitious Girls* and Annie M. McLean's *Wage-earning Women* were among the many books advising girls on the choice of careers.
10. *New York Times*, October 21, 1871.
11. *New York Times*, May 23, 1890.
12. *New York Times*, September 29, 1878.

13. *New York Times*, July 30, 1893.
14. *New York Times*, July 14, 1912.
15. *The Philanthropist*, September 1, 1859, p. 464.

Chapter 11

1. George Brown Goode, *The Fisheries and Fishing Industries of the United States*, Section 4, *The Fishermen* (Washington, DC: Government Printing Office, 1882), p. 50.
2. Samuel Eliot Morison, *The Maritime History of Massachusetts, 1783–1860* (Boston: Houghton Mifflin, 1922), p. 137.
3. Nathaniel Philbrick and Thomas Nickerson, *The Loss of the Ship "Essex" Sunk by a Whale and the Ordeal of the Crew* (New York: Penguin, 2000). The manuscript remained unpublished until 1984.
4. *Niles Weekly Register*, vol. 30 (Baltimore: Franklin Press, 1826), p. 356.
5. Thomas Goin, *Remarks on the Home Squadron and Naval School* (New York: Warner, 1840), pp. 1–3.
6. William Brady, *The Kedge Anchor, or Young Sailor's Assistant* (New York: Brady, 1852); J. Grey Jewell, *Among Our Sailors* (New York: Harper, 1874).
7. *New York Times*, July 1, 1861.
8. *New York Times*, August 26, 1865.
9. *New York Times*, October 22, 1876.
10. *New York Times*, February 21, 1895.
11. *New York Times*, June 30, 1907.
12. Charles Poole Cleaves, *A Case of Sardines: A Story of the Maine Coast* (Boston: Pilgrim Press, 1904), p. 13.
13. Everett W. Lord, "Child Labor in the Textile Industries and Canneries of New England" (paper delivered at the 5th annual conference of the National Child Labor Committee, Chicago, Illinois, January 1909).
14. A. J. McKelway, report to the 6th annual conference of the National Child Labor Committee on the topic of Child Employment Industries (Boston, 1910), p. 235.
15. Lewis Hine, "Report on the Oyster and Shrimp Canneries," in *Publications of the Committee for 1911 National Child Labor Committee*, p. 15–17.
16. Gifford Pinchot, "Child Workers Increasing: Million Are Now Employed. State Laws Often Evaded," *New York Times*, September 2, 1923. Article written by two-term governor of Pennsylvania. In 1914, Pinchot ran for the United States Senate on the Progressive Party ticket but later returned to the Republican Party. Pinchot called for federal action to stop child labor. In 1933 he supported the children strikers of the Pennsylvania garment industry.

Chapter 12

1. Criticism of the Dyottville Glass Works comes from William C. Woodbridge, ed., *American Annals of Education and Instruction for the Year 1833* (Boston: Allen & Ticknor, 1833). Also Edwin Markham, *Children in Bondage* (New York: Hearst, 1914).
2. Florence Kelley, *Fourth Annual Report of the Factory Inspectors of Illinois, for the Year Ending December 15, 1897* (Springfield, IL: Government Printer, 1897), p. 15.

3. Florence Kelley, "A Boy-Destroying Industry," in *The American Monthly Review of Reviews,* vol. 28 (New York: Review of Reviews, 1903), pp. 221–222.

4. *New York Times,* April 24, 1902. Payment to workers comes from United States Senate, 53rd Congress, 2nd session, *Report of Committees, 1893–95* (Washington, DC: Government Printing Office, 1895), p. 124.

5. Florence Kelley, "The Needless Destruction of Boys," *Charities Magazine* 14 (June 3, 1905).

6. *New York Times,* August 10, 1903.

7. Bonnie Stepenoff, *My Father's Daughters: Silk Mill Workers in Northeastern Pennsylvania* (Cranbury, NJ: Associated University Presses, 1999).

8. Rick Halpern, *Down the Killing Floor: Black and White Workers in Chicago's Packinghouses, 1904–54* (Champaign: University of Illinois Press, 1997). Also Ernest L. Talbert, *Opportunities in School and Industry for Children of the Stockyard District* (Chicago: University of Chicago Press, 1912). These books discuss children working in the packinghouses.

9. Florence Kelley, *Third Annual Report of the Factory Inspectors of Illinois for the Year Ending December 15, 1895* (Springfield, IL: State Printers, 1896), p. 11.

10. Upton Sinclair, *The Jungle* (New York: Doubleday, 1906).

11. W.J. Rorabaugh, *The Craft Apprentice: From Franklin to the Machine Age in America* (New York: Oxford, 1986).

12. Investigation by the 44th Congress into the influx of Chinese workers to San Francisco, Report #680 (Washington, DC: Government Printing Office, 1877).

13. United States Bureau of Education, *Bulletin,* no. 52 (Washington, DC: Government Printing Office, 1913).

14. Isaac A. Hourwich, *Immigration and Labor: The Economic Aspects of European Immigration in the United States* (New York: Huebsch, 1922).

15. Estelle Reed, *Course of Study for the Indian Schools of the United States — Industrial and Literary* (Washington, DC: Government Printing Office, 1901).

16. State of Missouri, *Annual Report of the Bureau of Labor Statistics of the State of Missouri for the Year ending November 5, 1910* (Jefferson City, MO: Sterns, 1911).

Chapter 13

1. Christopher Hawkins, *The Adventures of Christopher Hawkins* (New York: private printing, 1864). Also Ebenezer Fox, *The Adventures of Ebenezer Fox* (Boston: Fox, 1847).

2. David Rose, *Armies of the Young: Child Soldiers in War and Terrorism* (Piscataway, NJ: Rutgers University Press, 2005).

3. Jim Murphy, *The Boys' War* (New York: Houghton Mifflin, 1990).

4. Bell Irvin Wiley, *The Life of Billy Yank: The Common Soldier of the Union* (Baton Rouge: Louisiana State University Press, 1952).

5. Mary A. Gardner Holland, *Our Army Nurses* (Boston: Wilkins, 1895), p. 230.

6. Richard Hall, *Women of the Civil War Battlefield* (Lawrence: University Press of Kansas, 2006).

7. William E. Doster, *Lincoln and Episodes of the Civil War* (New York: Putnam's Sons, 1916), p. 159.

8. Virginia Perry, *The Employments of Women* (Boston: Wise, 1863).

9. Doster, *Lincoln and Episodes of the Civil War,* p.240.

10. Judith E. Harper, ed., *Women During the Civil War: An Encyclopedia* (New York: Routledge, 2007), pp. 414–415.

11. James Alan Marten, ed., *Children and Youth During the Civil War Era* (New York: New York University Press, 2012). Also James Alan Marten, ed., *Civil War America: Voices from the Home Front* (Santa Barbara: ABC-CLIO, 2003).

12. Cecile Freamux Garcia, *Remembering Louisiana, 1850–1871* (Athens: University of Georgia Press, 1987). Also James Marten, *The Children's Civil War* (Chapel Hill: University of North Carolina Press, 1998).

13. *New York Times,* January 21, 1893.

14. *New York Times,* September 25, 1942. Charles Dorn in his book *American Education, Democracy and the Second World War* (New York, Palgrave, 2007), reviews the relationship between mother's work and child delinquency.

Chapter 14

1. Gilbert L. Campbell, *Industrial Accidents and Their Compensation* (Boston: Houghton Mifflin, 1911).

2. *Industrial Conference Called by the President, January 19, 1920,* Section 5 on Child Labor (Washington, DC: Government Printing Office, 1920), pp. 32–34.

3. Report of the Treasurer of the Committee of Relief for the Sufferers of the Fall of the Pemberton Mill in Lawrence, Mass. on the 10th January, 1860. Lawrence, June 1860.

4. Slade & Franklin, *A Complete History of the Great Fire at Granite Mill No. 1, in Fall River* (Fall River, MA: Slade & Franklin, 1874).

5. Florence Kelley, *Hull House Maps and Papers* (New York, Crowell, 1895).

6. Florence Kelley, *Modern Industry in Relation to the Family, Health, Education and Morality* (New York: Longmans, Green, 1914).

7. Helen S. Woodbury, "Working Children in Boston," *Monthly Labor Review* 12 (1921), pp. 45–59.

8. George P. Barth, "Health Supervision of Working Children," *Wisconsin Medical Journal* 9, no. 17 (February 1919).

9. *Every Child in School* was publication #64 of the Children's Bureau of the U.S. Department of Labor, issued in 1919. *Stay-in-School* was issued in 1928.

10. Lucile Eastes, "One Thousand Industrial Accidents Suffered by Massachusetts Children," *American Child* 2 (November 1920), pp. 222–232.

11. Raymond Garfield Fuller served as director of research for the National Child Labor Committee and wrote *The Meaning of Child Labor* (1922) and *Child Labor and the Constitution* (1923).

12. Amy Hewes, "Study of Accident Records in a Textile Mill," *Journal of Industrial Hygiene,* 1921, p. 187.

13. U.S. Department of Labor, Bureau of Labor Statistics, *Monthly Review* 12, January-June 1921.

14. *New York Times*, January 7, 1915.

15. Rosa M. Barrett, "Child Hawkers," *The Hospital*, September 20, 1902, p. 437.

16. Thomas A. Smith, *Ninth Annual Report of the Bureau of Industrial Statistics of Maryland, 1900* (Baltimore: Sun Book, 1901), pp. 176–179.

17. United States General Accounting Office, *Child Labor in Agriculture*, B-278488 (report submitted to Congress on August 21, 1998).

Chapter 15

1. Edgar Gardner Murphy, *Problems of the Present South* (New York: Macmillan, 1904), with several reprints.

2. Another member of the German-Jewish elite associated with Temple Emanu-El was Jacob Schiff, the benefactor of the Henry Street Settlement House, aimed to uplift the poor Jews of Eastern European heritage.

3. Edgar Gardner Murphy, *The Federal Regulations of Child Labor: Criticism of the Policy Represented in the Beveridge-Parsons Bill* (Montgomery, AL: Alabama Child Labor Committee, 1907).

4. Josephine C. Goldmark and Florence Kelley, *Child Labor Legislation: Schedules of Existing Statutes and Standards* (New York: National Consumers' League, 1907).

5. *New York Times*, May 11, 1966.

6. Owen R. Lovejoy, "Child Labor in the United States," *Current History* 16, no. 4 (1922), pp. 617–620.

7. *New York Times*, March 9, 1945.

Chapter 16

1. Lewis W. Hine, "Child Labor in the Gulf Coast" (talk at the 7th annual meeting of the National Child Labor Committee in Birmingham, AL, March 1911; published in "Uniform Child Labor Laws," New York: National Child Labor Committee, 1911, pp. 118–121).

2. Lewis W. Hine, "Child Workers in the Tenements," Pamphlet 181 (New York: National Child Labor Committee, 1912).

3. Lewis W. Hine, "Child Labor," in *Child Welfare in Oklahoma* (New York: National Child Labor Committee, 1918), pp. 106–117.

4. Lewis W. Hine, "The High Cost of Child Labor" (presented at the 10th annual conference of the National Child Labor Committee, New Orleans, 1914; printed New York: National Child Labor Committee, 1914, pp. 63–71).

5. Lewis W. Hine. *Some Local Child Labor Problems in California* (presented at the 11th annual conference of the National Child labor Committee, Washington, D.C. 1915. Printed by NCLC, 1915, pp. 114–116).

Chapter 17

1. *New York Herald*, January 2, 1907.

2. George Taylor Winston, *Daniel August Tompkins: A Builder of the New South* (New York: Doubleday, 1920), p. 278.

3. James A. Emery, with F.C. Schwedtman, *Accident Prevention and Relief* (New York: National Association of Manufacturers, 1911). Emery's 1924 criticism of the child labor amendment appeared in the *New York Times*, August 18, 1924. During the first half of the twentieth century he was one of the leading lawyer-lobbyists to oppose the trade unions.

4. Stephen A. Knight, "Seventy-One Years in Cotton Mills," *Charities* 16, no. 21 (August 25, 1906), p. 352.

5. Sixteenth annual meeting of the National Association of Manufacturers, New York, May 1911, reported in Department of the Interior, *Congressional Edition*, vol. 1 (Washington, DC: Government Printing Office, 1911), pp. 245–246.

6. *New York Times*, January 26, 1913.

7. Thomas Robinson Dawley Jr., *The Child that Toileth Not: The Story of a Government Investigation* (New York: Garcia, 1913).

8. United States Commission on Industrial Relations, Final Report and Testimony, vol. 12, (Washington, DC: Government Printing Office, 1916), pp. 10927–10928.

9. "The Child Labor Bill," *Pearson's Magazine* 35 (March 1916), p. 207.

10. "The Child Labor Bill," *The Outlook*, January 26, 1916, pp. 168–169.

11. The views of Ellison A. Smyth were printed in *The Survey* 36 (April 15, 1916), p. 69, and United States Congress, Committee of Interstate Commerce, *Interstate Commerce in the Products of Child Labor* (Washington, DC: Government Printing Office, 1916).

12. *Manufacturers Record 1924*, a magazine published in Baltimore and dedicated to the development of the South and Southwest.

13. Florence Kelley, "The Young Breadwinners," (speech before the National American Women Suffrage Association convention, Portland, Oregon, June 28, 1905). The speech was widely reported in the press.

14. Florence Kelley, *Some Ethical Gains through Legislation* (New York: Macmillan, 1905).

15. Theodore Roosevelt, *Theodore Roosevelt: An Autobiography* (New York: Scribner, 1920), pp. 491–92.

16. Albert J. Beveridge, quoted in "The Blighting Curse," *Journal of the Switchmen's Union* 9, no. 5 (March 1907), pp. 259–267.

17. John Van Vorst, *The Cry of the Children: A Study of Child Labor* (New York: Moffat Yard, 1908).

18. Florence Kelley, *Modern Industry in Relation to Family, Health, Education, Morality* (New York, Longmans Green, 1914), p. 88.

19. Eleanor Roosevelt, "Insuring Democracy," *Collier's Magazine* 105 (June 15, 1940), p. 70, 87–88.

20. Charles W. Bacon and Franklyn S. Morse, *The Reasonableness of the Law* (Washington, DC: Beard, 1924), pp. 364–366.

21. Helene C. Hoerle and Florence B. Salzberg, *The Girl and the Job* (New York: Holt, 1919), p. 28.

22. *New York Times*, March 12, 1945.

Chapter 18

1. *New York Times*, April 23, 1908.

2. *New York Times*, April 27, 1913.

3. *New York Times*, December 6, 1912.

4. Kristin Downey, *The Woman behind the New Deal* (New York: Doubleday, 2009).

5. *New York Times*, June 11, 1933,

6. *New York Times*, June 13, 1933.

7. Russell Buhite and David W. Levy, *FDR's Fireside Chats* (Rockville, MD: Arc Manor, 2009), p. 33.

8. *New York Times*, March 24 1935.

9. *New York Times*, March 22, 1936.

10. Frances Perkins, comments before the joint hearings on S.2475 and H.R. 7200, Fair Labor Standards Act of 1937, 75th Congress, 1st session, 1937, part 1, pp. 185–186.

11. Richard D. Polenberg, *The Era of Franklin D. Roosevelt, 1933–1945: A Brief History with Documents* (New York: Bedford-St. Martin's, 2000), p. 19.

12. *New York Times*, September 18, 1935. Also Burton W. Folsom Jr., *New Deal or Raw Deal: How FDR's Economic Legacy has Damaged America* (New York: Threshold, 2008), p. 132.

13. Eleanor Roosevelt, *You Learn by Living: Eleven Keys for a More Fulfilling Life* (New York: Harper, 1960).

14. Eleanor Roosevelt, *Courage in a Dangerous World: The Political Writings of Eleanor Roosevelt*, ed. Allida Mae Black (New York: Columbia University Press, 1999), p. 75.

15. House of Representatives, *Life and Ideals of Anna Eleanor Roosevelt* (Honolulu: University Press of the Pacific, 2001), pp. 107–113.

16. *New York Times*, obituary, May 15, 1965.

Chapter 19

1. Rowland Hill Harvey, *Samuel Gompers* (Palo Alto, CA: Stanford University Press, 1935).

2. *New York Times*, May 2, 1940.

3. *New York Times*, September 4, 1950.

4. *New York Times*, December 3, 1951.

5. *New York Times,* July 22 1962.

6. Cassandra Stockburger, *New York Times*, September 4, 1972.

7. *New York Times*, August 9, 2000.

8. *New York Times*, June 18, 2010.

9. *New York Times*, May 7, 2012.

10. Child labor enforcement statistics from the Wage and Hour Division of the U.S. Department of Labor provided by Michael Kravitz, director of communications. I am grateful to him also for sending me case histories of recent violations of the federal child labor laws.

11. Gail Hershatter, *The Workers of Tianjin, 1900–1949* (Stanford, CA: Stanford University Press, 1988).

12. *New York Times*, April 18, 1926.

13. International Labor Organization, "Labour Practices in the Footwear, Leather, Textile and Clothing Industries (Geneva: International Labor Organization, 2000).

14. *China Labour Bulletin*, "Small Hands; A Survey Report on Child Labour In China," Research Report No. 3, September 2007. www.clb.org.hk.

15. *China Labour Bulletin*, July 25, 2007.

16. *New York Times*, May 1, 2008.

17. *New York Times*, February 23, 2012; *The Telegraph*, February 15, 2011.

18. "By the Sweat & Toil of Children," Vol. 2 (report issued by the U.S. Department of Labor, Bureau of International Labor Affairs, a Report to the Committee of Appropriations, Washington, DC, 1995).

19. S. Wal, ed., *Child Labour in Various Industries* (New Delhi: Sarup, 2006).

20. Usha Sharma, *Child Labour in India* (New Delhi: Mittel, 2006).

21. World Bank, *World Development Indicators, 2011* (Washington, DC: World Bank, 2011). Gamini Herath and Kishor Sharma, *Child Labor in South Asia* (Aldershot, England: Ashgate, 2007). See Charita L. Castro, "A Review of Child Labor Statistics," in *Child Labour: A Public Health* Perspective, ed. Anaclaudia Gastal Fassa, David L. Parker, and Thomas J. Scanlon (New York: Oxford, 2010).

22. Eric V. Edmonds, "Public Health in the Economics of Child Labor," in *Child Labour: A Public Health* Perspective, ed. Anaclaudia Gastal Fassa, David L. Parker, and Thomas J. Scanlon (New York: Oxford, 2010). Also Eric Edmonds and Nina Pavcnik, "Child Labor in the Global Economy," *Journal of Economic Perspectives* 19, no. 1 (2005), pp. 199–220.

23. Herath and Kishor, *Child Labor in South Asia*.

24. U.S. Bureau of Foreign Commerce, Consular Reports, Vol. 34 (Washington, DC: Government Printing Office, 1890), p. 467.

25. *New York Times*, April 4, 2012.

Bibliography

Abbott, Edith. *Women in Industry: A Study in American Economic History*. New York: Appleton, 1910.

Abernathy, Byron R., ed. *Private Elisha Stockwell Jr. Sees the Civil War*. Norman: University of Oklahoma Press, 1985.

Addams, Jane. *My Friend, Julia Lathrop*. New York: Macmillan, 1935.

___. *Twenty Years at Hull-House; With Autobiographical Notes*. New York: Macmillan, 1911.

Adler, Felix. *The Moral Education of Children*. New York: Appleton, 1908.

Agee, James, and Walker Evans. *Let Us Now Praise Famous Men*. Boston: Houghton Mifflin, 1941.

Alfred [Samuel Kydd]. *The History of the Factory Movement from the Year 1802 to the Enactment of Ten-Hour Bill of 1847*. London: Simpkin Marshall, 1847.

Alger, Horatio. *Dan, the Newsboy*. New York: Burt, 1893.

___. *The Erie Train Boy*. New York: United States Book, 1891.

___. *Farm Boy to Senator: Being the History of the Boyhood and Manhood of Daniel Webster*. New York: Ogilvie, 1889.

___. *Mark Mason's Victory: The Trials and Triumphs of a Telegraph Boy*. New York: Burt, 1899.

___. *The Telegraph Boy*. Boston: Loring, 1879.

___. *Tom, the Bootblack*. New York: Burt, 1889.

Appleton's Annual Cyclopedia for 1897. New York: Appleton, 1898.

Bedford, Henry F. *Their Lives and Numbers: The Condition of Working People in Massachusetts, 1870–1900*. Ithaca, NY: Cornell University Press, 1998.

Beecher, Catharine E. *The Evils Suffered by American Women and American Children: The Causes and the Remedies*. New York: Harper, 1846.

___. *A Treatise on Domestic Economy: For the Use of Young Ladies at Home and at School*. New York: Harper, 1842.

Bircher, William. *A Civil War Drummer Boy: The Diary of William Bircher, 1861–1865*. Mankato, MN: Capstone Press, 2000.

Bishop, John, Edwin T. Freedley, and Edward Young. *A History of American Manufactures from 1608 to 1860*. Philadelphia: Young, 1864.

Blackwell, Emily. "The Industrial Position of Women." *Popular Science Monthly* 23 (July 1883), 388–399.

Brennen, Margaret L. *The Irish Bridget: Irish Immigrant Women in Domestic Service in America, 1840–1930*. Syracuse, NY: Syracuse University Press, 2009.

Brisbane, Albert. *Fournier's Social Science*. New York: Greeley & Elrath, 1843.

Brooks, Eugene C. *The Story of Cotton and the Development of the Cotton States*. Chicago: Rand McNally, 1911.

Brown, Martin, Jens Christiansen, and Peter Philips. "The Decline of Child Labor in the U.S. Fruit and Vegetable Canning Industry: Law or Economics?" *Business History Review* 60, no. 4. (1992), pp. 723–770.

Calhoun, Arthur W. *A Social History of the American Family from Colonial Times*. Vol. 1. Cleveland: Clark, 1917.

Campbell, Helen, Thomas Wallace, and Thomas Bymes. *Darkness and Daylight; or Light and Shadows of New York Life*. Hartford: Worthington, 1892.

Carnegie, Andrew. *Autobiography of Andrew Carnegie*. Boston: Houghton Mifflin, 1920.

Chambers, Clark A. *Seedtime of Reform: American Social Service and Social Action, 1918–1933*. Ann Arbor: University of Michigan Press, 1963.

Chernow, Ron. *Washington: A Life*. New York: Penguin, 2010.

Cleaves, Charles A. *A Case of Sardines: A Story of the Maine Coast*. Boston: Pilgrim Press, 1904.

Cody, W.F. *Biography of Buffalo Bill*. New York: Cosmopolitan, 1922.

Davis, Anita P. *North Carolina During the Great Depression: A Documentary Portrait of a Decade*. Jefferson, NC: McFarland, 2003.

Dawley, Thomas R. *The Child That Toileth Not: The Story of a Government Investigation That Was Suppressed*. New York: Garcia, 1912.

De Graffenried, Clare. *Child Labor*. Baltimore: Guggenheimer, Weil, 1890.

Dorr, Rheta C. *Inside the Russian Revolution, 1917.* New York: Macmillan, 1917.

Doster, William E. *Lincoln and Episodes of the Civil War.* New York: Putnam's Sons, 1915.

Downey, Gregory J. *Telegraph Messenger Boys.* New York: Routledge, 2002.

Downey, Kirstin. *The Women Behind the New Deal: The Life and Legacy of Frances Perkins.* New York: Anchor, 2009.

Drysdale, William. *Help for Ambitious Girls.* New York: Crowell, 1900.

Dunaway, Wilma A. *Slavery in the American Mountain South.* New York: Cambridge University Press, 2003.

Ely, Richard T. *Introduction to Political Economy.* New York: Hunt and Easton, 1884.

Engels, Friedrich. *The Condition of the Working-Class in England in 1844.* London: Swan, Sonnenschein, 1892.

Flannery, James L. *The Glass House Boys of Pittsburgh: Law, Technology and Child Labor.* Pittsburgh: University of Pittsburgh Press, 2009.

Forbes, Esther. *Johnny Tremain: A Story of Boston in Revolt.* New York: Houghton Mifflin, 1943.

Freedman, Russell. *Children of the Great Depression.* New York: Clarion, 2005.

Fuller, Raymond G. *Child Labor and the Constitution.* New York: Crowell, 1923.

_____. *The Meaning of Child Labor.* Chicago: McClurg, 1922.

Gallop, Alan. *Children in the Dark and Death Underground in Victoria's England.* London: Sutton, 2003.

George, Henry. *Progress and Poverty.* New York: Appleton, 1879.

Glasco, Laurence A. *Ethnicity and Social Structures.* Buffalo: State University of New York in Buffalo, 1973.

Goode, George B. *The Fisheries and Fishery Industries of the United States.* Washington, DC: Government Printing Office, 1887.

Gordon, Linda. *The Great Arizona Orphan Abduction.* Cambridge, MA: Harvard University Press, 2001.

Greene, John O. *The Factory System in its Hygienic Relations.* Boston: Massachusetts Medical Society, 1846.

Grimshaw, Robert, and Lewis S. Ware. "Suggestions Worth Considering of Interest to Farmers and Agronimists." *The Sugar Beet* Vol. 27 (1906): 74–77.

Gundtvig, Svend. *Fairy Tales from Afar.* New York: Hartrap, 1914.

Hall, Richard. *Women on the Civil War Battlefield.* Lawrence: University Press of Kansas, 2006.

Herndon, Ruth W., and John E. Murray, eds. *Children Bound to Labor: The Pauper Apprentice System in Early America.* Ithaca, NY: Cornell University Press, 2008.

Hillstrom, Laurie C. *The Muckrakers and the Progressive Era.* Detroit: Omnigraphics, 2010.

Hine, Lewis W. *Child Labor in the Gulf Coast Canneries.* New York: National Child Labor Committee, 1910.

___. "Child Workers in the Tenements." *Child Labor Bulletin,* no. 181 (1912).

___. "The High Cost of Child Labor." *Child Labor Bulletin* 3, no. 4 (1914).

Hoerle, Helen C., and Florence B. Saltzberg. *The Girl and the Job.* New York: Holt, 1919.

Hogg, James. *Men Who Have Risen: A Book for Boys.* London: Hogg, 1859.

Honeyman, Katarina. *Child Workers in England, 1780–1820.* Aldershot, England: Ashland, 2007.

Hourwich, Isaac A. *Immigration and Labor: The Economic Aspects of European Immigration to the United States.* New York: Huebsch, 1922.

Hunter, Robert. *Poverty.* New York: Macmillan, 1912.

___. *Tenement Conditions in Chicago.* Chicago: City Homes Association, 1901.

Illinois Department of Factory Inspection. *Third Annual Report, Illinois Department of Factory Inspection for 1895.* By Florence Kelley. Springfield: State Printer, 1896.

Jacoby, Johann, and Florence Kelley. *The Object of the Labor Movement.* New York: International, 1899.

Katzman, David M. *Seven Days a Week: Women and Domestic Service in Industrializing America.* New York: Oxford University Press, 1978.

Kelly, Edmond. *A Practical Programme for the Working Man.* London: Swan, Sonnenschein, 1906.

Kelley, Florence. *Modern Industry in Relation to Family, Health, Education, Morality.* New York: Longmans, 1914.

___. "The Needless Destruction of Boys." *Charities Magazine* 14 (June 3, 1905).

___. *Our Toiling Children.* Chicago: Women's Temperance, 1889.

___. *Some Ethical Gains Through Legislation.* New York: Macmillan, 1905.

___, and Florence Kelley. *Twentieth Century Socialism: What It Is Not, What It Is, How It May Come.* New York: Longmans Green, 1910.

___, Kathryn K. Sklar, and Beverly Palmer. *The Selected Letters of Florence Kelley.* Champaign: University of Illinois Press, 2009.

Larcom, Lucy. *A New England Girlhood.* Boston: Houghton Mifflin, 1889.

Lord, Everett. "Child Labor in the Textile Industries and Canneries of New England." Fifth Annual Conference of the National Child Labor Committee, Chicago, January 21–23, 1909.

Lumpkin, Katharine D., and Dorothy W. Douglas. *Child Workers in America.* New York: McBride, 1937.

Markham Edwin. *Children in Bondage.* New York: Hearst, 1904.

Martin, Edward W. *The Secrets of the Great City.* Philadelphia: Jones Brothers, 1868.

Martin, William. *The Adventures of a Sailor Boy, by an Old Sailor.* London: Darton and Hodge, 1862.

Marx, Karl. *Free Trade.* Florence Kelley Wischnewetzky, trans. Boston: Lee & Shepard, 1888.

___, and Friedrich Engels. *Capital: A Critique of Political Economy.* Chicago: Kerr, 1915.

Massachusetts Department of Labor and Industries. *Annual Report on the Statistics of Labor,* Vol. 4. Boston, Wright & Potter, 1875.

McGrath, Patrick J. *John Garfield: The Illustrated Career in Films and on the Stage.* Jefferson, NC: McFarland, 1993.

McLean, Annie M. *Wage-Earning Women.* New York: Macmillan, 1910.

McNeill, George E. *Factory Children: Report Upon the Schooling and Hours of Labor of Children Employed in the Manufacturing and Mechanical Establishments of Massachusetts.* Boston: Wright & Potter, 1876.

Morison, Samuel E. *Maritime History of Massachusetts, 1783–1860,* Boston: Houghton Mifflin, 1922.

Munroe, Kirk. *Cab and Caboose: The Story of a Railway Boy.* New York: Putnam's, 1892.

Murphy, Edgar G. *Problems of the Present South.* New York: Macmillan, 1904.

Murphy, Jim. *The Boys' War: Confederate and Union Soldiers Talk about the Civil War.* New York: Clarion, 1990.

New York Department of Labor. *First Annual Report of the Commissioner of Labor, Department of Labor, 1901.* Albany: Lyon, 1902.

Otely, Elizabeth. *Report on the Conditions of Women and Child Wage-Earners in the United States.* Washington, DC: Government Printing Office, 1910.

Paradise, Viola I. *Child Labor and the Work of Mothers in Oyster and Shrimp Canning Communities on the Gulf Coast.* Washington, DC: Government Printing Office, 1922.

Parrow, Charles. *Organizing America: Wealth, Power, and the Origins of Corporate Capitalism.* Princeton, NJ: Princeton University Press, 2002.

Pennsylvania Inspectors of Mines. *Report of the Inspectors of the Coal Mines of the Anthracite Coal Regions of Pennsylvania for the Year 1871.* Harrisburg, PA: Pennsylvania Inspectors of Mines, 1872.

Penny, Virginia. *The Employments of Women.* New York: Walker, Wise, 1863.

Phelan, Craig. *Divided Loyalties: The Public and Private Life of Labor Leader John Mitchell.* Albany: State University of New York Press, 1994.

Philbrick, Nathaniel. *In the Heart of the Sea: The Tragedy of the Whaleship Essex.* New York: Penguin, 2001.

Phillips, Ulrich B. *American Negro Slavery.* New York: Appleton, 1917.

___. *Life and Labor in the Old South.* Columbia: University of South Carolina Press, 2007.

Prentice, Harry. *Ben Burton: The Slate Picker.* New York: Burt, 1888.

Residents of Hull-House. *Hull House Maps and Papers.* New York: Crowell, 1895.

Riis, Jacob A. *How the Other Half Lives.* New York: Charles Scribner's Sons, 1890.

Ripper, William. *Bread and Butter Studies and Their Relation to the Higher Education of Workmen.* New York: Longman, Green, 1906.

Rorabaugh, W.J. *The Craft Apprentice: From Franklin to the Machine Age in America.* New York: Oxford University Press, 1986.

Rothbard, Murray N. *Power and Market.* Auburn, AL: Ludwig von Mises Institute, 2006.

Sallee, Shelley. *The Whiteness of Child Labor Reform in the New South.* Athens: University of Georgia Press, 2004.

Sampsell-Willmann, Kate. *Lewis Hine as Social Critic.* Jackson: University Press of Mississippi, 2009.

Schmidt, James D. *Industrial Violence and the Legal Origins of Child Labor.* New York: Cambridge University Press, 2010.

Sewell, Samuel. *The Diary and Life of Samuel Sewell.* Boston: Bedford, 1998.

Seybolt, Robert F. *Apprenticeship and Apprenticeship Education in Colonial New England and New York.* New York: Columbia University Press, 1917.

Sklar, Kathryn K. *Florence Kelley and the Nation's Work: The Rise of Women's Political Culture, 1830–1900.* New Haven, CT: Yale University Press, 1995.

___, and Beverly W. Palmer. *The Selected Letters of Florence Kelley: 1869–1931.* Champaign: University of Illinois Press, 2009.

Spargo, John. *The Bitter Cry of Children.* New York: Macmillan, 1906.

Smith, Thomas A. *Ninth Annual Report of the Bureau of Industrial Statistics of Maryland.* Baltimore: Maryland Bureau of Industrial Statistics, 1901.

Stanley, Maude. *Clubs for Working Girls.* New York: Macmillan, 1890.

Sumner, Helen L., and Ellen A. Merrill. *Child Labor Legislation in the United States.* Issue 10. Washington, DC: Government Printing Office, 1915.

Trattner, Walter I. *Crusade for the Children: A History of the National Child Labor Committee and Child Labor Reform in America.* Chicago: Quadrangle, 1970.

U.S. Bureau of Labor Statistics. *Employment of Children in Maryland Industries.* By Marie L. Benanger, and Mary Loryngton. Issue 96. Washington, DC: Government Publishing Office, 1912.

U.S. Congress. House Committee of Rules of the House of Representatives. *The Strike at Lawrence,*

Mass. Hearings before the Committee of Rules of the House of Representatives. 62nd Cong., 2nd sess., March 2–7, 1912.

___. House Committee on Mines and Mining. *Conditions in the Copper Mines of Michigan: Hearings before the Committee on Mines and Mining,* 63rd Cong., 2nd sess., February 16–21, 1914.

U.S. Immigration Commission. *Report of the Immigration Commission: Immigrants in Industries.* Senate Document 633. Washington DC: Government Printing Office, 1911.

Vickers, Daniel. *Farmers and Fishermen: Two Centuries of Work in Essex County, Massachusetts, 1630–1830.* Chapel Hill: University of North Carolina Press, 1994.

Wald, Lillian D. *The House on Henry Street.* New York: Holt, 1915.

Walker, Francis A. *Our Domestic Service.* New York: Scribner's, 1875.

Weaver, Eli W. *Profitable Vocations for Girls.* New York: Laidlow, 1913.

Weld, Theodore Dwight. *American Slavery as It Is: Testimony of a Thousand Witnesses.* New York: American Anti-Slavery Society, 1839.

Werner, Emma E. *In Pursuit of Liberty: Coming of Age in the American Revolution.* Westport, CT: Praeger, 2006.

Wickersham, John. *Boy Soldier of the Confederacy: The Memoir of Johnnie Wickersham.* Kathleen Gorman, ed. Carbondale: Southern Illinois University Press, 2006

Wiley, Bell I. *The Life of Billy Yank: The Common Soldier of the Union.* Baton Rouge: Louisiana State University Press, 2008.

Willoughby, William F., and Mary C. de Gravenried. *Child Labor.* Baltimore: Guggenheimer, Weil, 1890.

Winston, George T. *A Builder of the New South: The Story of the Life Work of Daniel Augustin Tompkins.* New York: Doubleday, 1920.

Index